The symposium held by
The Commission of the European Communities
Directorate-General "Information Market and Innovation"
Luxembourg, 23-25 November, 1983

Coordinators of the symposium:
John Michel Gibb
Commission of the European Communities
and
Siegfried Neumann
INFOBRIEF Luxembourg S.A.R.L.

Symposium secretary:
Pier Paolo Rotondò
Commission of the European Communities

Zusammenfassungen der Vorträge, Empfehlungen der Arbeitsgruppen und Zusammenfassung der Symposiumsergebnisse in deutscher Sprache Seite 193

Résumé des exposés, recommandation émises par les groupes de travail et résumé des conclusions du Symposium en langue française page 243

Riassunti delle relazioni, raccomandazioni dei gruppi di lavoro e sintesi dei risultati del Simposio in lingua italiana pagina 291

VENTURE CAPITAL MARKETS FOR THE REGENERATION OF INDUSTRY

Proceedings of the symposium held by the
Commission of the European Communities,
Directorate-General "Information Market and Innovation"
Luxembourg, 23-25 November 1983

Edited by

John Michel GIBB
Directorate-General "Information Market and Innovation"
Commission of the European Communities
Luxembourg

1984
NORTH-HOLLAND
AMSTERDAM · NEW YORK · OXFORD

ISBN: 0 444 87567 0

Published for the:
COMMISSION OF THE EUROPEAN COMMUNITIES
Directorate-General "Information Market and Innovation"
Bâtiment Jean Monnet
Luxembourg

by:
ELSEVIER SCIENCE PUBLISHERS B.V.
P.O. Box 1991
1000 BZ Amsterdam
The Netherlands

Sole distributors for the U.S.A. and Canada:
ELSEVIER SCIENCE PUBLISHING COMPANY, INC.
52 Vanderbilt Avenue
New York, N.Y. 10017
U.S.A.

EUR 9153 EN/FR/DE/IT

LEGAL NOTICE
Neither the Commission of the European Communities nor any person acting on behalf of the Commission is responsible for the use which might be made of the following information.

PRINTED IN THE NETHERLANDS

CONTENTS

OPENING SESSION

Opening Address 3
E. MUHLEN
Deputy Minister for Finance (Luxembourg)

Welcome Address and Progress Report 7
H. BURGARD
Director for New Technologies and Innovation Policy,
Directorate-General "Information Market and Innovation",
Commission of the European Communities (Luxembourg)

Venture Capital in Europe 12
C. CLEIFTIE
Deputy Director-General, SOFINNOVA, Paris (France)

SESSION I:
NON-BANKING VENTURE CAPITAL INVESTORS
Experience, Constraints, Solutions

Superannuation Funds as Venture Capital Investors 17
D.J. PROSSER
CIN Industrial Investments Ltd., London (United Kingdom)

Industrial Venture Capital Investors 26
R.A. ONIANS
Director, Business Development, Monsanto Europe S.A.,
Brussels (Belgium)

Insurers as VC Investors. A Dutch View 34
D.S. VAN HOUT
General Manager, Investments and Corporate Finance, Ennia N.V.,
's-Gravenhage (The Netherlands)

Collective Investment and Mutual Funds 48
G.D. DEAN
Managing Director, Electra Risk Capital P.L.C., London (United Kingdom)

SESSION II:
TAXATION AND INNOVATION FINANCING
Positive and Negative Impacts of Taxation

Taxation and the Financing of Innovation. Comparison of the Different Rules in Force in the European Community 57
P. FONTANEAU
Professeur Agrégé des Facultés de Droit, Avocat à la Cour d'Appel de Paris (France)

The Taxation of Collective Institutional Investors 70
D. O'HOGAN
Partner, Arthur Young & Company, Chartered Accountants, Dublin (Ireland)

Tax Treatment of the Individual Investor 75
C.A.M. RASENBERG
General Manager, Tax Department, Amsterdam–Rotterdam Bank N.V., Amsterdam (The Netherlands)

Impact of Tax Changes on Venture Capital Investments and Innovation in the USA 86
P.T. KAPLAN
Tax Consultant, Weil, Gotshal Manges, New York City (United States of America)

SESSION III:
EUROPEAN SECONDARY-LEVEL SHARE MARKETS
Exit Mechanisms and Access to Equity Capital for Small Industries

Special Stock Market Segments for Small Company Shares. Situation and Perspectives 97
H. SCHMIDT
Direktor, Institut für Geld- und Kapitalverkehr, University of Hamburg (Federal Republic of Germany)

Access to European Markets by Medium-Sized Companies 107
Y. FLORNOY
Syndic de la Compagnie des Agents de Change, Paris (France)

European Secondary Level Share Markets – The Entrepreneur's View 117
R.G. HODGSON
Managing Director, Granville & Co. Ltd., London (United Kingdom)

The Venture Capital Investor's View 122
J.P. DE BLOCQ VAN KUFFELER
Director, Brown, Shipley & Co. Ltd., London (United Kingdom)

The American Over-the-Counter Markets 129
A.E. YOUNG
Professor of Finance, School of Management, Syracuse University, Syracuse (United States of America)

The London "Unlisted Securities Market" 142
R. STORMONTH-DARLING
Chairman, Laing & Cruickshank (inc. McAnally Montgomery & Co.), Stockbrokers. Chairman, Quotations Committee, The Council of The Stock Exchange, London (United Kingdom)

SESSION IV:
PARALLEL WORKING GROUPS

WORKING GROUP 1
Developing Venture Capital Exit Mechanisms at an EC Level 153
Chairman: H. SCHMIDT
Direktor, Institut für Geld- und Kapitalverkehr, University of Hamburg, Hamburg (Federal Republic of Germany)
Rapporteur: D.L. ADAMSON
An Investigation of Inquoted Holdings of United Kingdom Financial Institution, Nuffield College, Oxford (United Kingdom)

WORKING GROUP 2
Improving the Capital Environment Affecting VC Investments 156
Chairman: P. FONTANEAU
Professeur Agrégé des Facultés de Droit, Avocat à la Cour d'Appel de Paris (France)
Rapporteur: P. WECKEL
Assistant, Université de Strasbourg III, Strasbourg (France)

WORKING GROUP 6 AND 3
Stock Options for Managers in Companies with Growth Potential 161
and
Mobilizing Non-Banking VC Investors on EC Level 161
Chairman: R.G. HODGSON
Managing Director, Granville & Co. Ltd., London (United Kingdom)
Rapporteur: S. NEUMANN
Infobrief Luxembourg S.a.r.l., (Luxembourg)

WORKING GROUP 4
Governmental Schemes Stimulating the Venture Capital Market 164
Chairman: K. NATHUSIUS
IVCP – International Venture Capital Partners S.A. Holdings, London (United Kingdom)
Rapporteur: P. DOURNEL
Expert, Directorate General "Information Market and Innovation", Commission of the European Communities, Brussels (Belgium)

WORKING GROUP 5
EC Infrastructure to Link VC Markets 170
Chairman: C. CLEIFTIE
Deputy Director General, SOFINNOVA, Paris (France)
Rapporteur: R. GUTH
Directorate General "Information Market and Innovation", Commission of the European Communities, Brussels (Belgium)

WORKING GROUP 7
Venture Capital through Collective Investment 174
Chairman: J.D. INCLEDON
Chairman, Hilger Analytical Ltd., London (United Kingdom)
Rapporteur: E. PHILLIPS
Directorate General "Information Markets and Innovation", Commission of the European Communities (Luxembourg)

WORKING GROUP 8
Venture Capital Management 176
Chairman: I.N. MOMTCHILOFF
General Manager, Investors in Industry Group P.L.C., London (United Kingdom)
Rapporteur: J.M. GIBB
Directorate General "Information Market and Innovation", Commission of the European Communities (Luxembourg)

SESSION V: REPORTING BACK SESSION

Subjects for Future Meetings 183
D. WATSON
Directorate General "Information Market and Innovation", Commission of the European Communities, Brussels (Belgium)

Summing-Up 187
I.N. MOMTCHILOFF
General Manager, Investors in Industry Group P.L.C., London (United Kingdom)

Zusammenfassung der Vorträge 193

Arbeitsgruppen 1, 2, 6–3, 4, 5, 7, 8 205

Zusammenfassung der Symposiumsergebnisse 237
I.N. MOMTCHILOFF
General Manager, Investors in Industry Group P.L.C., London (United Kingdom)

Résumés des Exposés 243

Groupes de Travail 1, 2, 6–3, 4, 5, 7, 8, 255

Résumés des Conclusions du Symposium 285
I.N. MOMTCHILOFF
General Manager, Investors in Industry Group, P.L.C., London (United Kingdom)

Riassunti dele Relazioni 291

Gruppi di Lavoro 1, 2, 6–3, 4, 5, 7, 8, 303

Sintesi dei Risultati del Simposio 330
I.N. MOMTCHILOFF
General Manager, Investors in Industry Group, P.L.C., London (United Kingdom)

LIST OF PARTICIPANTS 333

OPENING SESSION

Opening Address 3
E. MUHLEN
Deputy Minister for Finance (Luxembourg)

Welcome Address and Progress Report 7
H. BURGARD
Director for New Technologies and Innovation Policy,
Directorate-General "Information Market and Innovation",
Commission of the European Communities (Luxembourg)

Venture Capital in Europe 12
C. CLEIFTIE
Deputy Director-General, SOFINNOVA, Paris (France)

Venture Capital Markets for the Regeneration of Industry
J.M. Gibb (Editor)
Elsevier Science Publishers B.V. (North-Holland)

OPENING ADDRESS Mr Ernest MUHLEN

Deputy Minister for Finance

Grand Duchy of Luxembourg

It was an excellent idea of the European Commission to organize a symposium on venture capital markets for the regeneration of industry, from 23 to 25 November 1983 in Luxembourg. I regard it as a privilege that I have been given the opportunity, as Deputy-Minister for Finance, to open this symposium and to welcome all the eminent speakers who have come rot only from European countries, but even from the United States, to relate their experience for the benefit of a select international audience, to whom I also extend a warm welcome. I would like to present the apologies of the President of the Government, Mr Pierre WERNER, who is unable to open this symposium himself owing to other engagements.

Secondly, I would like to congratulate the European Commission and in particular the Director-General, Mr K. APPLEYARD, and his collaborators, Mr H. BURGARD, Director of the New Technologies, Directorate - Information Market and Innovation - , and Mr J.M. GIBB, for taking the initiative to hold this symposium.

As is well known, the European Commission is constantly active in the field of innovation, sparing no effort to stimulate the growth of new technologies and to contribute to generating the capital indispensable for financing the related investments.

At a time when the international economy continues to show signs of weakness - the crisis even being extremely acute in some countries - it is more important than ever to stimulate investment. This is a prerequisite for recovery and for a new period of growth. The object of this symposium is precisely to act as a stimulus in this area, particularly in relation to investments in industries which use advanced technology and which involve frequently obvious risks for the capital invested.

It is stated in the preamble of the programme of this syposium that 'the establishment of new companies providing new jobs is a basic and urgent necessity. There is one major obstacle, however : a shortage of capital markets making it possible to provide companies with the type of financing they mainly require, namely venture capital invested in a perspective of growth'.

Consequently, the aim of this symposium is to examine the prerequisites for meeting the demands for funds of this kind on the capital markets, to perfect the instruments for collecting capital and to adapt these to the tasks awaiting them.

It cannot be denied that as regards research and development, Europe lags behind other countries, particularly behind the United States, even if this gap is starting to close, as Mr Guido CARLI, former Governor of the Bank of Italy, took pains to demonstrate in 'Investing in Europe's Future', published to commemorate the 25th anniversary of the European Investment Bank.

The author arrived at the rather surprising conclusion that the difficulties experienced by the Community countries 'are not due fundamentally to a lack of human or financial resources' but that they arose 'mainly from the inefficient use of resources'.

Be that as it may, it must nevertheless be recognised that a rethink is taking place in Europe, in that both politicians and businessmen are beginning to realize that it is necessary to explore new ways of generating venture capital, particularly where the capital is required for investment in advanced technology industries. The term 'venture capital funds' is heard more and more frequently in connection with such investments.

In this context I am pleased to note that, on the model of the policy pursued in the USA, a group of 36 finance companies and banks from Community countries which provide venture vapital have just created an association which aims to promote this type of financing in the EEC and thereby to support companies launching export orientated innovative projects. As such, this initiative is in line with the guidelines recommended by the European Commission.

Furthermore, I make no secret of the fact that my country is following these developments with great interest. The first company with such objectives was set up on 29 April 1983 in Luxembourg. Since the activity of financial intermediaries of this type can be considered as complying with the objectives of the financial market, we are currently examining the conditions under which venture capital funds catering for private savers should be encouraged in Luxembourg.

However, if I may, I should like to raise a few points concerning the structural problems which should concern us at European level.

For about the past ten years, alas, our countries have been experiencing very great structural problems which we must solve without delay in order to revive our industries, otherwise our economic future and the prosperity of our peoples may be permanently undermined.

At world level, historic readjustment of the division of labour between countries and continents is currently taking place, with more and more young nations developing profitable and competitive industrial sectors and beginning to rival our traditional companies. Our wage and social security costs are often many times greater than theirs, with the result that manufacturers have an uphill struggle, which in the case of many products does not lead to an automatic victory - far from it.

We have already, and will have to again in the coming years, had to relinquish one after the other a number of products to our competitors in the Third World, owing to our lack of competitiveness.

At the same time, fortunately, we are witnessing the advent of new products, manufactured by more sophisticated processes and requiring greater investment. In other words, countries with advanced know-how, if they have adequate financial resources, can in the final analysis readapt and create new activities which are less vulnerable to competition from the young continents.

At the same time our Western societies are undergoing considerable changes in relation to consumer choice and are witnessing increased demand for services at the expense of consumer goods. New advanced technology industries, such as electronics and robot technology, data processing and office automation, nuclear energy and satellite communications, represent growth sectors, whereas steel, textiles and many other traditional products seem likely to be doomed to decline.

Needless to say, the resultant fundamental economic changes create an enormous need for investment, and particularly for venture capital in the service of innovation and the regeneration of the industrial fabric of our countries. Our production tools, our working methods, research and the technical progress of our companies will decide the future of our civilization. It is against this background that your two-day discussion in Luxembourg is taking place.

Ladies and gentlemen,
I deliberately chose not to enter into the heart of the subject. Indeed I have not broached the problems related to capital markets, which you will have ample time to analyse. For my part, I shall confine myself to wishing you a fruitful discussion.

Lastly, I wish to thank the organizers for choosing our capital city as the meeting place. Luxembourg, as you know, is the seat of Community institutions, in particular the financial bodies and departments. An I should just like to point out that in addition Luxembourg, and particularly its capital city, has always tried to be a haven for capital and to play a part as 'financial intermediary' at international level.

Ladies and gentlemen,
I wish all of you who have come here from other countries a very pleasant stay in Luxembourg, and I hope you have a chance to take ful advantages of these few days.

Venture Capital Markets for the Regeneration of Industry
J.M. Gibb (Editor)
Elsevier Science Publishers B.V. (North-Holland)

WELCOME ADDRESS AND PROGRESS REPORT

Dr. Hermann BURGARD,

Director for New Technologies and Innovation Policy,
Directorate-General "Information Market and Innovation",
Commission of the European Communities

I would like to begin by welcoming all participants to this symposium, which is one of a series being held by the Commission of the European Communities in order to examine the question of financing innovation. Within the general context of innovation financing there are three themes which at present particularly merit time and effort devoted to their analysis. These are:

- non-banking venture capital investors,
- the fiscal climate for innovation,
- secondary-level share markets.

It is these themes which we proposed to examine during this symposium. There have been a record number of people wanting to attend, demonstrating that the topics chosen for discussion are widely seen as important and that this symposium series is well appreciated as a forum for an exchange of views among all parties involved in the financing of innovation. We are therefore looking forward to lively debates.

By way of introduction to the presentations and discussions, I propose to review various initiatives and developments bearing on innovation financing which have taken place at European Community level. First I will briefly describe work done on the three specific topics which I have just mentioned.

Non-banking venture capital investors

As part of a continuing analysis of the development of venture capital investment, a comparative study of venture capital for new technology-based firms in the United-States and in Europe, sponsored by the Commission (Directorate-General "Information Market and Innovation", has just been completed. A study on the holdings of unlisted securities by United Kingdom financial institutions, cosponsored by the Commission, is at present under way.

Fiscal climate for innovation

A paper on "Tax and financial measures in favour of investment" (COM(83)218 final) was communicated from the Commission to the Council on April 28, 1983. In parallel with this generalised approach, the more specific aspects of the fiscal climate for innovation have been analysed in collaboration with other services of the Commission (Directorate-General for Fiscal Institutions and Taxation) and with officials from Member States. Questionnaires have been circulated, the results analysed, and two outside studies sponsored on "Fiscal aspects of possible options for financial interventions in favour of innovative enterprises" and on "The tax system and the stimulation of industrial innovation in the Community". The reports of theses studies have been distributed to all participants as an input to the discussions, although the Commission does not necessarily endorse the views expressed in the reports.

Furthermore, the "Directory of direct and indirect public measures for promoting industrial research, development and innovation in the Member States of the European Communities", sponsored by the Commission, has been revised by an outside consultant and recently published on behalf of the Commission. The directory covers many relevant fiscal measures.

Work is continuing in this important field, both within the Commission and in consultation with officials of the Member States.

Secondary-level share markets

Comparisons are often made between the situation in the United States, where an informal secondary-level share market has been developing for some years, and Europe where this trend is of a much more recent date. These markets are however beginning to be established in the Member States, notably in London (the Unlisted Securities Market) and Paris (Second Marché). The Commission has expressed a positive attitude towards these developments, and has asked Professor Schmidt of Hamburg University to undertake a review, looking especially at the potential of such markets for providing an exit mechanism for initial investors and as a source for second-round financing. An executive summary of Professor Schmidt's report is available to participants, and he will be presenting his conclusions during the symposium.

Meanwhile the Commission, through the Directorate-General for Financial Institutions and Taxation, is continuing to pursue consultations with the national stock exchange authorities and with Member State officials.

I would now like to summarize several further aspects of the Commission's work which have a bearing on the financing of innovation, beginning with two initiatives in the area of venture capital.

Venture capital

A pilot scheme for transnational cooperation between venture capital companies was started by the Directorate-General "Information Market an Innovation" in October 1980 with the aim of checking the feasibility of such cooperation and the advantages which it should offer to client enterprises - the new technology-based firms. The scheme was run for three years and included representative venture capital companies from all Member States with the exception of Greece and Luxembourg. Experience with the scheme has demonstrated that cooperation at the European level between venture capital intermediaries is indeed both feasible and desirable. The concept has therefore been included in the Transnational Innovation Infrastructure Plan (recently approved by the Council) and as the basis for the establishment, by the venture capital industry, of the European Venture Capital Association. Having thus served its purpose, the pilot scheme was terminated on September 30, 1983. Mr. Adam, who ran the liaison office in Brussels for the pilot scheme, has produced a report drawing provisional conclusions from this experiment, and copies are available to participants.

The European Venture Capital Association, thus created on the basis of the pilot scheme, was set up provisionally on August 31, 1983, following a meeting which was held in Brussels in June 1983 involving a fair number of representatives of the venture capital industry from several Member States. The inaugural general meeting was held on November 9, 1983, and among the board members elected is Mr. Cleiftie (the chairman) who will present a paper at this symposium.

Transnational Innovation Infrastructure Plan

This plan, aimed at improving the competitiveness of Community firms, small firms especially, through the rapid penetration of the Community's economies by new technologies, was first proposed to the Council by the Commission in June 1982. An amended version was submitted in May 1983 and received Council approval on October 26. The final formal Council Decision is due on November 25, and the Decision takes effect on the day of its publication in the Official Journal of the European Communities*. The Decision mentions the sum of 10 million ECU as the amount deemed necessary for the implementation of the plan, and there is a possibility of requesting further funds after 18 months. The priority actions for the initial period of the plan include start-up support for the European Venture Capital Association, but a formal commitment to this support must await the opinion of the Consultative Committee which will be established to aid the Commission in the implementation of the Decision.

---

*The Decision was published in the Official Journal on December 15, 1983, No. L 353, page 15.

Financing innovation in small and medium-sized enterprises - the European Innovation Loan

This proposal, communicated by the Commission to the Council on June 7, 1983 (COM(83)241 final), involves the authorisation of a tranche of borrowings in order to fund innovative projects in sectors which introduce new products, devise new processes or apply innovatory technology. The loans are to benefit small and medium-sized enterprises in the Community, and are to be granted through financial intermediaries. The proposal is being discussed by the Economic and Social Committee, by the European Parliament and by the Council. The criteria for selection of intermediaries are under discussion with the European Investment Bank.

Other developments

I have only had time to cover those developments which are directly related to finance for innovation. Within the general field of industrial innovation there are many other relevant Commission initiatives. I can mention research programmes, such as the ESPRIT programme on information technologies and the biotechnology programme, guidelines for R & D cooperation, industrial property rights and so on. Nevertheless I hope this progress report will provide a starting point for the symposium, and I am looking forward to the presentations and the discussions which are to follow.

Venture Capital Markets for the Regeneration of Industry
J.M. Gibb (Editor)
Elsevier Science Publishers B.V. (North-Holland)

VENTURE CAPITAL IN EUROPE

Christian Cleiftie
Deputy Director-General
SOFINNOVA

While preparing this paper, I asked myself why Venture Capital has received so much attention in Europe during the last few years and whether the profession is today in a position to fulfil the hopes that it raises.

It seems to me that one of the prime reasons for this interest is that Venture Capital means a return to grass roots, the resurgence of a phenomenon which was very important from the end of the 19th century onwards for the growth of industry in Europe, namely the association of a man with an idea or a technique and an enterprising financial backer. The legal form this kind of association would take would be a limited partnership, a form which has since fallen into disuse.

The limited partnership emphasized the importance of individual people working together in an atmosphere of mutual confidence, concepts which it is difficult to institutionalize. It is, moreover, significant that in the United States, modern Venture Capital has been the brainchild of a few individuals on the fringes of the financial institutions and in particular the banking system.

A second reason in my opinion is that Venture Capital has shown, particularly in the USA, that in a favourable socio-economic climate, this concept can have an impact on industry far beyond the scope of the small and medium -sized businesses with which the profession is so often associated in Europe.

DIGITAL EQUIPMENT, FAIRCHILD, INTEL, APPLE COMPUTERS, which were all created with Venture Capital, were small businesses and are now large multinationals.

Finally, there is a ready association between Venture Capital, technological innovation and the setting up of businesses, since the most striking examples have sprung up in the rapidly developing technological sectors, a field in which Europeans are daily finding it increasingly difficult to make headway against American or Japanese competition.

However, American Venture Capital has provided a lifeline for many sectors of the economy, - distribution, services in general - by supporting businesses to the point where the financial market could take over. Thus, to consider Venture Capital simply as a financial technique for analysing risks, specializing to a greater or lesser extent in small technological businesses but capable of adapting to any socio-economic context, is to misunderstand the driving force behind it and deprive it of its deeper meaning.

Venture Capital has therefore to find fertile ground and it is significant that it has grown up in the United States, the prime example(if ever there was one) of a market economy, free enterprise, mobility and personal initiative.

In Europe, the profession has developed in a rather different fashion owing to local conditions and it was really not until the start of the 1980s that Venture Capital began to emerge after a long period of gestation, thanks to the fillip given by certain Member States to the profession either by introducing tax incentives or by partly covering the risk.

Although, in the whole of Europe, the profession transacts only about a quarter of the volume of business of its American counterpart - which is not to say that it is negligible - it must nevertheless be emphasized that there are wide differences between the various countries of Europe - between the United Kingdom, which alone represents more than half of the profession, France, the Netherlands, where Venture Capital is finally emerging as a force to be reckoned with, and Germany or Italy, where Venture Capital is still in its infancy.

Factors which are known to stunt the growth of Venture Capital, such as the fact that hiving off is a rare phenomenon, the idea that capital should be handed down, the limited scope of our national markets, all restrict the growth of emerging companies which cannot, by the same token, attract the talent necessary to further their growth internationally.

It is our job - and an honourable objective for our profession - to promote the setting up of businesses, help them to expand at national level and thus encourage the growth of small and medium-sized companies, but with stakes at their current level, we must have loftier ambitions if we, for our part, wish to make our contribution to the emergence of important companies at European level.

It seems to me, therefore, that the European Venture Capital Association, recently initiated by representatives of the profession from eight European Community countries with the backing of the Commission of the European Communities, has been set up at just the right time.

With 36 full members and 7 associate members, the Association has 1500 million ECU of capital invested in industry and seems to me, therefore, eminently representative of the profession in Europe, both in terms of the number and the quality of its members, and as regards the financial institutions behind them.

The EVCA will have three basic objectives :

- publicizing the idea of Venture Capital in its sphere of activity, making out profession known and promoting its image, particularly in those countries where it is still in its infancy ;

- furthering personal contacts and the exchange of ideas and information and helping to set up pools for transnational financing, thus enabling the companies which are financed to expand more rapidly on the external markets ;

- representing the profession at Community level in order to help solve the various kinds of problems which affect it directly.

These are, admittedly, ambitious objectives and we realize that they will not be quickly or easily attained, but are convinced that we have no choice but to learn to work together.

The EVCA is not a closed shop, it is an association open to all, Venture Capitalists or representatives of other professions, who are involved in its development and who, aware of the formidable challenges facing Europe, have resolved to broaden their national horizons by promoting in their own sphere the mobility of men, ideas and capital.

SESSION I:
NON-BANKING VENTURE CAPITAL INVESTORS
Experience, Constraints, Solutions

Superannuation Funds as Venture Capital Investors 17
D.J. PROSSER
CIN Industrial Investments Ltd., London (United Kingdom)

Industrial Venture Capital Investors 26
R.A. ONIANS
Director, Business Development, Monsanto Europe S.A., Brussels (Belgium)

Insurers as VC Investors. A Dutch View 34
D.S. VAN HOUT
General Manager, Investments and Corporate Finance, Ennia N.V., 's-Gravenhage (The Netherlands)

Collective Investment and Mutual Funds 48
G.D. DEAN
Managing Director, Electra Risk Capital P.L.C., London (United Kingdom)

Venture Capital Markets for the Regeneration of Industry
J.M. Gibb (Editor)
Elsevier Science Publishers B.V. (North-Holland)

SUPERANNUATION FUNDS AS VENTURE CAPITAL INVESTORS

D. J. PROSSER

CIN Industrial Investments

Summary

Superannuation funds are neutral regarding income and capital return so far as tax is concerned. This allows greater flexibility in the structuring of a proposal. The long term nature of pension funds means that they do not necessarily have to seek a short term flotation tc realise their gain on successful investments.

Our investment in the USA although small provided a window on technology as well as a window on structuring deals. The American venture capital market is so much larger and longer established than the British market. It will be difficult for international venture capital funds to develop in Europe. The language, legal and acounting problems mean that investment in small unquoted investments are best made at local level. While there will obviously be the individual exceptions in general the 'pro-active' element would be missing from a broadly based fund without the establishment of a local office. In most cases this would be too expensive for a foreign fund.

CIN Industrial Investments regard venture capital investments as referring to development capital and project finance as well as 'start-ups'. Approximately £180m. is invested in this area and there are fifteen executives in the management team. In 1983 £26m. was invested and realisations of £13m. were made.

CIN Industrial Investments which is the direct investment arm of the NCB Pension Funds have been involved in Venture Capital investments for about six years. Compared to some investors, particularly in the USA and perhaps one or two in the United Kingdom our experience is still relatively short. However, most of the United Kingdom investors have entered the market more recently. Indeed, the rate at which money has been committed to Venture Capital either from the public or allocated by institutions over the last year or so has been quite amazing. For example 16 funds have been formed so far this year under the United Kingdom Government's Business Expansion Schemes, and another 12 are in the course of formation. At the same time several intermediaries have started new funds solely for institutional investors.

Coming back to the experience of CIN Industrial Investments, perhaps I had better start by saying what we regard as a Venture Capital investment.

Personally, I do not regard Venture Capital as only referring to 'start-up' finance ie financing a project which is still in the concept or patenting stage. Obviously, 'start-ups' come within everyones defination of Venture Capital but most of the principals that I have met in this business do not restrict themselves to 'start-ups'. Most people would agree that 'development capital' or 'second stage finance', which is where a small company with a short trading record is seeking additional finance to expand its activities, is Venture Capital. In fact, most Venture Capitalists seem to have more money involved in 'development capital' and probably rightly so. After 'start-ups' and 'development capital' we come to areas which some investors do not regard as Venture Capital. 'Project Finance' is an obvious example where Superannuation Funds can invest for a long-term return but where some other Venture Capital funds would find it difficult to invest because of the lack of an obvious exit. I suppose that this is one of the major differences between a Superannuation Fund investor and any other Venture Capitalist. Because, in general, Superannuation Funds have a positive cash flow they can consider long-term returns from a growing income as attractive as a shorter term capital appreciation. Perhaps this is why I can regard 'project finance' as properly belonging under the Venture Capital heading and others do not. "Management buy-outs" seem to have created a niche of their own, I would regard both 'Management buy-outs' and 'leveraged buy-outs' as Venture Capital.

It may appear that I am going to include the whole of the Pension Fund portfolio under this category, but this is not so. Obviously, quoted security investments would normally be excluded. Also property would normally be excluded. I say normally because sometimes we have made investments in both areas where the risks, the potential returns, and the high level of management involvement have been similar to Venture Capital investments. However, I would follow the accepted reasoning that these two areas would not form part of a new Venture Capital portfolio. I am intrigued about how we will all deal with mature portfolios. At the moment we only have a small number of companies that have come to the public market and in our portfolio these are being left under their original categories. At some stage these investments will need to be treated like other parts of the quoted portfolio. My initial thoughts were that this should not be done for two years but obviously each case may require a different approach. I suppose in theory if there was a limited pool of money available for Venture Capital investment the investors should realise the investment at an early stage after quotation in order to finance further unquoted investment. Fortunately, we do not have that problem and can afford to continue with the quoted security.

After spending so long in discussing what I regard as a Venture Capital investment you will be pleased to know that as far as I am aware there is no dispute on the term 'Superannuation Funds', from now on I shall refer to them as 'pension funds'. It is worth considering the nature of pension funds compared with other types of investors. There are four particular characteristics I would mention, namely:- investments do not bear tax on either income or capital gain, the liabilities emerge over a long period of time; most pension funds have positive cash flow; the liabilities are generally linked to inflation.

The fact that pension funds are neutral regarding income and capital return, so far as tax is concerned, means that a pension fund investor can be completely flexible in structuring a proposal to suit the needs of the company. As I am sure you know in most Venture Capital deals the investor provides a mixture of equity capital plus some kind of loan or preference package. The need for this package approach is because in some cases an all equity package would put too high a valuation on the equity, or insufficient money would be raised to meet the needs of the business. This high equity valuation might mean that the entrepreneurs could not contribute for as much equity as either they or the investor might wish. This ability to tailor the financial structure of each individual deal to the needs of the business is one of the most attractive features of pension fund involvement in the Venture Capital area. At CIN Industrial Investments we have provided finance with equity participations which have ranged from loans secured on specific equipment in a 'high tech' process to loans subordinated to the bank and practically everyone else. In each case we looked at the investment on its merits, what the needs were, what the potential returns were and what the probability of success was. The analysis of the potential return often involves an estimate at some point in the future of the value of the business and our interests in it and in putting a value on the business we are not restricted to a particular time-frame.

Because the liabilities emerge over a long period of time CIN Industrial Investments and other pension fund investors are able to agree disposals on a flotation at the time that best suits the company. There is not the pressure that there might be in other funds, particularly funds with a limited life to realise dthe whole of the investment by a specific date. It is true that we do like to see companies coming to the public market and generally we like to make some of our holding available for other investors at that time. We believe that when a company becomes public it is better for the company to have wider ownership of the shares. However, we still have 14.6% of Tunstall Telecom an electronic/service industry company that came to the Unlisted Securities Market in June 1983. The public issue raised £1.4m. in new money for the company and allowed founder shareholders and the sole institutional investor, ourselves, to reduce our holdings from 26% to 14.6%. We were not under any pressure to reduce our holding. Everyone was able to agree on the needs of the company for new finance and the needs of the market place for a sufficient number of shares.

The fact that most pension funds have positive cash flow is well known and in itself probably attracts a continuous stream of proposals. "Deal flow" is not really a problem for large pension funds. Indeed the NCB Pension Funds had a significant "deal flow" in the Venture Capital area before the formation of CIN Industrial Investments. At that time the proposals tended to come from intermediaries. The change that has taken place over the last few years means that a large number of potential investments now come directly rather than just from stockbrokers and merchant banks as in the past. There is a need for the direct approach, and if pension funds are intending to be committed to this investment area over the long-term then they have to attract entrepreneurs to make direct approaches the funds. It was for this reason that we formed CIN Industrial Investments and the sister company CIN Industrial Finance.

These companies have a profile and investment style that is diferent fromn the NCB Pension Funds while at the same time being able to draw on the strengths of the main funds. One of the problems of attracting a large number of proposals is that they require considerable analysis. Often an entrepreneur needs advice in order to put his business plan into a shape that can be analysed. While we do some of this work in-house we are not able to do the whole exercise and prefer that the entrepreneur works with a firm of accountants. However, this need for advice does point to the major requirement of Venture Capital investment, good quality staff and I would like to come back to staffing requirements later.

The fourth characteristic that I mentioned for pension funds was that their liabilities are inflation linked. This means that there is a preference for inflation linked assets. This aspect can be quite important, if one can obtain a well secured inflation linked investment on a project it can be made quite attractive for a pension fund. It is sometimes possible to incorporate such a loan with a very low initial cost as part of a package. The use of low cost loans is limited but it can be a useful variation for the investees and we are talking to a company at the moment on the structure of such a package.

A portfolio need that I have not mentioned earlier is the requirement for diversification within the Venture Capital portfolio. Although this area will in general only be a small part of the total portfolio it is desirable to obtain a spread of risk within the portfolio. Most institutional funds, certainly insurance companies and pension funds, will recognise this requirement, but for other specialist Venture Capital funds it may be unsuitable. I do not believe our portfolio should only contain home computer companies, or film companies or be limited to any other narrow sector. Because most small companies are not vertically integrated it is necessary to look at the end product use to ensure that not too many companies in the portfolio are dependent upon one product or sector within the market. Within our portfolio we have companies in very basic industries as well as high growth "high-tech" companies. There are many companies that while providing a basic service within the economy can earn a good return on capital. Some of them can expand to quite decent size companies while remaining in their niche, others can sometimes expand into other related areas, sometimes with higher technology and higher value added content. These companies provide balance for our exposure to the computer, electronics and other potential high growth areas.

Since this is a European Community Symposium on Venture Capital it is relevant that I put some views on international Venture Capital and how our approach to Europe might develop. I must say that the problem I see for pension funds in international Venture Capital, is the ability of management to evaluate and monitor the investments. I think that it would be very difficult for a United Kingdom based pension fund to invest directly in small unquoted companies in the European countries. The language, legal and accounting problems would add to the commercial difficulties and make the exercise too time consuming to manage directly from the United Kingdom and it would probably be too expensive to establish a local office. The "hands on" or "pro-active" element is an important part of any Venture Capital investment and it would be missing without a local presence. It would be possible to invest through intermediaries and we do use this approach in the USA. Our approach in the USA has been to establish a close working relationship with one Venture Capitalist. We have a fund established in Santa Clara and Boston which gives us a presence in two strong high-technology Venture Capital areas. Not only do we receive a good 'deal flow' via our general partners; we have a constant window on the technology itself and on the largest market for high technology products. We also have a window on the structuring of deals. This latter point was particularly useful in our early years. The technology window is very useful now and will I am sure continue to be useful in the future. More and more of the technologically advanced products will be suitable for the whole of the developed world and the USA economy is such a major component. What is important about our American involvement is that there is a good reportimg and monitoring system which ensures we receive the insights as well as the commercial return.

One of the ways in which I think the European relationships between Venture Capitalists might develop is through the development of international markets for products. For example we would welcome approaches from small companies in Europe wishing to expand a United Kingdom subsidiary or seeking to develop additional products in the United Kingdom. Similarly, it would be useful for us to know of Venture Capital funds prepared to finance the expansion of United Kingdom companies within their own national boundries. I think that by having an economic involvement and by taking a "hands-on" approach the local Venture Capitalists can add substantially to the strength of a local subsidiary for the benefit of all concerned.

In entering the Venture Capital area some pension funds will wish to invest via specialist funds or using specialist intermediary management groups. CIN Industrial Investments have invested via specialist funds as well as developing our own internal team. The external funds initially provided a good window on deals and we have continued our involvement with them. The great advantage with these specialist funds is that they immediately provide experienced staff to evaluate and monitor investments. The quality of staff is important in all areas of investment but is particularly so in Venture Capital. As in other financial areas a variety of skills are required but because of the rapid growth of this area recently there sometimes are not enough good experienced people to go round. Some of the Business Expansion Schemes for example have not yet recruited their own managers but are using specialist external managers who had previously built up their experience with earlier institutional funds. The Business Expansion Schemes add to their funds under management and there may well be some synergy in having both types of investment funds under one house. While we do not have a Business Expansion Scheme under management at CIN Industrial Investments (we only manage NCB Pension Funds money) we have considered whether we should have formal links with such a fund. The obvious problem of such a link is we might end up in competition with ourselves. However, we have found with the existing external funds with which we are involved we are rarely in competition on individual deals and I would regard it as even less likely for a Business Expansion Scheme.

It may be of some interest if I tell you how we manage CIN Industrial Investments. I have mentioned the difficulty of obtaining good quality staff and I believe we have been very lucky in recruiting and retaining our executives. These operate in teams, usually three people to a team, one director, a manager and an assistant. This structure seems to work quite well both for monitoring and evaluating new investments. The director of each team has had a broad range of experience, is professionally qualified, sometimes with an MBA, and in each case has spent some years making Venture Capital investments. The managers and assistants are younger, less experienced but nevertheless do their share of both monitoring and evaluation. They do, of course, both work closely with their director. Each team has its own portfolio which is not specialised but has a wide spread of holdings. For initiating investments and building up a portfolio it is not necessary to have such a team structure. However, having invested in a company the investor has a greater responsibility to monitor and advise the small companies in the portfolio than would be the case for a portfolio of quoted companies. This "hands-on" or "pro-active" element varies from company to company but can at times be quite intensive in the use of management time. Obviously, it is important to us that we deal effectively with both the existing investees and new proposals. We have found that this team structure works very well for our style of long term investment and allows the right level of management involvement.

This 'hands-on' involvement is said by some to lower the risks involved in Venture Capital investment; I am not so sure. It seems to me that the greater risks with small companies are that in general they only have one product, in their early years their equity capital base is thin and they rarely have depth of management. The presence of a good Venture Capital investor can help on the management side by suggesting the right kind of non-executive directors and can certainly contribute themselves on the financial aspects. However, the success of the business will ultimately depend upon whether it can sell enough of a product at the right price. If the market disappears for a period of time these small companies often do not have the reserves to support themselves through to the next upturn. The investors can help and frequently do provide additional support but it must be on the basis of an early return to profitability. So I would say "hands-on" involvement can help but it does not eradicate the risks and the risks remain higher than an investment in a large multiproduct company with a good balance sheet. You must accept that I am generalising and these same risks can also produce corresponding rewards.

An aspect of American Venture Capital investment that does not appear to have shown its presence in the United Kingdom yet is the concept of a first round financing, with the sole intention of only providing enough capital to a second round financing. The idea is that the second round financing is done at a much higher price because the company is better established, but generally with negative cash flow and loss making on an on-going basis. This faith, in the ability to raise second round finance on better terms and the fact that it does happen, is probably a reflection of a much larger established Venture Capital market and of the continuing and steady flow of funds into Venture Capital. My impression of United Kingdom investors and our own fund in particular is that we try to finance a company through to the profitable phase. At the present time I think most investors would be reluctant to enter into an investment without feeling that they could deal with the financial commitments necessary to bring the company to profitability.

The number of people we have employed on Venture Capital investments, fifteen executives plus support staff, may seem large, certainly in comparison to the numbers employed in managing a quoted securities portfolio. The team we have are responsible for nearly £180m. of investments, of which approximately £50m. is in projects. The balance are in 120 company investments most of them involving some kind of equity/debt package. In many cases we have board representation sometimes we have nominated external directors, in other cases our own executives sit on the boards. We try to balance the needs of the company for a broadly balanced board with our own needs. The ideal is for us to recommend a non-executive director who has knowledge of a particular area of the business which would otherwise not be represented on the board. Often the entrepreneur has his own ideas about board structure and it is sometimes a delicate balance to obtain the best non-executive director.

When our own executives are involved on the board it does mean additional monitoring and for that reason we do try to limit the number of directorships each executive takes. We do not want to miss new viable deals because of the monitoring and so far this has not happened. In the year to April 1983 £26m. was invested and there were realisations of £13m. While the comparison with a quoted securities portfolio will not look good in terms of total funds under management or turnover, relative to management costs, the portfolio is quite large and quite active in comparison to other Venture Capital funds. While it is difficult to be exact I believe that the costs of managing investments in this area are at least 10 times more than managing a quoted securities portfolio for each £1 invested, if it is to be done properly. CIN Industrial Investments and the NCB Pension Fund trustees believe that the returns will justify these higher costs and we have faith in the Venture Capital investment area.

Venture Capital Markets for the Regeneration of Industry
J.M. Gibb (Editor)
Elsevier Science Publishers B.V. (North-Holland)

INDUSTRIAL VENTURE CAPITAL INVESTORS

Richard A. ONIANS, Director, Business Development,
Monsanto Europe S.A., Brussels

I am going to talk about corporate venturing, which is how our own corporation, an American corporation, has entered, and enjoyed being in the venture capital business - in Europe. Although corporate venturing is still in a relatively early stage of development, I will be presumptious enough to give advice to any corporate representatives here on how to get involved in this type of business in Europe.

I would like to start by defining what we mean by venture capital, because there are still a number of definitions and I think that, from a corporation's point of view, it is quite important to know what sort of venture it is embarking upon. In our terms, we are talking about equity capital investments, each investment being relatively small. The name of the game is wealth creation through capital gain, involving venture capitalists with minority holdings who are prepared to roll up their sleeves and indulge in some "hands-on" management. That is our basic definition of venture capital. As it relates to Monsanto, as you will see in a moment, we are dealing exclusively with high technology investment. That, of course, is just our particular preference, and it does not have to apply to everybody. My main theme will be the role of the corporation in the venture capital business and the benefits it can bring to itself and all concerned by playing this role.

Monsanto is a 6 billion dollar corporation - though that is not necessarily a qualification for anything, including being in venture capital. However, I suppose it is quite important to know that we spend over 300 million dollars a year in basic research; that is relevant to our venture capital activities. We are technologically an eclectic corporation; we indulge in a very wide range of activities, and each of those activities has its own technology component. For instance, being involved in animal nutrition means knowing about amino-acids, in agriculture about plant genetics, in health care about blood chemistry, and therefore bio-technology. We have 55,000 employees and have had the same number of employees for over ten years, even though the size of the company has trebled. Our first experience in venture capital was in the United States in 1972. At that time we took a partner, another industrial corporation called Emerson Electric; since we had very little involvment in electronics at that time, we considered there was no conflict of interest, and that has proved to be true. Our fund in the United States is called "Innoven", it is managed "at arms' length" outside the corporation, as will be explained later, by a group called L.A.R.. They are compensated by 20 % of the realized capital gains over an established period of time; we, of course, as prime investors, take 80 % of the capital gain. They have made 33 investments since 1972 and their current portfolio has 22 investments. Over the whole period - and I am talking here of realized gains -, we have made a 25 % return per year after tax on average. It may be the best thing we have consistently done over the last 12 years.

We started looking at Europe in 1979, but decided then that the climate was not quite ready. However, we kept a watching brief, and decided in 1982 to come into the market. We did it in partnership with the Advent Group, which of course is associated with T.A. Associates of Boston, Peter Brooke's organization. We linked up with the London end of that group, which was run by David Cooksey. We put in 50 % of a 10 million pound fund; a number of universities, namely, Cambridge, Oxford, Imperial College London, Harvard University and Boston University, together with the Nuffield foundation, put in 17 % as a group; financial institutions picked up the rest. We have made 14 investments to date, which I actually consider to be quite a rapid rate of investment, considering the short period we have been in business. We have not any real gains yet, though there are some paper gains. We are thus now well entrenched, we believe, in venture capital on both sides of the Atlantic.

If one subscribes to the Boston Consulting Group theory, then one knows that a corporation needs to be constantly renewing its portfolio of businesses. The more intelligence can be got from outside the organization to help decide what the corporation should become, the better. That is really the role that venture capital plays.

It is not done in isolation, of course; we do a number of other things. Many corporations going into this current recession, or should I say this past recession, have made a lot of money by divesting; in other words, by taking losses off their income statement, they have managed to show an overall greater return, and we have certainly used that method. We also maintain large internal research and development activities. We have many arrangements with the universities around the world, we buy technology in, acquire companies and, of course, constantly train and retrain our people and change the technology and people mix as that can also improve the income statement.

Venture capital is on an equal footing with any of those activities. What is its role for us in rather more specific terms?

First of all, it speeds up our decision process. I mean, as a 6 billion dollar corporation, we run internal management systems designed to make 100m. dollar decisions on average; trying to make 1/2 m. dollar decisions involves the same amount of paperwork, the same number of people; so, by using a venture capital vehicle, which is outside the corporation, it is possible to delegate authority and therefore speed up that decision-making process considerably.

It also gives us a "window" on small business growth patterns. When you are in a vast management complex, you tend to forget some of the basic and fundamental principles of business. How do you actually pay people on a Friday? I have operated many businesses in Monsanto and have never had to worry about legal implications or the mechanics of looking after people; it is more the motivation aspects that the management look after in a large organization, and you tend to forget what it is like to be actually running a small business, day after day, and having to decide every 24 hours whether or not the next day is going to bring you what you would expect. It is good for us to get that rejuvenation every so often.

Thirdly, it helps us to identify acquisition candidates because, when you see a small company at an early stage of development, you can imagine what it will be like in the future, and how it might fit your corporate strategy.

Curiously enough though, very rarely does acquisition actually take place. In the United States, in that portfolio of 33 investments over the last eleven years, we have in fact only bought into three of them, and have only bought one of them totally. So the strike rate is fairly low.

Of course it also gives you a window on other companies who live in the same environment as the small company within the venture capital portfolio. For instance, if the small company in the portfolio fails, it is usually for a competitive reason. You can then look at the competitor who was successful and judge whether he is a worthy acquisition candidate.

It gives you a window on emerging technologies - that is a fairly obvious thing to say. It does, however, also give you a window on technology interaction, in other words you can see how technologies come together in order to create businesses, and even how one of your technologies can interact with the technology of a small portfolio company to create an even bigger business in the future.

It also helps us to identify licensing options. Obviously, we can buy licenses from the portfolio companies or can sell them licenses.

It is an outlet for "management buy-outs". If we have a group of managers in the company who wish to buy a business from us, we have access to the venture capital community who arrange for them to be suitably financed.

There is no such thing as a deal where both sides should not be treated fairly, and we have to consider what we, as a corporation, do for the venture capital business itself. In the case of both our funds, we believe that we do provide a very useful service in technology assessment capability. Spending as much as we do on research and development, we have sophisticated information systems in technology, we have many people with in-depth knowledge of specific areas of technology. We make those resources available freely to both the funds in which we are involved, because it is in our interest to do so. This can also help the development of the portfolio companies.

Moreover, we can provide specialized management skills. One of the drawbacks of a large corporation can here be turned to an advantage. When you have large legal and patent departments, for instance, they tend to become fixed costs for large corporations. From our point of view, they can be as helpful as they wish to the portfolio companies and the venture capitalists, because they can provide their services at a very modest cost. I can't even think of an example where we have charged those services to an organization in which we have an equity stake. We can help them in things like professional project management in building a plant, or developing a project, we can help them with accounting techniques, etc. In other words, the corporate staff departments, which to us are basically fixed costs, can be made freely available through the venture capital funds to the portfolio companies.

We can provide product distribution capability in various countries. If a company in the U.K., for example, in which we have invested, wants to distribute its products in other countries, then we have large sales forces then can be prevailed upon to help.

That was the rationale for the corporation getting involved in venture capital at all. However, one can draw up a list "of do's and dont's", which are specific to manufacturing corporations and we believe are extremely important.

First of all the things that one should do:

You should certainly employ an "arms' length" management vehicle. We, in Europe, are using the Advent Management Group. They have a contract with the shareholders of our fund which is called "Advent Eurofund" and that contract is written in such a way that they have the maximum amount of autonomy in making the decisions needed to manage the portfolio. They are in the business of creating wealth for themselves and, of course, for their shareholders, but not to have their activity diluted by the whims and fancies of a large corporation.

The management contract has to make absolutely clear the rules of the game. The rules of the game are to invest in a venture capital situation where the wealth creation process for the entrepreneur and for the venture capital manager is paramount in the whole process. So, anything that we get out of it, such as our research and development window on the world, are really by-products and must be seen as such.

The fund has to be big enough. We in Monsanto believe that less than 15 to 20 million dollars as a fund size is probably inadequate to support the people who are needed to run such a fund.

One should also provide inexpensive, preferably free consulting resources out of your fixed costs. Also provide a competent and objective receptor mechanism. In other words, do not create a situation where the fund managers have to spend an inordinate amount of time finding their way around your organization. If they want a particular point discussed or agreed, appoint a person or a group who can be the entry point to the corporation and who does the internal legwork for them.

Commit your money over a significant period of time; do not say: "We will try you out for a couple of years". Ten years is in fact probably a good minimum period.

Compensate generously. The American formula of 20 % of realized capital gains over the trading period seems a good formula. As a guideline for the percentage of the value of the fund that could reasonably be devoted to the annual management fee I suggest 2.5 %.

Now, what should one not do?

You should not lay the same reporting requirements on your fund managers as you would lay on an internal division or operating unit. They should not be wasting their time on meeting your reporting requirements.

Secondly, do not panic when an investment fails; corporations have a way of having post-mortems whenever one of their own operating units fails. In the venture capital business it is par for the course. The U.S. statistics show that 15 % of portfolio companies fail anyway; so you will be crying on average one day per week on that basis!

There are some other activities that may be important to you as a corporate investor, but resist the temptation. Do not distract the managers from the task they have set out to do, do not steal their people and dilute their power or their wealth creation ability, and do not steal people from the portfolio companies.

Do not compete directly with them. Do not, when you see something in which they are about to invest, say: "Oh! That looks interesting, it is too good for venture capital", and then go in with an offer that obviously blows them out of the water. Do not demand an inside track on acquisitions. It is truly an arms'length process. The people who should be getting wealthy out of this process are the entrepreneur who had the guts to start a business, the venture capitalist who has taken the risk of investing in him and working with him to the point of success. They deserve to get at least the market rate when they decide that they want to be bought out by a major corporation, or take the business to a public market. Do not, I repeat, expect to have an inside track on acquisitions.

Let me just review the reasons why it is a very solid idea for a corporation to invest in venture capital.

It keeps you young as an organization; it enables you to go through the renewal process that every large organization should go through; you can see how the world of small business is operating and innovating; it costs you nothing if you do it well. Have good managers running the fund and leave them alone to do it; you can actually make money at it. It is a window on your technology options and the technology options of your competitors, which is also important.

It will help you, if you want to go to these extremes, to look at very long term trends and even the development of industrial society. I would say that one of the reasons why Monsanto has been interested in venture capital in Western Europe, in the last year or so, and will remain interested for many years to come, is because for us it is an evolving Europe that we see, a better Europe. Entrepreneurship is starting to happen, albeit slowly, and venture capital is an integral part of the process. In other words, we hope we can develop our business in Europe perhaps more rapidly than we originally intended to do by using the window on Europe provided by Venture Capital.

How should you do it? It is difficult, but in this case a big corporation has to discipline itself to be modest. Admit that there are people who can manage this particular situation better than you will ever be able to do it. Then employ them, or rather fund them and let them employ themselves. Create an efficient interface between yourself, as the corporate investor, and the fund management. Be generous, don't resent their success, fund their success and be patient. Be more patient than you would ever be with any of your own internal management groups. I thoroughly recommend Venture Capital for any corporate investor. I would certainly recommend it in Europe today. There are very few corporate investors, but there is a rapidly growing venture capital climate. We believe that it is going to be very significant to be in this business particularly if you are using high technology, and need to be more aware of your external options.

Thank you for your attention.

Venture Capital Markets for the Regeneration of Industry
J.M. Gibb (Editor)
Elsevier Science Publishers B.V. (North-Holland)

INSURERS AS VC INVESTORS.

A DUTCH VIEW

D.S. van Hout

General Manager Investments and Corporate Finance
Ennia N.V.

Summary

While Venture Capital is seen as a solution for structural problems facing the industry in the EC, there appears to be a wide gap between demand and supply.
Moreover, the ability of potential suppliers should not be overestimated. Despite their assistance in rebuilding the industry, the attraction of VC is considered to be not great enough to let traditional capital Market participants invest heavily.

After analysing the Dutch situation, the characteristics of the Dutch assurance business are explained. The main complexities faced are

- The contradiction between maximalisation of profit sharing and high risk equity loan financing.
- Underdeveloped stock markets.
- Experience and knowledge as suppliers of risk capital.

Analysis of the Dutch situation learns that a voluminous inflow of new risk-capital is needed to stimulate employment to a sufficient and acceptable level and further that in various sectors of the industry can be searched for hidden demand. However, on the supply as well the demand side a great number of obstacles have to be removed, of which taxation exit-instruments and operational support to young entrepreneurs are crucial

The attitude of (Dutch) Insurers to VC will despite the under-development of this new financing instrument, reflect their social, but also their corporate responsibilities.

1. INTRODUCTION

Following years of stagnation, recession, or at least in terms of unemployment, depression with perhaps more to come, in the ten member countries of the European Community there is a growing consensus of opinion: new ways to stimulate activity have to be sought. There is now widespread acceptance that wealth and employment can only be created in a lasting manner by the private sector and that throwing government money at problems does not solve them. Endeavours are being made to halt and reverse the growth of the public sector. Since November 1982, the European Commission has been urging the Governments of the Common Market Countries to overhaul their tax systems to improve private investment incentives and the flow of risk capital. The revival of productive investment is now seen as an economic priority by all governments.

So in most member countries governments, entrepreneurs and the financial communities began to seek ways of creating a more attractive environment for expanding young business. In my country, The Netherlands, plans are being executed now in which both insurance companies and institutional investors play an important role.
In what follows, I will briefly outline the Dutch situation, the formal position and policy-based responsibility of insurance companies in order to put our present and future role into prespective.

2. THE NETHERLANDS

For centuries, The Netherlands was an agricultural and trading nation. It is probably because of this that the greater number of companies are privately owned. One consequence is that we, unlike Great Britain, for example, do not have a very well-developed stockmarket and that could be the reason why Dutch investors are much more risk-averse than their British colleagues and always commit themselves to equity-investment on a very limited scale. There are, of course, other reasons for this attitude as well, such as the profit-sharing system of most Dutch life-assurers and the existing system of accounting rules that makes it attractive to invest in bonds, but it cannot be denied that the general investment environment in Holland has not been very equity-minded for a long time.

In so far as there was a willingness for equity investment this was opposed by the trend, which has existed since the end of the 1960's of high interest rates, shrinking international demand and the penalising of sound and healthy financing by our taxation systems all of which gave rise to a situation in which there was financially no longer any incentive to take more investment risk.
Because of very low to negative net returns, but also by leveraged debt financing in times when interest rates were relatively low, the average equity ratio decreased from 36% in 1970 to only 22% in 1982. Share issues were rate events even in the prosperous period which is now past.
Investors, private as well institutional, became professional risk-avoiders, which is not surprising, taking into account a spread between coupon rates and dividend yields of 6-8%! This situation made fairy stories of all textbooks on time management! More and more manager's schedules were filled up with financial management, thus paralysing commercial decisions. This trend was further aggravated by the strongly supported "welfare" policy in The Netherlands. The wealth-economy, based on theory, and which was popular in the second half of the sixties, took care of a considerable increase in public spending.
In my view, the turning point was not only the two recessions we have suffered of late, but also and to a greater extent the recently growing awareness that a structural unemployment problem was emerging, caused by maturing industries, a falling demand, automation and demographic factors as postwar baby booms.

In this context the Netherlands is facing some specific problems. Though 50% of total employment is found in the smaller industries, a notable part is offered by the so-called large and key-industries. Those industries contributed heavily to the growth and wealth of the sixties and seventies. Nowadays however the petrochemical, shipbuilding, steel and construction industries are more or less mature and without large capital spending programs.

The availability of gas protected some of those industries somewhat against total disruption. Large, subsidy-schedules were offered by the government to save employment (RSV, Ogem are large examples).
For 3 years now the Dutch government has been becoming more and more convinced that we need a rejuvenation of commercial business and that the time to stress an expansion policy as a solution and to bail out mature industries is over.

Measures have been taken or proposed by industry to stimulate investments generally in 3 ways:

1. Lowering the tax and social security burden:
   * corporate taxes will be reduced from 48% to 40%,
     As a first step they will be reduced to 43% in 1984.

   The contribution of industry to the welfare schedules is to be transferred to the employees.
   * subsidies on capital investment (5 billion) (negative taxation).

2. Simplification or withdrawal of many restrictive regulations.

3. Specific measures
   * P.P.M. (Particuliere Participatie Maatschappij = Private Venture Investment Company)
     In 1981 the Dutch government announced that for a certain class of venture capital companies it was prepared to bear up to 50% losses realised.

     Since then 25 companies have been founded.
   * M.I.P. (company for industrial projects)
     Instigated by the ministry of Ec. Affairs, this investment

company was founded in 1982 with support from institutional investors, banks etc.
The capital base, which will grow up to ƒ 1 billion, will be used to assist financially sound larger industrial projects on commercial terms.

3. THE INSURANCE INDUSTRY

3.1 General

Notwithstanding a broad social security system in the Netherlands, the insurance industry in my country is well developed. The industry controls app. Dfl. 100 billion in assets, of which some Dfl 25 billion are abroad to take case of foreign liabilities.
Despite this, funds available for venture capital companies are not large. This is not due to any unwillingness on the part of the insurance industry to make such funds available, but reflects the way the insurance industry in the Netherlands is accustomed to operate.

Like any industry with a normal social behaviour pattern one of our short and long term goals is social acceptability, which may be translated as follows:

* to meet the needs of the consumer
* to have an acceptable investment policy
* to achieve sound and healthy solvency, which in turn is to be assured by the realisation of profits
* to provide employment.

One of the very important consequences of "meeting the needs of the consumer" is that the major life insurance companies in the Netherlands offer profit-sharing schemes to their policyholders, mostly with a guaranteed level of interest, or interest rebates on premiums. You will understand, ladies and gentlemen, that this has a considerable influence on the investment attitude of these companies. At Ennia we do this (on a voluntarily basis in the legal sense and on an obligatory basis in the economic sense) by matching assets and liabilities.

Or to put it into a banking perspective, life insurance companies are becoming to a greater and greater extent an interest margin industry.

This economic necessity is reflected in the company's balance sheet:

only 6% and a maximum of 15%, of the assets of the insurance industry is in stocks and real estate respectively, the remainder being invested in fixed income securities such as bonds, private loans and mortgages.

So here is the problem:

On the one hand, our clients ask for profit-sharing on an earned interest basis to assure and secure their pension-schemes on an economically justified basis.

As insurers we acknowledge our clients wishes and without intending to run into severe solvency problems the resulting code-word is then matching. On the other hand our clients ask us, through their democratically elected members of parliament to contribute to the restructuring of the country, a considerable proportion of whose savings (some 20%) is in our custody .

But this restructuring of investments, in general, does not cope with the above mentioned matching-requirements, of course.

So far, the supply problems. Incidentally, insurers, are not the only ones facing these problems.

For mostly the same basic reasons bankers are no more willing than we are to take high risks on assets meant as a hedge against high yielding liabilities. However, an exemption is to be made, or least in theory, for Pension Funds. Their liabilities are for the greater part also interest-bearing but on a lower yield basis.

3.2 Insurers and Innovation

Let me first of all make a few of remarks to avoid any misunderstanding.

* An inflow of money is too simple a solution.
  Although research in Canada by M.I. Kostuck and also in the Netherlands shows that those starting up in business believe financing to be their main problem.

I do feel that it is mostly the expected return/interest ratio that breaks up financing negotiations.

* Innovation is not made by venture capitalists, but by well trained entrepreneurs in existing companies or those just starting up.

* Venture capital is commercial business. It is profit-oriented for the sake of investors and entrepreneurs. It guarantees correct competition and prevents misallocation of production means. Capital-cost reductions are only acceptable in the short term, to be corrected afterwards with the infant industry argument, borrowed from the "theory on international economics", in mind.

* Venture capital is not the only way of financing the restructuring.
It is a good idea to understand that the path of progress and restoration will be walked for the greater part by existing innovative industry. Financing means for new necessary projects will be found in existing, renewed and new instruments:
- retained profits
- share issues
- issues of preferences shares
- convertibles
- subordinated loans
- long term borrowings, in combination with warrants.

* Without a major investment cycle -(in the sense of capital spending)- there will be no rejuvenation of the international economy on a sustained basis.

The basic conditions for such a cycle are the same for the past as for the future, namely:
- low interest rates
- deflation
- stability

Back to the insurers position.
In making available longer term corporate loans, insurers accept their social rèsponsibility. Although demand from industry has been very low in recent years, my company for instance, stayed in that market all the time. But can we go further; can we expand our investments in the equity market and even more, can we search aggressively for opportunities in emerging industries? In answering my first question, apart from my remarks on matching requirements, we face some technical difficulties in the Dutch market.

Table: Market Value of quoted shares and total investment, as % GNP.

	Investments	Market value
Belgium	10	10
Germany	10	12
France	14	11
Netherlands	70	21
U.K.	50	47
U.S.A.	42	40
Switzerland	87	113

In comparison with other industrialised countries, but also in a strictly Dutch analysis, The Netherlands is a country with large savings and an underdeveloped stock market.
So from a technical point of view, Dutch institutions can hardly enlarge their stockholdings as a percentage of their assets without disturbing an entire stock market. Anyhow I see one solution for participating on a larger basis: if double taxation (on profits and dividends) were to be abolished, we should see a whole series of new issues and it is my opinion that nor only private individuals but almost certainly institutions as well, would easily absorb the new issues against share prices reflecting a bearable cost of capital to the issuer.

4. VENTURE CAPITAL IN THE NETHERLANDS

4.1 An Overview

Young entrepreneurs are once again appreciated in the Netherlands. This new climate has not accelerated their activities. As in the end of the fifties in the USA, at least 3 problems need to be solved:

- Profit expectations of existing industries are too low or, without a comparatively good success ratio of existing industry, who will take the risk of starting up young companies?
- Security. After a period of fast wealth growth, technicians and scientists prefer security with governments or multinationals as employers;
- Lack of financing instruments to set up new technology companies.

Except perhaps for the security argument we are facing these problems in every economic cycle, knowing that unemployment has risen to unacceptable levels and that there is at least a need to equal the progress in technology of other industrialised countries; the old instruments are just not enough.

This evaluation is not new. There is broad consenus in the Netherlands that we need a large number of new enterprises each year. The report of the Committee on Venture capital in 1982 with the title "Start and Innovation" gave the following figures. In employment terms: the Netherlands needs at least 300.000 - 400.000 new jobs plus - according to research done by Prof. Birck in the USA - approximately 8% of the industrial workforce a year of job obsolescence. In my country that means a requirement of another 150.000 jobs a year.

Given a planning period of 3 - 4 years, some 250.000 jobs a year must be created, of which 50% must be created by emerging industry if statistics of the past may be extrapolated.
In creating these 125.000 jobs statistical research gives the following data:

Jobs	Investment per job	equity need yearly
125.000	app. Dfl. 35000/ equity capital	Dfl. 4,00 billion
	Jobs per company	Companies needed yearly
125.000	4	30.000

So studying the theoretical demand two questions arise:

1) Is there some Dfl 4 billion available in the risk capital market on a yearly basis?
2) Knowing that nowadays only 15.000 companies a year start up, is there any chance of stimulating entrepreneurship, so as to create another 15.000 companies?

The first question ladies and gentlemen is easily answered. My reply to it would be "yes".
But in transferring the available capital stream problems arise:

- there is a lack of commercially viable projects
- the traditional investing community (banks, pension funds, insurers) are not equipped for venture investing
- attractiveness of venture capital in terms of the return.

With this in mind, one is justified in being afraid to answer the second question. With the present state of the economy and the resulting investment / climate, we fear that there is little chance of realising that objective (30.000 starters a year).

Let me make a short analysis of factors that are holding back achievement:

* The demand-side

- almost 50% of potential starters lack enough equity to set up their own business

- incomplete management: most starters do not have commercial and financial management skills as well as organisation. Often this is an important barrier to founding an enterprise
- though basis-innovation is the prime responsibility of existing larger industry, there is more room for spin-off's
- young enterprises especially in the technology sector must absorp huge development and research costs. Starting losses up to as much as 80% of the equity are normal, while pay-back periods are long (up to 6-8 years)
- starters know they are almost on their own. Support at reasonable cost is essential
- regulation / overregulation kills activity.

* Supply-side

- professional captains of finance are not too enthusiastic about financing enterprises or projects whose main characteristics are little equity and almost no collateral
- the cash requirements of emerging industry are mostly immediate. Without a clear corporate strategy and a trustworthy return perspective it is difficult to demand quick decisions
- returns on financings in the early years are too moderate to cover the capital costs of banks or institutions (matching)
- private capital is difficult to obtain, except from entrepreneurs
- risks: research shows that only 40% of starters (industrial and non-industrial) survive the first 6 years.

What has been done so far in the Netherlands to eliminate these problems?

1. "Particuliere Participatie Maatschappij" have been in existence since 1981. These investment companies, once admitted by the Dutch Central Bank, enjoy a guarantee of up to 50% of paid-up capital. Within slightly more than two years 25 PPM's were founded. Shareholders of these companies are mostly banks, institutional investors and some industries.
2. MIP: for large commercially viable projects the "Maatschappij voor Industriële Projecten" was founded in 1982 by the Dutch government. Co-participants are once again members of the

capital market (Banks, Pension Funds, Insurers).

3. Government Program for deregulation.
4. Specific expertise is (going to be) offered by a large number of governmental and private institutions. The transfer of knowledge on marketing, electronics, management techniques and operational support is growing fast.

4.2 The Future

Having 30.000 starters and 50.000 jobs a year as an objective I do feel that notwithstanding a brighter outlook than some years ago, more can be done to stimulate new growth by specific incentives and measures, which remove in part the aforementioned stumbling-blocks. Some recommendations are to be made to the government about tax matters: it would be wise to allow starters a period of 5 years during which they could make good their losses even with income earned in the past as individual employees. On the Supply side I would suggest making investments in VC tax deductable, thus encouraging private institutions and individuals to invest in less secure projects. But there is also work to be done for capital markets participants: there is a strong need for specific financing instruments to help entrepreneurs in the critical stage of their companies. In the field of Support here is a lot to be learned from America's SBIC's. I think that the support of shareholders is more important than the employment of consultants, who are working for these companies on too free a basis.
And very important : disposal procedures, or how to get rid of your successes: in the USA in the past 20 years an active over-the-counter-market has developed. Except perhaps in the U.K. there is almost no opportunity in Europe for realising capital gains on theoretically well appreciated shares in successful companies. Reviving the almost forgotten organisations of our post-capitalistic society without the chance of a proper reward is far from attractive.

4.3 Insurers and VC

Perhaps the best way to illustrate this is to tell you about our own activities in the VC-area.
Although my company is among the most active in this field in the Netherlands, I think our investment behaviour is comparable with that of our colleagues.

After the second world war we tried to help restore the economy by investing in the share capital of smaller companies. Speaking of disposal procedures, I can tell you that over 50% of them are still in our portfolio. To our great satisfaction the majority are real survivors. During the long growth period after the war, there was almost no call for our capital funds, other than normal industrial bonds and private loans.

Some 3 years ago, we concluded that one of the ways of restructuring our economy was to participate in emerging industry by means of venture capital. Although we had the money, we did not feel ourselves well equipped.
The analysis of opportunities seemed to be the lesser problem, but giving operational support would sooner or later prove to be extremely difficult if not impossible and too labor-intensive. That was also, one of the lessons we learned in the fifties by the way. We decided, not yet having sophisticated venture financing opportunities in the Netherlands, besides using common, but somewhat in flexible, financing instruments, to start learning projects. Our first project was to invest in a USA based venture-capital Partnership. One of our conditions was to learn on the sideline about selecting, screening and following up interesting projects. I am happy to say that our teachers were good; that means: not only were they friendly but they were also good commercially. Our second project was a research one in the Netherlands together with 2 other parties, neither of whom were institutional investors. After extensive study, we concluded that there were more than 10 areas in the Netherlands sufficiently attractive to invest in commercially. Among the developing areas we now include computer services, plastics, glass, metal stamping,

publishing, medical products, wholesaling, leasing, energy conservation, horticultural and agricultural technology and applications of electronics.

From the beginning we felt that, our own investment departments were not well equipped for managing Venture Capital Funds, if support was one of the objectives. These departments were staffed by people with financial and economic backgrounds, not entrepreneurs.

Therefore we decided to use our funds in two ways to activate these markets:

- we participate in 4 Dutch-based venture and small equity funds and the aforementioned MIP
- we reserve investment capital to supply companies directly with (subordinated) loans after the first stage of their existence.

At present total investments in this sector are approximately Dfl 25 millions.

That is not, in guilders, a very huge amount. Still I do think that relative to one size , we are the biggest VC investor among the Dutch institutional investors. However, we realise, ladies and gentlemen, that our efforts so far are relatively small. We think that there is a strong need to seek out demand and that suppliers require more incentives to make capital available.

Information for entrepreneurs, tax incentives and disposal procedures have to be developed to make VC a success in the Netherlands, a success that is needed to restore a growth economy with sufficient employment and return for the participants. And I am absolutely sure that under these conditions, the capital that is needed, will be there.

Thank your very much.

Venture Capital Markets for the Regeneration of Industry
J.M. Gibb (Editor)
Elsevier Science Publishers B.V. (North-Holland)

COLLECTIVE INVESTMENT AND MUTUAL FUNDS

Gordon D. DEAN

Managing Director of Electra Risk Capital P. L. C.,
London

Although the brochure describing this session refers to the growing venture capital industry in Britain, it is still in its infancy and I always use that excuse when I have to tell you that I have not yet graduated to slides or visual aids. Accordingly, I cannot therefore offer you any distraction from the tedium of my monologue.

Introduction to British Venture Capital

Venture capital in Great Britain until recently, was provided in small and spasmodic amounts by the merchant banks - usually if they were having a good year and felt justified in some speculation, particularly if they could write it off immediately against the profits. Such a write-off was usually justified because banks are principally in the business of lending money and never really understood the ramifications of venture capital. Having lost their money in the speculation, they then immediately withdrew from the market.

Over the last two years however venture capital in the U.K. has become established as a specialist financial operation and has been given considerable stimulus by the Government. There are some forty members of the newly formed British Venture Capital Association and they have under management approximatively £500m. invested in or available for venture capital investments.

This development has been greatly encouraged by the Government and, of course, the immense menu of grants and soft loans which the Government and the European Economic Community have made available in certain circumstances. However, I want today to dwell on one particular aspect of the British Venture Capital Industry and Government involvement. That is what is known as the Business Expansion Scheme.

Business Expansion Scheme - Legislation

Some 2 1/2 years ago the Government set up the Business Start-Up Scheme to stimulate investment by individuals - not institutions - in new or young companies and the Scheme involved providing tax relief against the individual's income for the relevant year up to the amount of the qualifying investment. In the course of placing this legislation on the Statute Book, the United Kingdom Inland Revenue Authority came close to heart failure but eventually succeeded in introducing so many convoluted and tortuous measures to prevent the abuse and misuse of the relief that finally nobody understood it, let alone was able to take advantage of it to any significant extent. As a result, of this poor response, the Government broadened the scope of the legislation this year into what is now known as the Business Expansion Scheme. The principle paradoxically results from the extortionate tax rates experienced in recent years in Britain and assumes that if the individual has any money left over at the end of the day, he will want to make a speculative investment. In fact, the top rate of personal tax on incomes (both earned and unearned) is 75% and the principle of the relief is to allow an individual investor to deduct from his assessable income, the amount of the qualifying investment. The main features therefore are : -

1. An individual can invest in aggregate up to £40,000 in any one tax year and , if he is in the top tax bracket, will get relief on the whole of that sum namely, £30,000.

2. The investment must be in the basic, common or ordinary share capital of the business and must not have attaching to it any preferential or unusual rights.

3. The investment cannot be sold for 5 years.

4. The shares of the company cannot be quoted on any recognised stock exchange.

5. The company's trade must be mainly in the United Kingdom and is defined by the legislation by exclusion. Most manufacturing and service operations qualify but activities relating to the provision of finance and dealing in commodities have been excluded. Profitting from cocoa futures or quite simply lending money are obviously regarded by the Government as nefarious activities which do not need their stimulus, I think, understandably.

Advantages of the Business Expansion Scheme

As you will appreciate, this is a generous and possibly unique fiscal incentive although it must be emphasised that it is not a tax scheme. The giving of the relief to individual investors is therefore designed to achieve three things : -

a) to encourage the making of risk investments which the individual would not otherwise make.

b) To enable the investment to be retained for a 5 year period and,

c) to compensate for the obvious lack of income which in any event would be of limited benefit ot the high rate tax payers.

The risk/reward ratio is significantly improved by the tax relief of up to 75% of the amount invested and you will appreciate therefore that even if the gross investment does not appreciate in value at all over the minimum 5 year period, or indeed any longer period, the investor will be making a straight profit on his residual investment of 300%, ignoring of course the carrying costs of the time involved.

Approved Investment Funds

The Government's original intention was that individuals should seek out and make their own separate investments but in general this has not worked because the opportunities, while they may have been there, have not been focused on the potential investors and the only point of contact really has been through the stockbroking community. The success of the Business Expansion Scheme so far therefore has been through investment funds which have been approved by the Inland Revenue for the purpose of investing under the Business Expansion Scheme. My own organisation Electra Risk Capital were the pioneers in this technique since we conceived the desirability of corralling as many individual investors as possible into a mutual fund and investing and managing the money for them. I will not bore you with the tedious administrative implications of this structure but the concept has been attractive to individual investors who, while investing through an approved investment fund remain the direct beneficial owners of the shares in all the underlying companies where we invest their money. These funds therefore have three advantages : -

1. They give the investor the opportunity to invest and consequently get the tax relief.

2. The high risk element is spread over a large number of investments.

3. The individual investors have the benefit of specialist and experienced management who negotiates and supervises their investments.

We ourselves have under management some £20m. to date and other funds are now springing up like the weeds in my garden. I estimate that during the current tax year - which incidentally for some reason I cannot possibly explain ends on the 5th April, 1984 - total investment under the Business Expansion Scheme will amount to some £50m. to £60m. This you will think is a relatively small figure but I should say that it only is part of the total venture capital industry in the U.K. and since the legislation will remain in place for a few years yet, it is expected that increasingly greater use will be made of it to invest in unquoted companies, bearing in mind that the relief extends to any companies whether they are starting-up or whether they have been in business for hundreds of years and are well established.

Our Experience, Constraints and Solutions

Our experience at Electra Risk Capital has not been dull. When we started in business under the Business Start-up Scheme as it was then known, the legislation was very limited and I felt that I was running a charity for beleaguered entrepreneurs. I learned very quickly that you do not simply draw a cheque on day 1 and hope that it pops up as a multiple of your original investment at the end of 5 years. The management of risk or venture capital funds is very intensive and cannot be undertaken without skilled and experienced people from industry. It bears little resemblance to the lending activities of a bank.

Also venture capital falls into a surprisingly large number of categories. For instance, it covers seed corn capital more or less to identify the operation, it covers the research and development stage, start-up capital is required to get a business off the ground, second stage capital is invariably required to achieve the break-through into profits although I am bound to say that this is very often a euphemism for the fact that they have quite simply run out of money, third stage capital is required to broaden the base of the business and expand operations, fourth stage capital just prior to a merger or a flotation, rescue capital where a business is being bought from a liquidator or receiver or is in serious trouble and capital for management buy-outs currently very topical to enable the managers of a business as the name implies to acquire that business from its existing owners.

Whichever category the investment initially falls into there is one common feature and that is that these 'whiz kid' managers are always running out of money and, as they will tell you, for reasons quite beyond their control. I have learned to expect telephone calls around the 25th of every month bearing in mind that the salaries and wages are payable at the end of the month.

The lesson from this as I have indicated already is that sophisticated experienced and intensive management is required on the part of the fund manager. The Americans have coined the description 'hands on' management, a title which to me indicates some form of obscure religious ceremony rather than close involvement in the venture capital industry. The management is required to cover three main areas : -

1. The investigation of the business and the negotiation of investment terms. Successful venture capital investments will be borne out of a thorough independent appraisal of the business, its technology and its market. Objective opinions are in fact difficult to obtain because those giving the opinions are usually frightened that you will blame them when the investment goes wrong. Part of the skill therefore is to arrive at a pragmatic and objective judgment of all facets of the business but of course the main criterion is

the quality of the entrepreneur and his team. A good balance between the disciplines is very difficult to achieve - many entrepreneurs have such faith in their product that they assume its magnificance will sweep the market. They often quickly find out that it is not that easy and part of the job of running a fund is to be prepared to augment and even replace the original management.

As to the technology, we live in an age when computers and communications represent the vast majority of our investment opportunities. I have had to adopt the investment standard myself that if I do not understand the product, it must be a good investment. As managers, you cannot achieve any degree of specialist knowledge in the technologies and to retain the services of, for instance, a computer software expert is not advisable because once he is out of his natural environment, he rapidly ceases to be an expert. The investigatory procedures therefore present many problems but must be given very great emphasis by the fund manager who must always be asking himself what can really go wrong and how can a young company insulate itself from all the dangers which beset it in establishing itself.

2. The second stage where the management is important is the completion of the negotiations, the agreement of terms and the making of the investment. Immediately I have agreed to make an investment, I fix the closing date because I know that the lawyers and the accountants will otherwise expand into infinite space and we will never make the investment. I sometimes think that the only people who are really making money in the venture capital market are the lawyers these days.

3. The third, and probably the most important management role involves the supervision of the investment. To do this the management organisation needs experienced industrial people who understand the problems of the small and medium sized company and people who can establish a good working relationship with the management of the company. A fund cannot rely on a meeting once a month followed by a big lunch and a chat about the future of the business. Almost continuous contact must be maintained with the company and financial reporting procedures are absolutely paramount. The company must be disciplined to producing detailed figures at regular intervals and, as part of those figures, must update its cash projection for the coming months and, of course, be able to justify the profile shown therein.

Conclusion

It has been demonstrated in the U.S.A. that investment in small companies is consistently more profitable. The object of Electra Risk Capital and the other funds in the United Kingdom is to make profit. We have no altruistic objective and we are using the Government legislative stimulus to make profit for the entrepreneurs, our investors and of course ourselves. Happily the days of the malingering corporate leviathans are beginning to pass and the Government's policy of returning some of these businesses to the private sector will hasten that process.

As fund managers, we are generally looking for the bigger deals very often involving not less than £250,000 and in our case, anything up to £5 m. in any one company. The mutual fund organisations in the venture capital industry are therefore not able to finance the very small businesses, the single unit retailer or the small engineering shop for instance. This area will continue to be starved of capital largely because the efforts of the smaller entrepreneur can usually not be sufficient to reward that capital. We are therefore looking to back people who by their own endeavours and skills want to be personally wealthy at the end of the day. If we are able to identify these entrepreneurs and the business is carried on with the right incentives and enthusiasm for all those in it, the knock-on effect will be considerable and the benefit to the U.K. economy in the fullness of time will materialise.

SESSION II:
TAXATION AND INNOVATION FINANCING
Positive and Negative Impacts of Taxation

Taxation and the Financing of Innovation. Comparison of the Different Rules in Force in the European Community 57

P. FONTANEAU

Professeur Agrégé des Facultés de Droit, Avocat à la Cour d'Appel de Paris (France)

The Taxation of Collective Institutional Investors 70

D. O'HOGAN

Partner, Arthur Young & Company, Chartered Accountants, Dublin (Ireland)

Tax Treatment of the Individual Investor 75

C.A.M. RASENBERG

General Manager, Tax Department, Amsterdam–Rotterdam Bank N.V., Amsterdam (The Netherlands)

Impact of Tax Changes on Venture Capital Investments and Innovation in the USA 86

P.T. KAPLAN

Tax Consultant, Weil, Gotshal Manges, New York City (United States of America)

Venture Capital Markets for the Regeneration of Industry
J.M. Gibb (Editor)
Elsevier Science Publishers B.V. (North-Holland)

TAXATION AND THE FINANCING OF INNOVATION

Comparison of the different rules in force in the European Community

P. FONTANEAU
Professeur Agrégé of the Faculties of Law and Economics
Avocat à la Cour d'Appel de Paris

Summary

Taxation plays an essential role in the financing of innnovation. Fiscal incentives towards innovation do exist in all the countries of the European Community.

In order to develop the market for risk capital, European countries have taken measures both for the reduction of the risk of such investment, and to improve its net return.

As a means to aid the financing of enterprises engaged in innovation, measures have been introduced to make the purchase of shares in such enterprises attractive, and to improve the capacity of such companies to finance investment from their own resources.

In order to improve their profitability, specific measures have been introduced concerning research and the early stages of innovation.

Nevertheless, fiscal incentives limited narrowly to assist innovation have shown themselves to be insufficient, where general rules for the taxation of individuals and companies impose such high levels of tax as to discourage the entrepreneur.

When all these matters are taken into account, and the importance of innovation for the growth of the European Community is realised, it becomes obvious that a tax policy must be developed, which takes account of the whole process of innovation, in a coherent manner.

This Tax Code for Innovation should be coordinated at Community level, in order to restore the competitive capacity of European enterprises vis à vis their principal competitors, namely the United States and Japan.

I. INTRODUCTION

Innovation is a complex process, which passes from a primary stage, that of research and invention, to the commercial stage : the sale of products or the licensing of patents. The process is long, one of very high risk, and one which implies serious investment. That investment must needs consist of own resources in very large part.

Thus, the examination of the effects of tax on the financing of innovation deals with three areas :
- the development of a market in risk capital ;
- aid to the financing of enterprises engaged in innovation ;
- improvement of the profitability of enterprises which innovate.

2. TAX AID TO THE DEVELOPMENT OF THE MARKET IN RISK CAPITAL

To give aid to the development of a market in risk capital, some countries have modified the rules for the taxation of dividends, or that of capital gains. Provision has been made for the deduction from taxable revenue of the value of new shares ; fiscal rules for institutional investment have been improved, as have rules for "venture capital" companies, and the tax status of financial investment, for example in the rules for the taxation of capital.

Broadly, these measures have sought :
- to reduce the risk element attached to the investment,
- and to improve its profitability.

21 The reduction of risk attached to the investment :

The principle actors in the reduction of risk have been investment companies and institutions.
Yet, these bodies cannot correctly carry out their task except to the extent to which they benefit from "fiscal transparence" : distributions arising to them must only be taxed at the level of shareholders or participators, who have a right to tax credits.

22 <u>Improvement of the net return on the investment</u> :

To this end, two kinds of fiscal incentives have been put forward :
- tax deductions for fresh investment in company stock ;
- limiting or suppressing the double-taxation of dividends.

221 <u>Deduction from income or tax due on investment in enterprises</u> :

This technique may permit the deduction of investment made, either from an individual's taxable income, or from the tax otherwise found due.

The first technique has been introduced in Belgium and the United Kingdom. The second has been instituted in France, under the Finance Act 1983. These techniques will be further gone into, below, n° 312.

222 <u>Reduction or suppression of the double-taxation of distributions</u> :

The double-taxation of distributions at a company level and at shareholder level, reduces the attractiveness of such investments.

The most widely practiced technique in E.E.C. countries for the reduction of this form of double taxation is the tax credit (1).

Those general rules have been supplemented by temporary and special measures in many countries.

In Belgium, companies freshly created or which make an increase in capital in 1982 or in 1983 enjoy a limited exemption from tax in respect of the new shares or other forms of participation which represent new liquidity brought into the enterprise (2).

Succession and gift duties are not exigible on certain shares and participations in Belgium (3).

In France, capital gains of minor importance on shares and participations are exempt from tax (4).

Where dividends are paid between companies, account must be taken of the tax systems applicable to groups (5). These special provisions exempt or limit the tax payable by the distributor company, leaving the tax to be paid by the distributee. Special rules have also been made, in some countries, to favour investment companies. In these cases, the tax is ultimately due on a consolidated result of the group (6).

3 TAX EFFECTS ON THE FINANCING OF ENTERPRISES ENGAGED IN INNOVATION

Under this head are to be included a number of different tax provisions. The taxation on increase of capital, rules for group taxation, provisions for deduction of dividends paid on new shares, for the tax deductibility of investments made in new shares, fiscal transparence among small and medium enterprises, all these measures play their part.

In this diversity, two lines may be distinguished which encourage new enterprise :
- provisions made to attract outside investors : all the rules in favour of new shares, in fact ;
- those provisions which aid the enterprise to finance its development from own resources.

31 Tax measures tending to encourage outside financing of enterprises which innovate :

311 Belgium :

Royal Decree n° 15, of 9 March 1982, contains new measures meant to encourage subscription or purchase of Belgian shares (7). These measures include :
- exoneration from corporation tax of dividends paid by companies -corresponding to the new, fully-paid, shares- and a correlative right of exoneration for individuals from income tax as well as taxes on successions and gifts.
- purchases or subscriptions of new shares are deductible within the framework of income tax.

As regards the company issuing the shares, the rules are as follows :

- the exemption from tax is equal to 8 % of the value of the newly created capital at par, whenever one of these operations is carried out, and is valid over 5 accounting periods from issue.

- the rate of exemption is raised to 13 % if the company formally undertakes and holds to its undertaking (which is to be set out in the prospectus, if there is a public issue, or in the formal documents for the original issue or increase in capital, if otherwise) to give the entire benefit of the tax saving to the holders of the new shares, or to redistribute the relevant portion of income realised by it in the same manner.

312 <u>France</u> :

The Finance Act 1983 has made changes in what was known as the "Monory" scheme : that scheme came to an end on 31 December 1982 (8).

Under the new law, the taxpayers may benefit each year by a reduction in tax equal to 25 % of his net purchase of French shares, made between 1 January 1983 and 31 December 1987 : such purchases must be placed in a share savings account with an authorised agent.

Further, Article 60 of Law number 76-1232 of 29 December 1976, which has become Article 214 A of the French Tax Code (C.G.I.) (9) authorises French share companies which issue or increase their capital between 1 January 1977 and 31 December 1987 to deduct from their taxable profits dividends paid on shares so issued : this may be done during the first 7 or ten accounting periods.

Article 16 of Law number 77-1467 of 30 December 1977, which has become Article 214 A II-C of the French Tax Code (C.G.I.) extends those rules to dividends distributed in respect of shares or other forms of permanent participation in companies, which have been issued in consideration of the incorporation into capital of the current loan accounts of participators active in the company. These dividends, too, are deductible during the first seven or ten accounting periods.

313 United Kingdom

Tax Deduction related to the establishment of new enterprises
(Business Start-Up Relief, created by the 1981 Finance Act and modified by the 1982 and 1983 Finance Acts).

The total amount of share purchases for the creation of new enterprise is, under certain conditions, deductible from the taxable income of private individuals. This system is also applicable to subsidiaries of British firms. The deduction is limited to £ 40,000 per annum.

314 Italy :

Law number 77 of 23 March 1983, Article one, authorises companies having a share capital paid up of not less than 2 billion lires, and whose exclusive object is portfolio management to set up fresh "open-ended funds", with the authorisation of the Treasury, after consultation with the Bank of Italy (10).

Article 9 of that Law deals with tax. These funds are not to be subject to income tax, nor corporation tax, nor to local taxes on income : withholding on the revenues of funds is made in full discharge from tax debt.

It is provided that the management companies will calculate the value of the fund annually, using a basis of monthly averages of net value and pay over to the Treasuries of the respective provinces before the 31 January in each year a sum equal to 0,25 % of the sum so calculated, by way of a compensatory tax.

The profits arising on participations held in these funds, save those obtained by persons engaged in commerce, are excluded from the taxable income of the participants.

Profits from the funds arising to companies mainly or exclusively engaged in commerce will carry a taxable tax credit of 10 %.

32 Dispositions favourable to the self-financing of innovating enterprises :

321 Belgium :

The Royal Decree of 26 November 1982 provides for total exemption from tax on profits, during ten years for defined new enterprises, whether industrial or service companies, which set up in what are called "employment zones" (11).

Similar dispositions are laid down for what are called centres of coordination for groups of companies. The "centres for coordination" are clearing houses exclusively devoted to the centralisation of publicity, purchases, information, scientific research, financial operations, etc....

322 France :

Tax reduction in favour of new industrial enterprises

For enterprises created between January first 1982 and 31 December 1983, the rate of reduction for the tax base has been fixed at 50 % of the profits made in the course of the year of creation of the enterprise, and the four following years (Article 44 bis of the French Tax Code (C.G.I.)).

323 Ireland :

Among various other measures, the Export Sale Relief consists of a temporary exoneration of profits realized on the export of certain goods (12).

A new tax incentive was introduced in 1981 which permits certain "industrial" enterprises to reduce the tax rate on profits to 10 % (up until 31 December 2000).

324 Italy :

Law number 240 of 21 May, 1981 has created a régime of exemption from tax on profits re-invested by a consortium of medium or small enterprises (at least 5 enterprises or corporations (13).

325 Luxemburg and the Netherlands :

The special tax privileges of holding companies in Luxemburg (14) and of investment companies in the Netherlands (15) are too well known to call for special mention.

4 THE EFFECTS OF TAXATION ON THE DEVELOPMENT OF PROFITABILITY IN ENTERPRISES ENGAGED IN INNOVATION WITHIN THE E.E.C.

The development of the profitability of European enterprises engaged in innovation is an essential aim. But the classical policy of attempting to increase investment by lowering taxation upon it shows itself, at present, to be ineffective : this policy is not adapted to the situation of world economic crisis, and long-term inflationary tension. European enterprises can only be aided to become more competitive, that is to say, more profitable, when engaged in innovation, by a tax policy which takes account of the entirety of the process which we call "innovation" : for research, invention, preparation or marketing, finance, production and selling. From this alone will follow interest in investment of this nature.

As at present constituted, the tax systems of the European Community countries are imperfectly adapted to the needs of innovation, as the examination of some of the main provisions of that legislation has shown.

41 Specific tax legislation relating to the first stage of innovation, research and development :

This class of legislation concerns the writing down of the value of patents and know-how, of investments for research ; other fiscal incentives to undertake research ; tax provisions for the expenses of research ; tax treatment of income arising from patents and know-how.

One can indicate only some of the broad outlines :

- the capital write-off of the value of patents, technical procedures and technical know-how : the rules are flexible in Italy and the Netherlands ; in France they tend to strictness, with a normal life of 20 years being considered ; they are average in Great Britain and Ireland, either 17 years, or the period of the patent, if this period is shorter than 17 years.

- depreciation of buildings used for scientific and technical research (16) : 75 to 100 % in Great Britain, 50 to 100 % in Ireland, 50 % during the first year in France (17), 50 % in Germany, elsewhere the normal regime is in force.

- writing-down of plant and material used for scientific and technical research (18) : 100 % in Great Britain and Ireland ; degressive depreciation with an increase of 40 % or more in France ; in Germany, there is an exceptional depreciation allowance of 40 % ; deduction of 20 %, non-deductible from the depreciation base used for the calculation, in addition to further degressive depreciation ; in Belgium, degressive depreciation, with a maximum of 40 %, in Luxemburg.

- specific provisions for investment in research : tax crecit ("crédit d'impôt") of 25 % in France ; deduction of 20 % from tax due ard exemption from tax in "employment zones" and in favour of the centres of coordination in Belgium (19) ; provisions for groups of small and medium enterprises in Italy (20), etc.

- tax regime applicable to scientific, technical and applied research ; regime of general expenses, also a special exemption of 100 000 F.B. per additional research worker, in Belgium (21) ;

- tax system applicable to revenues received from patents and know-how : under certain conditions, sales of patent rights and royalties are entirely exempt from tax in Ireland (22) ; reduced tax rate of 15 or 10 % in France (23) ; in certain cases, patent receipts may be spread over 6 years in Britain ; the private inventor has a specially reduced rate of 33 % in Belgium (24).

- there is variable taxation of the enterprise which may be carrying out research : this is the case of the "taxe professionnelle" in France.

42 - The limits of above Tax Incentives :

Specific tax measures are relatively favourable to innovation ; yet other heads of taxation work against it.

In the latter category are :

- liability to V.A.T. on operations relating to the creation of patents and know-how ;
- taxation of the enterprise so engaged.

Thus, the specific measures of aid to innovation do not suffice to accomplish their purpose. The enterprise planning innovation will decide to go ahead or not in function of its whole financial position (potential profit, cash flow, funds available from own resources or on loan). However, the general systems of taxation do not take into account the peculiar nature and requirements of the innovation process.

Two examples will suffice to demonstrate this fact :

- first, the taxation of dividends ;
- secondly, the taxation of enterprises' profits.

421 The taxation of dividends :

The multiplicity of special deductions and tax credits (deductions from income in respect of savings, tax credit in respect of tax deducted at source, or in respect of corporation tax already paid) have produced a very stimulating effect on modest investors.

Nevertheless, if one takes account of the highest rates of income tax on individuals and the general rules for the taxing of dividends, it becomes clear that net payment to shareholders is heavily marked by taxation : up to 72 % of the profit made by a company, when distributed, can be absorbed in taxation. This situation is troubling, when one takes into account the fact that the development of companies' own capital, presupposes dynamic financial markets, and correct returns to shareholders. At the level of shareholders'own taxation, the sum left after tax from gross dividends may vary from 28 % to 68 % country by country.

422 The taxation of small and medium enterprises :

It is common wisdom that the small and medium enterprises are a most important source of innovation, and all the tax measures directly in favour of innovation seek to grant them special advantages. But the small and medium enterprises are often too heavily and maladroitly taxed, especially in France, as the following table shows (25):

COUNTRIES	RATE	VALUE IN FRENCH FRANCS	DOLLARS
Germany	- 56 % on undistributed profits. - 36 % on distributed profits.		
Belgium	- 45 % on profits of more than 14.4 million Belgian Francs. - reduced levels for profits of less.	2 156 000	267 000
Denmark	- 40 % flat rate on all profits.		
France	- 50 % flat rate on all profits.		
Great - Britain	- 52 % on profits above 500 000 Livres - Reduced rates on profits less than that.	6 028 000	743 200
Ireland	- 50 % on profits of more than 35 000 Irish pounds. - Lesser rates on profits of less than £ 35 000. - 10 % on profits from "manufactured goods".		
Italy	- 30 % on profits plus local tax of 16.2 % deductible from Corporation Tax.	Effective rate : 41.3 %	
Luxemburg	- 40 % on profits superior to 1,312.000 Florins. - Lower rates on lesser profits.		
Netherlands	- 48 % on profits superior to 50 000 Florins. - Lower rates on lesser profits.	135 000	16 740

Thus, the general systems of taxation in the E.E.C. countries increase the risk attached to innovation, by the various distorsions which they create.

- a company's own funds, intended for re-investment may be withdrawn, and the possibilities of self-financing reduced.
- it may be difficult to carry over losses through the entire creative part of the cycle of innovation.
- the payment of various taxes and the difficulties of recovering some, such as V.A.T. and other taxes unrelated to the research and development may create problems of cash-flow.
- as said, the general tax régimes and the special inducements to innovation are ill adapted to a period of general crisis, and inflation.

In these conditions, the specific measures in favour of innovation are often nullified by the other factors.

CONCLUSION

Tax inducements limited specifically to assist innovation will remain insufficient to achieve their aim, so long as general bodies of tax rules on the taxation of companies and individuals hit innovators too hard. In the light of the importance of innovation for growth in the European Economic Community, what is required is the creation of a coherent basic policy, the aim of which will be to stimulate the innovation process at all stages : research, product design, financing, production and marketing. The policy should be created at Community level, in the form of a Tax Code for Innovation.

Such a common code is in fact, the only realistic framework for common action seeking to restore the competitive vigour of European enterprises vis à vis their principal competitors, such as the Americans or the Japanese.

NOTES

(1) Refer to "Tableaux Fiscaux Européens", Tome I, Pierre Fontaneau, I.P., Chapter II, Div. II, Sect. IV, p. 3/Sect. VII, p. 1 and pp., Editor : "Les Cahiers Fiscaux Européens".
(2) Ref. "Fiscalité Européenne Revue" 1983-4, "Encouragement Fiscal à la Formation du Capital à Risque, Modifications et Précisions", W. Lenaers, G. Bollen, p. 3 and pp.
(3) See above n° (2), p. 14.
(4) Ref. "Fiscalité Européenne France", Pierre Fontaneau, I.R., S. Part. I, Chap. II, Div. IX, p. 22 and pp., Editor : "Les Cahiers Fiscaux Européens"
(5) Ref. "Tableaux Fiscaux Européens", Tome II, Pierre Fontaneau, I.S., Chap. II, Div. I, Sect. III, p. 1, Editor : "Les Cahiers Fiscaux Européens".
(6) See above n° (5), p. 3.
(7) See above n° (2).
(8) Ref. "Fiscalité Européenne France", Pierre Fontaneau, I.R., S. Part. I, Chap. II, Div. XI, p. 7 and pp., n° 416 and further, Editor : "Les Cahiers Fiscaux Européens".
(9) See above n° (8), I.R., S. Part. II, Chap. II, p. 5 and pp.

(10) Ref. "Fiscalité Européenne - Italie", Pierre Fontaneau, I.R., S. Part. II, Chap. I, p. 5, n° 156 bis, Editor : "Les Cahiers Fiscaux Européens".

(11) Ref. "Fiscalité Européenne - Belgique", Pierre Fontaneau, I.R., S. Part. II, Chap. II, p. 19, n° 312, Editor : "Les Cahiers Fiscaux Européens".

(12) Ref. "Fiscalité Européenne Revue" 1983-3, "L'Irlande, une Excellente Possibilité d'Investissement", Don. Reid, F.C.A., p. 40.

(13) See above n° (10), I.R., S. Part. I, Chap. II, Div. II, Sect. III, p. 18, n° 78 ter.

(14) Ref. "Fiscalité Européenne - Luxembourg", Pierre Fontaneau, I.S., Chap. I, p. 7, n° 271 à 297, Editor : "Les Cahiers Fiscaux Européens".

(15) Ref. "Fiscalité Européenne - Pays-Bas", Pierre Fontaneau, I.S., Chap. II, p. 15, n° 204 to 208, Editor : "Les Cahiers Fiscaux Européens".

(16) Ref. "Le Régime Fiscal des Amortissements dans la C.E.E.", Etudes Jurif, Editor : "Les Cahiers Fiscaux Européens".

(17) See above n° (8), I.R., S. Part. I, Chap. II, Div. II, p. 20.

(18) See above n° (16).

(19) See above n° (11), I.R., S. Part. II, Chap. II, p. 19, n° 312, p. 21; n° 312 B, I.R., S. Part. I, Chap. II, Div. IV, Sect. II, p. 48.

Also, "Fiscalité Européenne Revue" 1982-6, "La Déduction pour Investissements", Henri-Robert Depret, p. 10.

(20) See above n° (10).

(21) See above n° (11), I.R., S. Part. I, Chap. II, Div. IV, Sect. II, p. 50.

(22) See avove n° (12), p. 43.

(23) Ref. "Le Régime Fiscal des Plus-Values dans la C.E.E.", Etudes Jurif, Tome II, p. 168-169, Editor : "Les Cahiers Fiscaux Européens".

(24) See above n° (1), I.P., Chap. III, Div. II, p. 7.

(25) Ref. "Fiscalité Européenne Revue" 1982-2, "Nécessité de l'Harmonisation des Systêmes d'Imposition des Sociétés dans la Communauté Européenne", Christopher Tugendhat, p. 3 and pp.

Venture Capital Markets for the Regeneration of Industry
J.M. Gibb (Editor)
Elsevier Science Publishers B.V. (North-Holland)

THE TAXATION OF COLLECTIVE INSTITUTIONAL INVESTORS

D. O'HOGAN

Partner, Arthur Young & Company, Chartered Accountants,
Portobello House, Dublin 8.

Summary

Mr. O'Hogan spoke about the taxation of the institutional/collective venture capitalist and, in particular, of the neutrality of the tax system in determining where investments should be made.

While I appreciate that this conference is concerned with tax regimes within the European Community, I will confine myself to the manner in which my country (Ireland) taxes this type of investor. The restriction is clearly necessary as fifteen minutes is too short to deal adequately with the taxation policies of each Member State. However, my understanding is that the adequacy or otherwise of the Irish tax system in attracting venture capitalists is reflected generally throughout the Community. There is nothing in our tax legislation which is specifically aimed at the venture capitalist but this is not to say that the general tax environment necessarily discourages him.

Obviously, it is for capital gains that the venture capitalist gets involved in any particular investment situation. Therefore, I will concentrate mainly on the manner in which the investor is charged to capital gains tax rather than income tax. I am not unaware of the fact that venture capital is made available to the entrepreneur in different forms and in particular in the form of convertible loan stock carrying an interest rate. Nevertheless it is when this loan stock is converted into ordinary shares and ultimately realised in cash form that the venture capitalist looks with trepidation to the tax man to see how much he will retain out of the realisation of his investment.

The main, and some might say the only, beneficial aspect of our capital gains tax system is that it allows for full indexation of original cost by reference to the increase in the overall consumer price index before any charge to capital gains tax crystalises. So at least the investor must make a real gain before this tax bites at all. However, once a chargeable gain does arise the rate of capital gains tax can be quite high with the lowest rate being 40% for assets held for more than 3 years. The rate of tax for assets held for less than a year is 60% but since venture capitalists would normally anticipate holding an investment for at least 5 years we can assume that the capital gains tax rate with which we are concerned is the 40% rate.

Before getting down to discussing how he is taxed I think it is important to identify who is the Collective or Institutional investor. I assume we are concerned with the pension funds, life assurance funds, general insurance funds, unit trusts and indeed in particular the venture capital companies. Many of these latter companies have been set up in the Republic of Ireland by banks and other financial institutions to engage exclusively in venture capitalism. Within the past few months, the Irish Industrial Development Authority which is a Government Agency charged with attracting manufacturing companies to Ireland has itself set up a venture capital company which is administered by one of the bigger financial institutions in the country. There are many companies which embrace many of the above functions and the manner in which these functions are separated for tax purposes would be a mathematicians dream or nightmare so I assume you do not wish me to go into these technicalities. I will deal with the way in which these functions are taxed after the separation has been accomplished.

1. PENSION FUNDS

Pension funds are exempt from capital gains tax and income tax provided they are approved by the tax authorities. There are a multiplicity of rules and regulations to be satisfied before this approval is available but once obtained the investment manager of the fund is not constrained by any fiscal considerations in making his decisions. You have already heard at one of this mornings sessions of the role which pension funds play in the venture capital market. However, it needs to be stressed that the tax exempt status of the fund applies irrespective of the type of investment made so the tax system neither encourages nor discourages venture capital investment as against the more conventional and less risky alternatives. Pension funds are becoming more involved in venture capital (certainly in the United Kingdom and Ireland) but we cannot say that the tax system has played any part in this. While their involvement is there and is increasing, it still accounts for a very small percentage of the total deployment of funds and given its present very attractive tax position it is difficult to see how the tax system can be used to encourage the investment managers of these funds to commit a greater proportion of their funds to this area. In addition to the activities of the funds being generally tax exempt all contributions whether by employees or employer are fully tax deductible and it is only when the benefits are paid out to the employees on retirement that any tax becomes payable at all. I think it is unlikely that granting more favourable tax treatment to pensions paid out of the gains from venture capital investments is likely to get a positive response from the legislators in my country nor I suspect from yours.

2. LIFE ASSURANCE COMPANIES

The manner in which the income and capital gain allocated to policy holders of life assurance funds is taxed differs very little from the normal tax regime. The main difference is that any investment income allocated to policy holders is effectively pegged at the standard rate of income tax at 35% and the capital gains tax rate is the same as any other corporate investor. There is limited income tax relief to the individual policy holder on his life assurance premium and the proceeds of the maturity of the policy is totally exempt from income tax and capital gains tax. The absence of any tax incentive to persuade the investment managers of these funds to look beyond the blue chip investment is clearly to be regretted. If this is general throughout the Community then perhaps this could be one of the more positive recommendations to come out of this conference.

3. UNIT TRUSTS

The tax system applied to unit trusts is very similar to that of life assurance companies with one main distinction. The Revenue authorities have recognised the difficulty associated with having the unit trust charged to capital gains tax on any gains which it makes on its investment and the unit holder being charged to capital gains tax on the sale of his units. To overcome this difficulty the capital gains tax system is modified by reducing the rate of capital gains tax on the unit trust by 50% and having a similar reduction in the rate of capital gains tax on the unit holder. While the mathematicians among you will presumably see that this does not add up to a full capital gains tax charge on the sale of the asset it was considered preferable to exempting either the trust or the unit holder.

4. GENERAL

Rather than get involved separately in how venture capital companies are taxed and how general insurance such as aviation, marine, car insurance funds etc. are taxed I thought it would be preferable to deal with all of them under the one heading since the tax treatment in the Republic of Ireland is the same. The income, if any, from any venture capital investment is charged to corporation tax at a 50% rate and to capital gains tax at 40%. I have already mentioned the existence of indexation relief. This means that the capital gains tax is levied only after the original cost of the investment is uplifted by reference to the increase in the consumer price index from the date the investment is made up to the date it is sold (provided the investment is held for at least 12 months). For example an investment made in the tax year 1974/75 and sold in the tax year 1983/84 would be multiplied by 3.759 to arrive at the cost of the asset for computing any tax payable. Clearly, the reason for this is that inflation in Ireland during this period came to 275.9%. The recognition by the tax authorities in my country of the incidence of the double taxation within a unit trust is not reflected in the legislation relating to individual shareholders of companies. The venture capital company pays its tax on any capital gains which it realises and the shareholder in the venture capital company has to pay his tax as well. Again, if this is general throughout the community we should consider whether we should recommend some special consideration be given to the venture capital company in the tax laws of each member state.

5. CONCLUSION

I know that the manner in which the Republic of Ireland taxes the collective or institutional investor is not of the greatest interest to you but I suspect that the absence of any discrimination in the tax treatment between investments giving rise to employment and those which are totally passive is common thoughout the Community. I know that we can point to specific instances where this positive discrimination does exist in selected areas of our tax code e.g. the U.K. gives a tax deduction for certain types of investment but the role of the venture capitalist may not have been sufficiently considered by those who draft the tax legislation of each member state. In the Republic of Ireland, the institutions or collectives have the cash and invest it but the tax system is neutral in persuading them where these investments should be made.

Venture Capital Markets for the Regeneration of Industry
J.M. Gibb (Editor)
Elsevier Science Publishers B.V. (North-Holland)

TAX TREATMENT OF THE INDIVIDUAL INVESTOR

CORNELIS A.M. RASENBERG

General Manager, Tax Department
Amsterdam-Rotterdam Bank N.V.
(The Netherlands)

Summary

The nature of the venture capital market requires an individual investor to make a high-risk investment for a fairly long period of time. His current income from such an investment will almost always be fully subject to tax at ordinary rates; capital losses are only in a few cases deductible from ordinary income while the taxation of capital gains differs substantially from country to country. Depending, inter alia, on whether the gain is treated as business income or other income, ordinary or reduced rates may apply. Tax-incentives aimed at reducing the after tax amount-at-risk of an investment in venture capital (deduction of or tax credit for the investment) are effective ways for generating venture capital. Existing tax-incentives for investment in equity capital tend to discriminate against investments in foreign enterprises. Many countries have unilaterally created privileged tax treatment for collective investment vehicles, but in varying ways. A community-wide unified legislation for Venture Capital Organizations eliminating double taxation of corporate profits, other tax obstacles and regulatory impediments for collective investment in innovation should be introduced.

1. INTRODUCTION

When considering how to finance the substantial innovation efforts that are required for the regeneration of industry in the countries of the European Community, the capital resources that may be provided by individual investors should not be overlooked. A very rough estimate of the private investor funds available in the Netherlands indicates that under optimal circumstances, that is if the incentives are sufficient, at least Dfls 1,000 million (ECU 390 million) might be invested in innovation.

An investor's decision to provide funds for this high-risk purpose will be made on the basis of the amount that has to be put at risk on the one hand and the benefits that may be expected to arise from the investment on the other. Both of these factors have a tax aspect and government or supranational measures to promote investment in innovation may be based on either of these factors or both. Most private investors will prefer some form of collective investment with other investors which provides a spread of risks, instead of an individual investment.

In the following pages, the tax situation in the Netherlands will be used as a starting point for illustrating some of the problems related to the financing of innovation by the private investor.

2. COLLECTIVE INVESTMENT VEHICLES.

An individual investor may decide to participate in a venture capital enterprise in the Netherlands in one of the following two ways:

a. Direct through the creation of a venture capital enterprise in whose management and trade the individual actively participates, or

b. Indirect through participation in a scheme of collective investment.

In case a. such an individual will receive business income from his investment. The general rules for business income as they are set out in the tax legislation of the Netherlands, including the exemptions and reduced rates applying upon certain forms of termination of a business enterprise, apply to such investment. No specific incentives for investment in innovation apply in this sphere. If the individual investor participates in some form of partnership which invests in innovation, he is normally for tax purposes deemed to be an entrepreneur and he will receive business income treatment for his share in the partnership. This will be the case if he is entitled to the proceeds of the hidden reserves of the partnership upon realisation of such reserves. If he does not meet this criterion he is deemed to receive investment income as described under b. The above rules providing for business income treatment apply equally to resident and non-resident individual investors although to the latter group this is only the case where the investors are deemed to conduct business in the Netherlands through a permanent establishment situated there.

In case b. an individual investor is deemed to enjoy investment income according to the tax legislation of the Netherlands. It is interesting to note in this respect that such legislation only provides for taxation of the current income from the investment. Capital gains are exempt from tax while capital losses are not deductible. Dividend income is taxed, in the case of residents at the progressive income tax rate which applies to net dividend income. Non-residents are taxed with a 25% Dividend Withholding Tax on gross dividends received, but such rate may be reduced by tax treaties. Resident individual investors may benefit from an allowance of up to Dfls. 500 (ECU 195) which is permitted on private dividends from shares from which Dutch Dividend Withholding Tax has been deducted in any one year. A supplementary dividend allowance of Dfls. 1,000 (ECU 390) is possible on dividends from certain companies whose purpose is to finance small businesses, the so-called "Particuliere Participatie Maatschappijen" (PPM's) (in English Private Equity Participation Companies).
Although no important specific incentives for venture capital investments are included in the individual income tax legislation there are some incentives from which certain companies may benefit. Individuals could invest in innovation through the intermediary of such companies and thus have indirect benefits. These companies are referred to as Investment Institutions and PPM's respectively. On the side of the individual investor the general rules applying to investments in shares which have been described above also apply to investments in both kinds of companies.

I Investment Institutions.

In the Netherlands entities qualifying as "Investment Institutions" receive privileged tax treatment because, in the opinion of the legislator, there should be no difference in tax position between an individual investor who invests directly or indirectly through an Investment Institution. From the investor's viewpoint the shares or participation in the Investment Institution are a substitute for the securities and other investments in which the Institution invests the funds subscribed. Qualifying Investment Institutions are taxed at a zero rate of Dutch corporate income tax if, and as long as, they distribute all their net current income to their shareholders or participants within eight months after the end of the accounting year. Net capital gains may be retained in a tax-free reserve. An Investment Institution must meet the following conditions in order to qualify for the favourable tax treatment.

- The Investment Institution must be resident in the Netherlands.
- The Investment Institution may be either a public limited company (N.V.), a private limited company (B.V.) or an - unincorporated-fund for joint account (fonds voor gemene rekening). It should be noted that Investment Institutions are ordinary companies and funds for joint account and are not regulated in the Dutch corporate or public law in a different way from similar entities which do not qualify for privileged tax treatment.
- Debt financing of the Institutions' investments is subject to restrictions.
- The articles of association of the entity must provide that its activities consist of investment wholly or almost wholly in securities, real property and loans secured by real property, and these must be its actual activities.

It is estimated that more than 1000 entities have acquired the Investment Institution status. Most of them are owned by a small number of investors and are used to finance and manage business interests of the same group of investors.*

The taxation system described below implies that resident individuals will be taxed on the net current income that is distributed by the Investment Institution. Net capital gains earned but not distributed by the Institution remain untaxed, both in the hands of the Institution and in the hands of the investor, as long as the Institution qualifies for privileged treatment. However, the general rules for tax on Substantial Interest gains (see below) and Dividend Withholding Tax are applicable to shareholdings in Investment Institutions and income therefrom. Investment Institutions may upon request to the Netherlands tax administration be granted relief for foreign withholding tax on their investment income. The relief is in the form of a cash payment of which the maximum is the amount that resident investors would have been able to credit against their income tax if they had owned the investments in foreign property directly. In order to prevent abuse of the double taxation treaties concluded by the Netherlands, privileged tax treatment does not apply if any non-resident individual, any non-resident fund for joint account or any non-resident company of which the capital is wholly or partly divided into shares owns an interest of 25% or more in the Institution.

II Private Equity Participation Companies.

In 1981 the Netherlands government introduced measures to encourage the provision of riskbearing capital (i.e. equity and - to a certain extent - subordinated convertible debentures) to middle-sized and small businesses.**

The measures apply to equity-type investments made by Private Equity Participation Companies (Particuliere Participatie Maatschappijen (PPM's)). Such a PPM may be either a public limited company (N.V.) or a private limited company (B.V.) or even a (limited) partnership and must be recognised as such by the Central Bank of the Netherlands. The measures are twofold:

(1) A recognised PMM may be granted a cash payment from State funds amounting to a maximum of the one-half of the investment in (partial) compensation of a loss incurred upon (partial) alienation of the participation taken, upon liquidation of the company in which it has participated, or - in the case of participation through subordinated convertible debentures - upon bankruptcy of such company. The loss compensation is available for minority participations only and is limited to cases where the total of the participations in a given company taken by all recognised PPM's for which the loss compensation benefit is claimed does not exceed Dfls. 4,000,000 (ECU 1,6 million).

(2) An individual shareholder receives an annual exemption of a maximum of ECU 390 for dividends received from his shareholdings in PPM's.

Until now 22 PPM's have been established, 7 of which operate jointly under one name so that, effectively, 16 PPM's exist.

None of these has issued shares or other participations to the public. The great majority of existing PPM's receive their funding from banks, institutional investors (insurance companies, pension funds) and large industrial groups. It is estimated that 10-20% of the funds so far raised have been invested in innovation.

Comparison with other EEC-countries.

Even though in many European countries measures against double taxation of company profits have been enacted and in some countries a general tax on capital gains is levied, often a tax regime similar to the Dutch rules for Investment Institutions exists. A major difference from the Dutch tax system is that privileged tax treatment is often only available to entities that meet the requirements of many non-tax regulations, e.g. dealing with spreading investment risks, management, availability of investment expertise, legal structure and number of participants in the collective investment. In some cases full attribution to the participants of the benefits accruing to the company is applied, while in other cases certain benefits are for tax purposes not passed on to the participants. The treatment of non-resident participants may or may not differ from the treatment of resident participants.

2. TAX POSITION OF THE INDIVIDUAL INVESTOR

(A) Situation in the Netherlands.

According to the individual income tax legislation in the Netherlands, income is only taxable if it is derived from one of the sources enumerated in the law. These sources are:

1. Income from a business or profession;
2. a. Income from employment (e.g. wage, salary, pension);
   b. Income from personal activities performed outside the framework of an employment contract;
3. Income from assets (i.e. investment income);
4. Income from certain regular payments (e.g. state benefits, maintenance payments);

5. Capital gains resulting from the sale of a substantial interest.
All sources of income apply to residents of the Netherlands.
Only sources 1, 2a, 3 and 5 are applicable to non-residents of which source 5 applies only in exceptional circumstances. In the context of this paper only source 1 (business income), source 3 (income from assets) and source 5 (capital gains) will be dealt with since only these are of significance for the subject. Under the income tax legislation there is a capital gain tax in the Netherlands on gains arising on the alienation of a "substantial interest" in the shares of a company. Capital gains arising from business activities are taxable as business income. Other capital gains earned by an individual are not taxable. Under the substantial interest rules, a resident investor is liable to tax on capital gains realised upon alienation of a shareholding when at the time of alienation of the shares or at any time during the five years preceding the alienation he, together with his spouse, owned more than 7% and, together with certain relatives enumerated in the law, owned at least one third of the nominal paid-in equity capital of a resident or non-resident limited company. Upon application, a flat 20% rate applies to such gains. Losses are taken into account in that 20% thereof may be credited against the income tax liability on other sources of income.

Business income and income from assets.

Business income and income from assets are taxable at the ordinary income tax rates (progressive, up to 72,75%). The income of a taxpayer from all sources is added together on an annual basis. Substantial interest gains are then upon request treated in accordance with the above rules (i.e. at the lower rate of 20%) and the remaining balance is taxed at the ordinary rate. A negative balance of income may be carried back to the two years preceding the year concerned and, if necessary, carried forward to the following eight years, for set-off against positive income earned during those years. A special rule applies to negative income of the first six years of operation of a business enterprise. Such losses may be carried forward indefinitely. Another feature of business income is the fact that, upon application, flat rates (minimum 20%, maximum 54%) instead of the progressive rate, and certain exemptions, may apply to those gains that are realised upon the termination or the transfer of a business enterprise.

The rules regarding deduction of expenses differ according to the source of income to which the expenses relate. In the business sphere all expenses directly connected with that certain business are deductible. They must be deducted in the period to which they pertain. This rule implies that it is generally not possible to accelerate deductions relating to a business by making prepayments of expenses. In the investment income sphere only expenses reasonably incurred in the production of the income are deductible. Deduction must be claimed in the year of payment of the expenses.

Non-residents are taxed on income from sources within the Netherlands. Although the rules for computation of the income from a given source do not differ from income earned by residents of the Netherlands, some sources are treated in a different way. As already stated, business income from an investment can only be taxed in the hands of non-resident individual investors if they conduct business in the Netherlands through a permanent establishment situated there and the investment is connected with such permanent establishment. Non-resident investors are taxable on investment income in the form of dividend declared on shares in resident limited companies and proceeds from profitsharing bonds issued by such companies. The applicable rate is 25% of the gross amount of such investment income, but this may be reduced by tax treaties. In exceptional cases (e.g. interest from loans secured by real property situated in the Netherlands) non-residents are liable to tax, at the progressive rate, on interest income from sources within the Netherlands. A tax treaty, however, may modify the rules that apply to such income. In addition to the taxation of dividends and interest, non-residents are liable to tax on the net income from real property situated within the Netherlands. Resident and non-resident investors have in common that double taxation of corporate profits remains fully intact: first corporate profits are taxed with corporate income tax and, upon distribution, again in the hands of the shareholder. An exception to this rule is the privileged tax treatment available to Investment Institutions that has already been discussed

(B) Situation in some other countries of the European Community.

The tax systems of the other countries of the European Community all differ in some respects from the situation in the Netherlands. Some countries do not have a general capital gains tax, others do; if they do, there may be various exemptions and/or reduced rates, depending on, inter alia, the nature of the investment and the length of the period that the investment is held; the deductibility of capital losses may be restricted, and the law may or may not provide for indexation of the cost price of the investment on account of inflation. Exemptions for dividends received from domestic companies exist (e.g. in France ECU 440, in Greece up to ECU 1370 if the shares are quoted on the Athens Stock Exchange). The rules for giving an investor business income treatment differ from country to country. A few countries have introduced sophisticated incentives for investment in equity capital of certain resident companies by resident investors. Under the Business Expansion Scheme in the United Kingdom, an individual who is not connected with the company in which he invests may receive a deduction from total taxable income for investments in new ordinary shares in unquoted resident companies exercising a qualifying trade. The minimum investment is ECU 875 and the maximum deduction is ECU 70,000 per individual or married couple per year. An individual may also invest through an approved investment fund. A qualifying trade is defined by exception; most industrial activities qualify. The relief may be (partially) withdrawn if the shares are sold within five years after the issue to the investor. In computing gains for capital gains tax purposes, the full amount of the investment may be deducted from the proceeds. However, where the sale proceeds are less than the original cost, no further relief is allowed for the loss.

In France, for taxpayers born after 1 January, 1932, the legislation on Shares Savings Accounts succeeded the well-known Monory Act. Resident individual investors who are not subject to the French net worth tax may receive tax relief for net investments up to ECU 2,000 per individual or married couple per year in shares and certain participations in French quoted or unquoted companies and certain investment funds. The relief is a tax credit equal to 25% of the qualifying investment, so that the maximum annual relief for an individual or a married couple is ECU 500. It is only available for investments made through a Share Savings Account with an approved intermediary. As in the U.K., the relief is subject to (partial) recapture during 5 years. Arrangements have been made to enable investment clubs formed by private investors to benefit from the tax relief.

3. EVALUTATION AND RECOMMENDATIONS.

From the above discussion it appears that no specific tax incentives for investment in venture capital exist in the Netherlands. The incentives created for PPM's are mainly of a non-tax character.

Although these measures have not been in effect for a long time, an interesting positive psychological influence can be noticed. Institutions which so far had no high-risk investments have now decided to invest indirectly in new equity venture capital. However, the incentives have so far not been able to direct individual investor funds towards the financing of innovation. The nature of the incentives is "defensive" in the sense that losses are partially compensated by payment in cash but if a PPM turns out to be successful then neither the PPM nor the investor in the PPM are treated in a sufficiently favourable way. A minor incentive is the higher dividend allowance permitted on PPM dividends received by an individual investor. The dividends received deduction is of little (potential) importance as venture capital rarely generates dividends in the first years of investment. A tax-deduction for the investment itself would be more effective. In the U.K., where there is a substantial tax incentive for investment in new shares in unquoted companies, the withdrawal of tax relief in the event of a sale within five years, with no corresponding relief to the purchaser, may be a disincentive. The relief available in France is restricted to a small amount.
Obviously there should be organizations which offer to the private investors investment proposals having interesting prospects. The following recommendations may provide an effective incentive system which may operate at the Community level:

- Innovation financing should be encouraged by the creation - at private or government initiative - of Venture Capital Organizations (VCO's) which are allowed to obtain funds from all countries of the European Community and are allowed to invest in all of these countries. Such VCO's could attract funds by issue of transferable participations wich may be bought and sold by individual investors in an organized market and could provide financing for research and development projects undertaken by third parties and could carry on such activities themselves.
- VCO's should be exempt from all income-, net worth- and business taxes, including taxes on their distributions, both in the country where they

are resident and in the countries where they operate, even if they retain their profits.

- Investments in new and existing VCO participations by private investors should be deductible from taxable income in the country of residence of the investor up to a high amount per year, e.g. ECU 70,000 per individual or married couple (as in the U.K.) There would need to be provisions for (partial) withdrawal of the relief in the event of sale within, say, five years. High income taxpayers and persons having a high net worth should no be excluded from enjoying this tax-incentive.
- Capital gains realized on the participations as measured by the difference between the purchase cost and the sale proceeds should be exempt from tax or taxed at a low rate, e.g. 20%; capital losses should be deductible. Distributions on VCO participations should be exempt from income tax and the participations themselves from net worth tax and inheritance and estate duties.
- The above tax-incentives for innovation financing should be introduced in all countries of the Community.

Notes

* More information on Investment Institutions can be found in P.J.M. Bongaerts: Het fiscale begrip Beleggingsinstellingen, Kluwer, Deventer, 1982.

** See for a detailed discussion C.A. Troost: The Dutch Scheme in The Needs of Technology Based Enterprises, Infobrief, Luxembourg, 1983.

Venture Capital Markets for the Regeneration of Industry
J.M. Gibb (Editor)
Elsevier Science Publishers B.V. (North-Holland)

IMPACT OF TAX CHANGES ON VENTURE CAPITAL INVESTMENTS AND INNOVATION IN THE USA

P. T. KAPLAN

Weil, Gotshal Manges
New York City

Summary

While generally, the United States has been generous in according tax incentives to venture-capital investments and to innovation, one cannot from this fact alone derive a corrolation between these incentives and the high level of innovation achieved in the United States in post-war years -- such a conclusion can only be drawn by observing the effect of relevant tax changes. Many such changes have occurred in the United States, but data are not yet sufficient to permit economists to quantify relationships. Proceeding in a less scientific manner, some tax changes, particularly in the capital gains tax, do seem to have induced changes in investment behavior, but other changes in investment behavior cannot be related to contemporaneous tax changes. Statistics apart, one can deduce the importance of tax incentives to innovation in the United States in specific cases by observing certain investment offerings which pass the tax deductions for research and development through to the individual investor; thus reducing the real cost of his investment by as much as 55%. Since such U.S. deductions have no geographical limitations, European investment opportunities could be structured to accord similar pass-through deductions to U.S. investors.

1. BACKGROUND

From the EEC report entitled "Tax and Financial Measures in Favour of Investment" (1) one can break down tax incentives to innovation into three categories:

(i) Category 1. Specific tax inducements for innovation -- generally consisting of tax rewards to the companies undertaking the research and development. Examples are full first-year deductions for the cost of qualifying research and development, tax credits providing direct reductions of the company's tax burden for expenditures on research and development, etc.

(ii) Category 2. Incentives for venture-capital investments that are not necessarily limited to innovative companies; generally taking the form of tax rewards to venture-capital investors. Examples are low taxes on capital gains; measures permitting taxpayers to claim ordinary (rather than capital) losses on venture-capital investments which do not succeed, direct reductions in a taxpayers tax burden for investments in new businesses, measures allowing the taxpayer to deduct on his personal tax return a part of the research and development costs incurred by a business in which he has invested.

(iii) Category 3. A generally favorable business-tax climate. Important factors in creating such a climate can be generous rules for depreciation of capital equipment and for the claiming of tax credits for the purchase of such equipment; reduction in aggregate corporation-shareholder taxation by the integration of tax systems as is done by many countries in the EEC; the encouragement of risk taking by allowing carrybacks and carryfowards of business losses; favorable tax treatment for schemes of collective investment in new businesses and for employee shareholding schemes.

While the United States practices nearly complete double corporation-shareholder taxation -- i.e., it does not follow the EEC norm of reducing the aggregate tax burden on distributed corporate income -- it does otherwise score well in all of these categories. As to category 1, the United States has, for many years, allowed full first-year deductions for research and development costs and recently has added a 25% incremental tax credit for qualifying research and development costs. In category 2, the United States currently imposes low taxes on capital gains, encourages venture - capital investments in smaller businesses by allowing ordinary losses when the venture does not succeed and, in defined circumstances, by allowing the costs of business research and development to be deducted on the individual returns of investors. In category 3, the United States does provide a generally favorable business-tax climate (with the exception of the extremely unfavorable and confusing network of taxes imposed by the individual states). Depreciation deductions for capital investment have been made progressively more favorable and the investment tax credit has been increased to 10%. The United States accords generous carryback and carryforward provisions for business losses and favorable tax treatment to schemes of collective investment and to employee-shareholder schemes.

While the United States has been one of the most innovative countries since World War II, one cannot conclude from these simple observations that the high level of innovative activity in the United States has resulted largely from the favorable tax climate. Nonetheless, it is only common sense to conclude that this was one of the contributing factors. The question whether tax incentives have been a major factor in encouraging innovation in the United States cannot properly be answered by a detailed study of U.S. law. It is only by studying the effects of **changes** in relevant features of U.S. tax law that the observer may hope to correlate tax trends with trends in venture-capital investment and in innovation -- changes that, in fact, have been quite frequent since 1965:

(i) Category 1. In 1982 (dates refer to the effective date of the change) a new 25% tax credit was added for increases in eligible research and development spending over a base-period amount -- a credit which is in addition to the immediate tax deduction for current costs of research and development.

(ii) Category 2. In 1969 the United States imposed a large increase in capital gains taxes which was then reversed, and capital gains taxes substantially reduced, in two bites in 1978 and 1981. It is interesting to note that the increases in capital gains taxes were imposed for purely ideological reasons -- a perception that the 25% tax on capital gains then in force constituted a "tax preference" that, in the interests of tax equity, should not generally be available. The increase took the form both of a direct increase in capital gains tax rates and of adding complicated layers of contingent additional taxes, notably a "minimum tax", on top of the ordinary capital gains tax, in some circumstances, and loss of the preferential (50%) top federal tax rate on "earned income" for taxpayers having too much capital gains income (a measure which alone could add greatly to the capital gains tax burden). The reductions in capital gains rates made in the late 70's and early 80's were made for pragmatic reasons -- easily imagined.

(iii) Category 3. In 1971 and 1982, the United States increased depreciation deductions available for investments in capital equipment and buildings and in 1975 increased the investment tax credit for investments in capital equipment from 7% to 10%. In 1979 the top federal tax rate on corporations (it must always be remembered that state taxes also exist in the United States and can be significant) was reduced from 48% to 46%.

2. CORRELATION BETWEEN TAX INCENTIVES, VENTURE CAPITAL INVESTMENTS AND INNOVATION

The United States is one of the principal statistics-keeping countries, and one would expect that the answer to the question posed in this paper would be found in the work of the social scientists -- the economists in particular. In fact, a number of studies have been made of the correlation between taxes and innovation in the United States. Regretably, the information available seldom has been sufficient to permit the drawing of meaningful conclusions. There has been a considerable amount of disagreement and much of the commentary has addressed itself to the question of how to improve methodology in making studies of this kind.

For example, Collins states in "Tax Policy and Innovation: A Synthesis of Evidence"(2):

> "Evidence is sparse about links between innovative activities and tax-induced changes in net-of-tax cost for innovation and in cash flow. There is no quantitative evidence specifically about tax variables; work in related areas is just beginning."

Similar statements are made by Professor Mansfield(3) and by Professor Nadiri.(4)

Professor Nadiri also makes the interesting point that the fact that tax incentives and cash-flow variables have been shown to have some effect on investment expenditures does not necessarily imply a similar effect on research and development investment since research and development activities are characterized by a high degree of uncertainty about their outcome and the usefulness of their benefits -- characteristics which may well lead to a different response to a given tax incentive then would have been the case for investment expenditures on plant or equipment.

If we cannot look to the work of the academic researchers to answer our question where can we look? One possibility is to attempt to examine the temporal relationships between tax changes and changes in relevant investment activity to see whether any rough and ready conclusions can be drawn -- conclusions which indicate a trend even though they might not be justified under the strict standards applied to academic research. The graphic presentation which appears at the end of this paper is an effort to identify apparent relationships.(5) The first six columns show the timing of significant changes in U.S. tax law that might be expected to affect venture - capital investments and investment in innovative activities. The final four columns give statistics as to investment in venture-capital firms, estimated disbursements by such firms to portfolio companies, and the amount, and percentage increase or decrease, of total U.S. research and development spending over a span of years. Some apparent relationships between the tax columns and the investment columns can be discerned; but often, expected relationships cannot be found.

Perhaps the most striking correlation is that between the increase, and the later decrease, of capital gains rates and investments in venture-capital firms. As can be seen, the major 1970 increase in capital gains taxes coincided with a dramatic drop-off in new investment in venture-capital funds and the 1979 reduction in capital gains rates (also a very significant movement in rates) was preceded only slightly by a nearly fifteen-fold increase in such investment! This sequence of events has been interpreted to be one of cause and effect.(6) In fact, it is likely that this was so. It is true that the 1969 Revenue Act, which increased capital gains rates, was preceded (in 1969) by a relatively large amount of investment in venture-capital firms but the history of that legislation was such that investors could not reasonably foretell the shape of the capital gains legislation much before December 30, 1969 when the Tax Reform Act of 1969 was signed into law.(7) On the other hand, the 1978 tax legislation which lowered capital gains rates was enacted on November 6, 1978 -- almost one year after the Carter Administration began to make public its plans on comprehensive tax legislation designed to encourage capital formation by reducing corporate income tax rates, liberalizing the investment tax credit and reducing the rate of taxation on capital gains.(8). It is not then surprising that investment in venture capital firms increased dramatically during the year 1978.

Other relationships are considerably more difficult to identify. A sharp drop-off in the rate of increase of research and development spending occurred in 1967 which was a year in which no major relevant tax change took effect. On the other hand, that trend was reversed in 1975 which was the year in which the investment tax credit increased from 7% to 10% and there may well have been some relationship between the two events.

3. SOME NON-STATISTICAL EVIDENCE

The fact that the relationship between tax incentives and innovation cannot yet be proved statistically, does not prevent some observers (including the author of this paper) from believing that the relationship often is a direct one -- a belief which arises in part from observed phenomena. An example is the recent offering circular for units of a California limited partnership, with 320 units being offered at $50,000 each for an aggregate issue price of $16,000,000. The purpose of the offering (which was dated July 1, 1983) was to raise funds for medical research and development in specific areas. The offering literally was built around the fact that, in general, the United States tax system is not a schedular system, so that deductions from one profit-making activity are available to offset income from another such activity.

The offering circular recites that investors' funds are to be invested in a matter intended to produce deductions, over a three-year period, equal to ninety percent of the funds committed to the venture. Hence a taxpayer in the 55% tax bracket (including state taxes) is to receive tax deductions having a value of $24,750, making the true cost of his "50,000 investment" only $25,250. At the end of the research cycle, assuming success, the partnership interest (and hence the processes developed) would be purchased by the company doing the research, probably in exchange for its own shares.

Interestingly, some of the investors in this venture are non-residents of the United States who, presumably, will not benefit from the tax deductions or will have a more limited benefit than will U.S. investors.

4. REVERSING THE INVESTMENT FLOW

If European investors are willing to invest in U.S. research and development projects without benefit of the related tax subsidy, it may well be that U.S investors would be interested in investing in European projects if they could import the deductions into the U.S for U.S tax purposes as, in fact, often would be possible. A venture-capital partnership, formed to carry on research and development activities in Europe in conjunction with a European company, could provide U.S investors with tax benefits comparable to those offered by the California limited partnership. U.S law does not contain a geographical limitation on deductions (although it does for the tax credit) for research and development expenses.

Obviously, European concerns seeking to raise investment funds in the U.S. in this fashion would have to comply with U.S. security laws, but this should not be a major impediment. In some cases, where the investor group is expected to be no more than 35 persons, recent changes in U.S tax law would make it possible for the offering to be made in the form of shares of a U.S-registered company (in place of a partnership) which would make an election to be an "S" company so that the research and development expenses incurred by the company would pass through as deductions to the individual shareholders.

5. CONCLUSIONS

It seems quite reasonable to conclude that the relationships between tax incentives, on the one hand, and venture-capital investments and investments in innovation, on the other hand, do exist and often can be directly observed. However, knowledge in the field is not yet fully systematized and it remains at times very difficult to distinguish effects arising from tax causes from those arising from other causes, or to quantify the tax input to an observed result.

References

(1) Commission of the European Communities, "Tax and Financial Measures in Favour of Investment" (COM (83) 218 final).

(2) Collins, "Tax policy and Innovation: a Synthesis of Evidence," (National Science Foundation, PRA Research Report 82-1).

(3) Mansfield, "Tax Policy and Innovation: Provisions, Proposals, and Needed Research" Tax Policy and Investment in Innovation (A Colloquium) (National Science Foundation, PRA Report 83-1).

(4) Nadiri, "Tax Incentives and Innovation Expenditures", Ibid.

(5) In the table, data on new investment in venture-capital firms and on estimated disbursements to portfolio companies are from the Venture Economics Division, Capital Publishing Corporation as reproduced in "SEC Government-Business Forum on Small Business Capital Formation"

(Final report, November 1982). Data on total U.S. research and development research spending are from the "28th Annual McGraw-Hill Survey of Businesses' plans for Research and Development Expenditures, 1983-86." Some of the data on tax changes are from New York Stock Exchange, "Federal Taxes in Historical Perspective" (Office of Economic Research, February 1982).

(6) This conclusion was drawn by Dr. Frank Press, President of The National Acadamy of Sciences as reported in the "Congressional Record-Senate of July 21, 1983 (S 10614).

(7) New York University, "1969 Tax Reform Act", Supplement to Twenty-Eighth Annual Institute on Federal Taxation (Matthew Bender, 1970) p. [iii].

(8) Ernst & Ernst, "Highlights of 1978 Tax Legislation", Introduction.

Year	Tax Treatment of R&D	Invest-ment Tax Credit	Depre-ciation	Top Tax Bracket: Corporate	Top Tax Bracket: Individual	Top Tax Bracket: Capital Gains	New Investment in Venture Capital Firms	Estimated Disburse-ments to Portfolio Companies	Total U.S. Research & Development Spending	R&D % Change
1965									14,185	
1966						25% (6 mos.)			15,548	10%
1967			Guide-line Lives						16,385	5%
1968									17,429	6%
1969							171	450	18,308	5%
1970		7%					97	350	18,067	(1%)
1971	Current deduct-ions				70%		95	410	18,320	1%
1972				48%			62	425	19,552	7%
1973					Earned Income	Approx. 50% (6 mos-1 yr)	56	450	21,249	9%
1974							57	350	22,887	8%
1975							10	250	24,187	16%
1976			ADR System		50%		50	300	26,997	12%
1977							39	400	29,825	11%
1978							570	550	33,304	12%
1979		10%					319	1,000	38,226	15%
1980						28% (1 year)	900	1,100	44,505	16%
1981				46%			1,300 (est.)	1,400		
1982	Current Deduct-ions plus 25% tax credit		3/5/10/15		50%	20% (1 year)	1,750	1,800		

SESSION III:
EUROPEAN SECONDARY-LEVEL SHARE MARKETS
Exit Mechanisms and Access to Equity Capital for Small Industries

Special Stock Market Segments for Small Company Shares.
Situation and Perspectives 97
H. SCHMIDT
Direktor, Institut für Geld- und Kapitalverkehr,
University of Hamburg (Federal Republic of Germany)

Access to European Markets by Medium-Sized Companies 107
Y. FLORNOY
Syndic de la Compagnie des Agents de Change, Paris (France)

European Secondary Level Share Markets – The Entrepreneur's View 117
R.G. HODGSON
Managing Director, Granville & Co. Ltd., London (United Kingdom)

The Venture Capital Investor's View 122
J.P. DE BLOCQ VAN KUFFELER
Director, Brown, Shipley & Co. Ltd., London (United Kingdom)

The American Over-the-Counter Markets 129
A.E. YOUNG
Professor of Finance, School of Management, Syracuse University,
Syracuse (United States of America)

The London "Unlisted Securities Market" 142
R. STORMONTH-DARLING
Chairman, Laing & Cruickshank (inc. McAnally Montgomery & Co.),
Stockbrokers. Chairman, Quotations Committee, The Council of
The Stock Exchange, London (United Kingdom)

Venture Capital Markets for the Regeneration of Industry
J.M. Gibb (Editor)
Elsevier Science Publishers B.V. (North-Holland)

SPECIAL STOCK MARKET SEGMENTS FOR SMALL COMPANY SHARES. SITUATION AND PERSPECTIVES

Prof. Dr. Hartmut SCHMIDT Director,
Institut für Geld- und Kapitalverkehr,
University of Hamburg

Summary

During the past decades the ideal stock exchange was believed to be a market organized on one single model that implied uniformly high disclosure, a standard trading procedure and securities issued by reasonably safe companies. As the recent and desirable emergence of special market segments for small companies shares has shown, a class of shares held by a limited number of investors may warrant a special trading procedures and a different disclosure regime. Unfortunately, the newly gained acceptance of small company public equity financing does not seem to extend beyond the segments recently created for companies that already can pass an advanced threshold of quality. The author pleads for the more frequent use also of the bottom level segment and for its recognition as an important component of any national equity financing system. To facilitate access of innovative high-risk companies to organized securities markets the recommends measures in areas such as investment banking, regulation of institutional investors and taxation.

About a year ago, Mr. WATSON of DG XIII asked me to do a study on secondary markets for small company shares. I was very much surprised, since I had submitted to the Commission a study on this matter in 1977. The 1977 report said: If you want to organize a stock market in the best interest of issuers and investors, you ought to offer four vertical market segments, two lower segments for small and medium sized companies and two upper segments for larger companies.

There are three reasons for a hierarchy of market segments:

1. Turnover characteristics of shares of large and small companies are different. Trading methods have to be geared to this. As elsewhere in industry, procedures for mass production differ from those used for small batch production.

2. Listing requirements concerning disclosure, dissemination of information and shareholder services can be linked to turnover characteristics since low turnover tends to imply a small number of shareholders. Obviously, dissemination requirements appropriate for a large national company tend to be onerous and inappropriate for small emerging companies with few shareholders.

3. Trading the shares of small companies with low market capitalisations implies high price volatility. In addition to this trading related risk, small innovative companies involve high business risk. The shares of high-risk companies should trade on segments other than those of mature and well diversified large companies. This enhances investor perception of differences in risk.

My current study focusses on the lower market segments. In the following I will use the term "bottom level segment" for the lowest segment that should be wide open and the term "advanced level segment" for the next higher vertical segment.

In recent years widespread and successful efforts have been made to create and to restructure stock market segments for companies of small and medium size. The probably best known junior stock markets are the unlisted securities market in the United Kingdom and Ireland, the parallel-markt in Amsterdam, the French second marché and the share market III in Copenhagen. However, there have been other important developments. In Italy a court ruled a long established lower market segment illegal in 1975, but in 1978 a new mercato ristretto was created. In addition, the terzo mercato developed as the third secondary market segment below the mercato ristretto. In the United Kingdom an over-the-counter market that focusses on small companies and dates back to the early seventies gained momentum as more securities firms entered this market. In Germany the two lower stock market segments were rediscovered as secondary markets for unlisted small young companies going public; more recently, plans for a second official market are being discussed. In Belgium, there are plans to reorganize the daily auctions of ulisted securities.

In Greece a new semi-official market for small company shares is being considered, all these new markets may become operative next year.

To a superficial observer all these developments appear consistent and aimed at facilitating access to the secondary market for small and medium sized companies. However, there are three different groups of reorganizations. The first comprises the unlisted securities market, the second marché and the proposed second official market in Germany. In the countries concerned, stock exchange facilities for small unlisted companies have been available for many years and, in principle, these facilities remain unaffected by the reforms. But for various reasons, these old facilities do not seem to provide the appropriate trading environment for those small and medium sized companies that have attained some stature. Unfortunately, requirements for access to the listed securities market appear to be onerous and too ambitious for these companies. Thus, special intermediate market segments have been designed for companies which can pass threshold of quality that is advanced although stiil below the threshold of full listing.

By contrast, attempts at reform in Belgium and Greece focus on the lowest segment in stock market hierarchy, in Greece a bottom level segment will be organized for the first time. In Belgium upgrading the bottom level segment and encouraging its use seem to be the central issues.

The third group comprises Denmark, the Netherlands and, less clearly, Italy. These countries traditionally enjoyed an inofficial market that was accessible to small companies. The traditional lower level segment was split up into two segments. As a result, an advanced level segment and a bottom level segment were created. This step was most pronounced in Amsterdam, where the former incourante Markt was split into the official parallelmarkt and the inofficial parallelmarkt. In Italy and Denmark the new regimes developed over an extended period. Quite appropriately, the final reorganization step in Denmark involved all market segments in order to bring about a convincingly segmented stock market.

As this brief survey of the present situation indicates, the advanced level segment of the secondary market and the bottom level segment aim at different kinds of companies.

Accordingly, entry requirements and other segment features have to be different. Advanced level segments are geared to those companies that have been in business for some years and achieved profitability before they apply for entry to the secondary market. These companies prefer to signal that they can pass some standard threshold of quality. The bottom level segment caters to young and high-risk companies that cannot meet this standard.

The new trend established by these recent developments is to welcome to stock exchanges advanced companies that were formerly considered too small and too young for public equity financing. Indirectly, this clearly contributes to private equity financing of young firms since it reduces the time venture capitalists and other early investors are locked in with their investments. However, direct benefits to young high-risk companies have been the exception. Their public equity raising still is widely met with outright opposition and with the call for upgrading regulation. In my opinion, it is the foremost future task to let the established trend extend down to the bottom level segment. It must not be stopped by regulatory or industry action.

Regulators hold the position that bottom level segments are highly undesirable. They believe in the principle that any investment vehicles available to the public should be reasonably safe and stable. High-risk investments, it is thought, should not be readily accessible to the public. Thus, any companies that do not pass a standard threshold of quality should not obtain funds from public investors, and existing bottom level segments should be upgraded in order to firmly establish this standard.

Bowing to this quality doctrine, many industry experts maintain that bottom level segments are not at all necessary for the equity financing of young and innovative small firms. Small and high-risk companies, it is claimed, should gradually establish an institutional shareholder base and should not go public before their high-risk characteristics fade. This opinion implies that there should be no secondary market for small and high-risk companies and that these companies should raise their equity privately.

However, many an entrepreneur strongly resents the high level of outside influence that comes with private capital raising and prefers public equity issues to a wide spread of shareholders at an early stage.

This not unrealistic as the experience in the United States has shown.

In addition to this control problem, private financing is impeded by the valuation problem. Prior to trading on an efficient secondary market a reliable valuation of equity instruments is not available. This adds to the well known reluctance of small companies to accept outside shareholders and considerably complicates external equity financing. To eliminate this impediment, small innovative companies should be able to enter a secondary market at an early stage in their development.

Raising equity capital publicly at an early stage and subsequent trading of the shares on a bottom level market segment is an important alternative and a useful supplement to financing privately. It is the encompassing approach. The resultant secondary markets benefit even companies that have yet to go public since the prices established in these markets provide guidance and facilitate the fair valuation of equity instruments which are to be used in private placements. Moreover,investors accepting minority interests in unquoted companies are well aware that the most profitable exit route is the public sale of their interest in a secondary market.

The existence of easily acessible bottom level segments assures participants in private financings that a secondary market could also be established for the shares in which they invest.

Ladies and gentlemen, after these pragmatic remarks in favour of wide open bottom level segments let me take on the fundamental regulatory opposition. The quality control doctrine and the principle of vertical segmentation agree on the need to provide the public with highly safeguarded investment opportunities such as bank deposits, government bonds and high quality stocks. Contrary to the traditional doctrine, however, vertical segmentation does not advocate minimum quality requirements beyond adequate disclosure. There are four reasons for this :

1. Individual and institutional investors in today's securities markets and their advisers seem to be well aware of the risk and return characteristics of available investments. Restrictions on the public availability of small company shares are unlikely to benefit any number of investors to speak of.

2. Diversification strategies now are widely followed by investors. The risk of a particular small company share may appear unacceptably high if one looks at it individually. Inspite of this, the share may well be most desiderable in a portfolio context. Restrictions based on risk characteristics of individual companies are misguided.

3. Even the average individual investor has ready access to a wide range of domestic and foreign high risk investment vehicles. As it is obvious in the case of options, the invested amount will frequently be completely lost. Against this background any regulatory efforts to restrict the investment in the shares of small companies appear discriminating.

4. The riskiness of small company shares is not artificially created. It reflects the innovativeness of the firm and other business characteristics. For employment and other economic reasons it is highly desirable to take advantage of the growth of independent small firms which assume these risks. This requires external equity financing. In contrast with former years of high employment, restrictions on small company equity financing are likely to carry a much higher economic cost.

To sum up, both advanced level segments and bottom level segments and the related public capital raising are most desirable components of any developed equity financing system. To improve the functioning of equity markets particularly at the bottom level I recommend seven sets of specific measures:

1. Initial and continuing requirements for entry to advanced level segments should be modelled on those that now prevail on the unlisted securities market. However, such entry requirements are not advisable for bottom level segments. Any requirements beyond those generally

Core requirements for access to advanced level small company segments

Segment (country)	Minimum amount to be held by the public in mio of local currency	Minimum percentage of stock to be held by the public	Use of flotation methods that tend to avoid underpricing	Press advertisement of prospectus	Interim reports	Standard minimum age of company in years	Accessible only to public companies
Unlisted securities market (United Kingdom and Ireland)	not required	1o%	rare	one or two box advertisements required	required	3	yes
Aktiemarked II (Denmark)	2.5	15%	required	one or two box ads. req.	voluntary	1	yes
Official parallelmarkt (Netherlands)	o.25	1o%	no	box advertisement required	required	o	no
Geregelter Freiverkehr (Germany)	not required	not required	no	voluntary, prospectus not required	voluntary	1	yes
Official market (Luxembourg)	5o	not required	no	voluntary	required	3	yes
Parketmarkt (Belgium)	not required	not required	no	voluntary	voluntary	5	yes
Second marché (France)	2-4[1)]	1o%	attempted	voluntary, prospectus not required	required	o	yes
Mercato ristretto (Italy)	2oo[3)]	2o%	no	full prospectus	voluntary	2[2)]	yes
Official market (Greece)	25[3)]	not applicable	no	voluntary	required	3[2)]	yes
Recommended	ECU 1 mio	1o%	incentive for use recommended	voluntary	required	3	yes

1) Tentative and preliminary.
2) Profits must have been reported for the latest two or three financial years respectively.
3) Calculated on the basis of related requirements.

Core requirements for access to bottom level small company segments

Segment (country)	Minimum amount to be held by the public in mio of local currency	Minimum percentage of stock to be held by the public	Use of flotation methods that tend to avoid underpricing	Press advertisement of prospectus	Interim reports	Standard minimum age of company in years	Accessible only to public companies
Broker-dealer OTC (United Kingdom)	not required	not required	no	voluntary	voluntary	1	yes
Occasional bargains facility (Ireland)	not required	not required	not applicable	not applicable	voluntary	1	no
Aktiemarked III (Denmark)	1	15%	required	one or two box ads. req.	voluntary	1	yes
Non-official parallelmarkt (Netherlands)	not required	not required	no	voluntary, prospectus not required	voluntary	o	no
Ungeregelter Freiverkehr (Germany)	not required	not required	no	voluntary, prospectus not required	voluntary	o	yes
Off-exchange trading (Luxembourg)	not required	not required	no	voluntary	voluntary	o	yes
Ventes publiques (Belgium)	not required	not required	not applicable	not applicable	voluntary	o	yes
Marché hors cote (France)	not required	not required	no	voluntary, prospectus not required	voluntary	o	yes
Terzo mercato (Italy)	not required	not required	no	voluntary, prospectus not required	voluntary	o	yes
Recommended	not required	not required	incentive for use recommended	voluntary, prospectus not required	voluntary	o	no

required by law are likely to be overshooting. As experience in the crucial area of disclosure has shown, voluntary action of capital raising companies is likely to be adequate. Moreover, growing companies do not stay long at the bottom level. They move up in stock market hierarchy and submit to advanced level requirements.

2. The strong desire to win independence is an important motive for becoming an entrepreneur. Fear of outside influence impedes ouside equity financing. For public equity financing I recommend a European participating certificate. Although it would not carry voting rights, it would be acceptable for stock market trading.

   Payments to holders should be based on dividends. They should be deductible for corporate income tax purposes. The European participating certificate may also foster equity financing of those companies that have yet to convert to public limited company status.

3. The most perfected small company segments are of little account if young innovative companies cannot find investment bankers that bring them to these markets. The successful investment banking activities of firms from outside the mainstream of investment banking and other indications point to gaps in investment banking service. To close this gap and to foster competiton in investment banking a licensed dealer status, as it is currently known in the United Kingdom, should be made available in all Member States.

4. At the time the decision to go public is taken the most important cost of going public is the impending cost of uncontrolled underpricing. It is the opportunity loss to the entrepreneur that results from selling the issue below market price. It is witnessed by oversubscriptions. There are a number of ways to remove this impediment to external equity financing. For first public offerings it is recommended to use discretionary tender offers and to calibrate underpricing to the preferences of the entrepreneur. The use of tender offers should be encouraged by exemptions from issue tax.

5. In most Member States investment of institutional investors in unlisted domestic and foreign shares is restricted or even prohibited. These restrictions impede equity financing and withhold from small companies the benefits or the priviliged tax status of investment funds, insurance companies and pension funds. To encourage the involvement of institutional investors in all segments of the stock market these restrictions should be abolished.

6. The reliability of share prices is a crucial factor for the entrepreneur and the investor. Since first public offerings are usually small, bottom level segments tend to suffer from poor marketability and poor price quality. The only way to overcome this natural disadvantage of small companies is to increase turnover. Therefore, it is recommended to exempt from corporate and individual invome tax all capital gains on small company equity instruments. In addition, all transactions in these instruments should be exempted from all indirect taxes.

7. A European innovation finance journal should be an effective means to improve the knowledge of investment bankers at home and abroad experienced in financing high technology. It also could be an excellent forum to champion the cause of innovative enterprise and to give public recognition to entrepreneurs who went public. Broad public acceptance of small enterprise and the example of successful entrepreneurs going public are most important. They assure more than any other remedy that special market segments for small company shares will actually perform the economic function for which they were skillfully designed.

Venture Capital Markets for the Regeneration of Industry
J.M. Gibb (Editor)
Elsevier Science Publishers B.V. (North-Holland)

ACCESS TO EUROPEAN MARKETS BY MEDIUM-SIZED COMPANIES

Y. FLORNOY
Syndic de la Compagnie des Agents de Change

The importance of small and medium-sized undertakings in Community economies continues to be decisive. Whether it be the number of companies or the labour employed by them, in relation to the total workforce of companies and the overall number of people in employment they constitute the real fabric of our economic life.

Since by virtue of this fact they are the recipients of a whole complex of manifold and varied development aid, the small and medium-sized undertakings have to date shown little interest in recourse to the stock markets. Of course, there are still considerable obstacles to their being granted quotation, but nevertheless, they are beginning to be aware of the advantages to be gained.

In this context, the present successful experience of a "Second marché" in France is evidence of the growing interest of medium-sized undertakings in gaining access to the stock markets.

At present small and medium-sized undertakings are regarded as one of the main motive forces of tomorrow's economy, either because they create employment, or because they provide a better working environment. Nevertheless little is known about them in most European countries as yet.

On the basis of the definition that SMUs are firms which employ from 10 to 499 persons, they represent about 13.8% of companies in Italy, 19.6% in Germany, 20.2% in Belgium, 27.5% in France and 29.5% in the Netherlands. The record is held by Ireland (68.9%), and Denmark (82.1%) but this is due mainly to the size of these countries.

From the point of view of employment, SMUs account for 40% of the labourforce in Germany, 49% in Italy and 54% in the Netherlands.

Logically therefore all European governments are concerned with supporting the activity of SMUs ; there are two main categories of aid to SMUs, firstly measures relating to existing companies, secondly measures encouraging company creation.

Aid to existing SMUs is increasing with every year, in most countries. In France it has been reckoned that there are more than 100 bodies which can come to the aid of a SMU. As regards encouraging the creation of companies, the general trend is to go beyond strictly financial support and to set up a network providing counselling, information and training.

Nonetheless there is an astonishing contrast between these various forms of aid to SMUs and the small degree of interest displayed to date by the state or the financial community in encouraging the companies to gain access to the Stock Exchange.

---

1. Undoubtedly considerable obstacles to the quotation of medium-sized undertakings on the stock exchange, remain.

2. However, companies are beginning to be aware of the advantages to be derived from the stock market.

3. The successful experience of the French Second Marché is proof of their growing interest in access to the stock markets.

---

1. Traditionally, SMUs are not spontaneously attracted by the stock market. First of all, the development of numerous more attractive sources of financing than those to be found on the stock market limits the advantage which it might have for these companies.

Furthermore, off-market transfers often offer better conditions to shareholders wishing to realize their capital, and the fiscal treatment both of assets and of dividends - particularly in France - discourages some heads of undertakings from introducing their company on the stock exchange.

This is particularly true in the light of the doubts engendered following the inadequate preparation of some introductions in the past which were due to insufficient precautions being taken as regards the quality of the company considered, the inadequate support arrangements, in a word to the absence of professional management of the introduction.

The fact remains, however, that the absence of a capital market for SMUs is felt increasingly. A number of medium-sized companies would like to expand and develop, but how? Some bodies are already taking an interest in this ; there have been various initiatives from time to time, but this is not adequate. It is now essential that a means be found cf bringing together potential investors and the SMUs seeking capital expansion.

For this, in my view, several conditions must be met. It is necessary, first of all to continue efforts to channel savings towards industry rather than towards less productive sectors such as real estate or totally unproductive sectors such as gold and works of art ; secondly, to avoid penalizing venture capital investors fiscally in comparison with the advantages offered to other traditional investments, and if necessary to provide specific incentives.

In addition to these structural obstacles, there are the cultural barriers affecting the behaviour of heads of undertakings.

In the United States, the quotation of a company on the stock exchange is for itself, its shareholders, and the general public, a lable of quality, the mark of success. Moreover, it is not necessary from the outset to aim at listing of the stock on the big board principally reserved for the largest companies and those with the best performance. In practice, there are several intermediate markets where small and medium-sized companies can make their shares available to the public.

In Europe, on the other hand, we know that companies dislike saying who they are, what they own, what they earn and what they hope to achieve. The reflex of keeping oneself to oneself, even of secrecy, is still too widespread amongst the heads of medium-sized companies. The information which quoted companies have to provide is generally considered excessive : listing on the stock exchange may furthermore involve a risk of losing control of the company, beyond the minimum number of shares which companies applying for listing are obliged, under regulations which are often too restrictive, to make available on the market ; the terms for listing are regarded as excessively strict and the stock exchange mainly appears as a club reserved for the very large companies.

2. Apart from the asset value which it may represent for majority shareholders, quotation also has many advantages for the SMU itself and its development.

First, the company applying for quotation, let us assume in a phase of growth, must acquire the additional shareholders' funds to finance both its working capital requirements and new equipment.

Quotation on the stock exchange and the issuing of securities to a large number of private or institutional investors enable the latter to take over this burden, at least in part, from the former shareholders.

The financial operations carried out to this end (the issuing of shares or convertible bonds, placing with new holders) may be the opportunity for a new distribution of capital.

Introduction on the stock exchange and the arrival of new partners may also provide an opportunity to enlarge the Board of Management, to strengthen the management if the need arises, which is often the case when a SMU begins to attain a certain level of maturity and development.

For such companies, quotation of the shares, publicity and comment by the financial intermediaries (press, analysts, banks and stockbrokers) are indispensible for gaining a reputation at national or international level. Quotation on the stock market is therefore part of the overall commercial and financial strategy of the company.

Thus, medium-sized companies in the United Kingdom profited on a large scale from the creation in November 1980 of the Unlisted Securities Market (USM). Their importance in the national economy prompted the authorities to create a new exchange market to suit their requirements.

In this context the USM ensures the mobility of the capital while reducing the risk of losing control, by reducing the cost of introduction and by offering less onerous conditions of access (at least 10% of the capital to be made available to the public, presentation of the accounts for the past three years and an undertaking to keep shareholders regularly informed of the development of activity, an annual admission fee of £1000).

In general, investors reacted favourably to this new structure. The average size of the companies, the organization of events designed to acquaint investors with the enterprises, the drive of the financial intermediaries are some of the positive factors which explain how more than 130 companies are at present quoted on the USM, which today constitutes a fully-fledged market.

Similarly, in January 1982 the Amsterdam Stock Exchange set up the 'Parallele Markt' which broadly resembles the British Unlisted Securities Market. Specially conceived to meet the capital requirements of SMUs, the 'Parallele Markt' offers mainly family companies less onerous access conditions (10% of the company capital to be made available to the public ; a required capital of 2.5 m guilders with the possibility of reducing this amount) and less stringent requirements (simplified information to shareholders which is less onerous for the companies ; an introduction cost which is lower than for the official market). In addition to this simplified access procedure there is a guarantee of market liquidity which better meets the needs of SMUs who wish to be quoted on the stock exchange.

Likewise the Federal Ministry of Finance in Germany is at present studying a report drawn up by a Stock Exchange Committee on the possible creation of a lower tier market. Although no official conclusion has been arrived at yet, the State Secretary has stated that he is in favour in principle and considers that legal provision could be made by amending the Framework Law on Stock Markets.

The Directors of the Bundesbank consider that a lower tier market, designed to meet the needs of the SMUs, would be beneficial to all German companies in that a structure would then exist within which the traditional relationship between private investors and industry could be re-established.

Similarly, Belgium does not intend to fall behind in the organization of a securities market for SMUs. A restricted working party is at present studying the technical problems involved (mainly as regards information to the public and the liquidity guarantee) and hopes to be able to conclude its work in the course of the autumn.

3. In this context, the present successful experiment with the French Second Marché demonstrates the growing interest of SMUs in gaining access to the stock markets. Traditionally, two paths were open to companies seeking introduction of the financial market : the official market and the Hors Cote market.

The former is subject to very strict conditions of access and requirements. On the other hand, access to the Hors Cote market is open freely to all companies wishing to be quoted on it.

Experience has shown that this structure was incomplete : it did not provide any market for companies who, while they could not satisfy the conditions of access required by the official stock exchange, nonetheless wished to avail themselves fully of the advantages of the financial market.

The creation in 1977 of the special segment of the Hors Cote market was designed to fill this gap. However, this 'antichamber of the official stock market' only partially fulfilled the hopes placed in it.

This is the reason why, following one of the recommendations of the Committee for the Development and Protection of Savings headed by Mr DAUTRESME, the Second Marché was created. This replaced the special Hors Cote segment on 1 February 1983 and will provide medium-sized companies with a permanent and easily accessible structure.

The rules governing its operation are more simplified than those of the official market.

The Second Marché will therefore be open to many companies without difficulty : there is no minimum threshold required for shareholders funds, turnover or profits. No examination for admission is required. It is simply stated that the applicant company must have real or estimated market, capitalization of an order of magnitude of tens of millions rather than millions of francs. Furthermore, to be admitted to the Second Marché, companies need not have paid dividends in the years preceding their introduction on the market, nor even indeed have shown a profit. This is particularly advantageous for growing companies which wish to reinvest all their profits.

Once they are quoted on a public market however, companies must make a certain number of essential commitments, even if these are considerably less onerous compared with those of the official listing.

Firstly, for their securities to be traded on the Second Marché, companies must place shares of a minimum value of 10% of their capital among the public. Thus they can apply for admission without the fear of losing control over this capital.

Secondly, the companies concerned must make a commitment to the Commission des Opérations de Bourse (Committee on Stock Market Transactions) to keep the public regularly informed of their activities and their results. Further, they must nominate a second auditor if they only had one and with the assistance of their auditors and of the Committee must make improvements, if these are considered necessary, in administrative and accounting procedures within a period of three years.

Finally, the Second Marché provides a guarantee of market liquidity for its stock.

Without it being required by any law, the profession has recommended the creation of two types of syndicates when new shares are introduced.

- a placement syndicate, composed of bankers and issuing brokers, intended to ensure the disposal of the shares made available on the market, a period of three years being allowed if all the stock was not absorbed by the market immediately on introduction ;

- a so-called 'liquidity syndicate', which must be composed of a broker and a banker, who may be joined by one or more original shareholders, as well as financial intermediaries such as regional development bodies, portfolio management firms and intermediate brokers.

To carry out the task of this syndicate successfully, the broker has been authorized to intervene directly on the market, making purchases to smooth fluctuations : his presence within the syndicate ensures that it does not collect any fees on these price stabilizing operations.

This important innovation in French Stock Exchange law authorizes the broker to intervene on the Market as 'principal'on his own behalf or on that of his syndicate, concurrently with his interventions as 'agent'.

The aim of this was to ensure as strong a correlation as possible between the company and the bank and broker introducing it, whose name and reputation will be closely associated with the success or failure of the introduction of their candidate on the Second Marché.

Conceived as the structure par excellence to permit medium-sized companies to enter the market, the Second Marché is particularly suited to certain types of undertaking. This is the case in particular :

-of family companies which would be in a position to gain access to the official listing, but which do not wish 25% of the capital to be held by the public ;

- companies which have already obtained a certain level of growth and have a certain reputation, which are unsuited to the Hors Cote, but which cannot aspire on the basis of current size and their prospects to an honourable place on the offical stock exchange ;

- companies which have succession problems and which are anxious to ensure long-term survival ;

- finally, the shareholders of some companies may wish them to be listed on the Second Marché for fiscal reasons, related for example to wealth tax.

Since it was officially launched on 1 February 1983, the Second Marché has listed a total of 34 companies (31 French and three foreign companies).

Thirteen stocks have recently been introduced on this market (of which 9 had never been listed previously and 4 came from the Hors cote).

Seven other companies have applied for admission before the end of the year. The volume of transactions carried out from the 1 January to 30 September 1983 amounted to 1250 million francs.

Thus the hopes placed in this new exchange structure are beginning to be realized, even if initially the level of profitability expected by the professionals is only very average.

The fact remains, however, that apart of some very large companies, the undertakings presently listed on the Second Marché have all the requisite characteristics (listed capital of some tens of millions of francs, growing activity).

On the basis of these examples, it is reasonable to believe that in three years about 100 companies will gradually overcome all reservations of a psychological, technical or fiscal nature which has to date stopped them from requesting a quotation on the stock exchange.

The success of the British, Netherlands and French experiments appears to be such as to encourage the European markets which have not already done so to consider the adjustments which could be made to the above models to ensure that the markets open to SMUs follow in the traditions of the national financial communities. However, in my view there are two points which must apply to all markets:

1. The attainment of 'stock exchange majority', for the share market of an SMU will only be achieved under the right circumstances if the development prospects which encouraged the first outside shareholders to share the risk of the original shareholders actually materialize. It should never be forgotten that the stock exchange, even at a time when money is scarce and expensive, is always ready to provide share capital to companies showing the best performance to help them to become even more successful.

Even when money is plentiful and cheap, the stock exchange will be very slow in providing assistance to companies which it does not consider to have a very secure future. On this point the stock exchange increases the gaps between companies and only the technocrats of financing complain. Its function is to exacerbate the conditions of competition : the stock exchange is the most pitiless censor of the allocation of resources, and, because this is so, guarantees the future of the free and capitalist economy which we value ;

2. Attainment of 'stock exchange majority' in the securities market of SMUs can only be obtained if, during the period which separates childhood from adulthood and adulthood from maturity, the financial intermediaries who have officiated at the baptism on the stock market, look after the establishment, liveliness and liquidity of the market and accept that their name and their reputation be for ever linked to the success of the company. In this respect decline and dullness of the market, once the popularity

attendant on the introductory celebrations has died away, are the first enemies to be combated.

To supporters of strict regulation, whose desire to protect savings should certainly not be flouted, let me say in conclusion that the relative 'deregulation' which appears to have assured the initial successes of the new market structure contains a quid pro quo which should ease their minds : before accepting an SMU applying for quotation into their 'stable', the bankers and issuing brokers will have weighed the chances of success and the risk of failure in a far more effective manner than any binding regulations could enforce.

Venture Capital Markets for the Regeneration of Industry
J.M. Gibb (Editor)
Elsevier Science Publishers B.V. (North-Holland)

EUROPEAN SECONDARY LEVEL SHARE MARKETS - THE ENTREPRENEUR'S VIEW

ROBIN G. HODGSON

Managing Director, Granville & Co. Limited, London

Summary

The entrepreneur's psychological make up determines his view of the various exit mechanisms which exist. Entrepreneurs can broadly be divided into two types - dynastic and non dynastic. European stock markets have concentrated on the needs of the latter; the needs of the former have been little considered.

In presenting a paper as to the view which is held by the entrepreneur of European share markets (and in particular the exit mechanisms they represent), one is inevitably forced to begin with some consideration of the psychological characteristics that go to make up a successful entrepreneur. For the view held by the entrepreneur (who is a user of venture capital) can differ quite dramatically from that held by the supplier of venture capital (the venture capital fund manager).

All entrepreneurs are different (that is why they are entrepreneurs) but psychological research, particularly in the United States, has disclosed certain threads of personality which keep recurring amongst successful entrepreneurs. In order therefore to concentrate my remarks on the essentials, I have to fall back on stereotypes and parodies.

In, analysing our mythical venture capital user, what do we find:

1. He is an obsessive character. The entrepreneur has to be obsessive in order to give his business the drive it requires to succeed. If he is starting a business from scratch, he has to build up organisational momentum which will mean working away for 2 or 3 years or indeed a great deal longer, during which time nothing much happens. He has to pick out and stick to the essentials of his plan - his financial resources will permit of no other approach. Above all, he has to have an obsessive (some would say a messianical, others less politely would say a maniacal) belief in the potential of his product, proposal or scheme.

2. He has to be a self contained character. The establishment of a new business is a lonely job. And no matter what the scale of the new business, it nearly always depends on the spark of the leadership provided by one man. That man is by nature a 'loner'.

   He has to have the self confidence to make decisions - decisions which are often of such fundamental importance as to radically affect his entire life thereafter - on his own.

Such a man is by his very nature 'a cat who walks by himself'.

3. He has to be a specialist. The entrepreneur has to be a specialist in his field of endeavour of which he will have a deep degree of understanding. But his degree of specialisation will have often left him ignorant of fields other than that of his chosen endeavour. In certain cases, this state of ignorance is not just a passive one but an aggressive one and extends to a dismissive attitude to areas other than his own.

   Thus all venture capital fund managers will have met the entrepreneur engineer who is dismissive of marketing men, the marketing entrepreneur who is dismissive of production men while all entrepreneurs can agree that the venture capital fund manager is at best an itch to be tolerated.

So we have this obsessive, self contained specialist who is struggling to build up his business and, before any entrepreneurs in the audience leave the hall to telephone their lawyers to sue me for slander, let me introduce two further stereotyped categories into which entrepreneurs tend to fall - those we can describe as having dynastic ambitions and those without - for these two categories have very different views and requirements of the exit mechanisms represented by stock exchanges and by over the counter markets.

The dynastically ambitious entrepreneur seeks to play the long and the big game - megalomania is therefore his bedfellow. Not for him the rapid build up of a business, the quick cashing in of all or at least part of his stake by means of a judiciously massaged share price at time of a market flotation. Even less unwelcome to him, is a high pressure marriage, closely akin to corporate rape, to a big daddy corporation with limitless supplies of funds and equally limitless layers of bureaucracy.

Entrepreneurs of this type certainly seek to build up their organisations but do so in a highly controlled way, picking staff with the right personalities, expanding the organisation steadily and planning always for the long term even to the extent of ignoring or missing some short term opportunities. Such long term plans can often include a particular role for the entrepreneur's sons (or perhaps even daughters) - 'the acceptable face of nepotism' as one of the clients of my bank once so charmingly and explicitly called it. Our dynastically minded entrepreneur will be equally careful with the equity of his company, it will be handed out sparingly and then only to individuals and financial institutions which he believes share his strategic views. Accordingly, in considering a market flotation, such individuals look for a market which has the following characteristics:

1. guarantees a high likelihood of independence preservation by ensuring that shares which are sold end up in 'friendly' hands.

2. affords more stable share prices against which the business can be planned by attracting long term investors.

3. offers access to shareholders with large financial resources to support the firm's dynastic ambitions.

4. requires standards of paperwork both as regards initial listing and subsequent trading which are 'commercial' as opposed to 'bureaucratic'.

On the other hand, our non-dynastically minded entrepreneur is prepared to take a much shorter term view. He often comes from a large company where he was working when he spotted a chink in the market place. He acted swiftly to take advantage of this opportunity and very often it will be found that, at root, even he is a little surprised at the extent to which he has succeeded in hitting the jackpot. Inevitably the way in which he has found success colours his subsequent approach. He tends to be very opportunity conscious and, just as our other stereotype's danger was megalomania, this stereotype has to guard against frittering away his own and his company's resources in a constant chase after fleeting market opportunities. A second influence on his further planning comes from the way in which he was able to exploit his success. He knows that this resulted from his leaving a large organisation to take advantage of that one opportunity and in his heart of hearts he believes that many of his own employees would leave him to do the same if the right opportunity occurred. He therefore has no particular loyalty to the organisation he has created. He also knows that the market which opened up to give him his opportunity could shift again this time to crush him. Accordingly, his perceptions of what is required of an exit mechanism is that it should afford the opportunity:

1. to realise part of his investment at the highest possible price by becoming involved in a market where private investors play a large part.

2. for potential bidders for the company to make approaches (always given that the price is right).

3. for the maximum publicity at time of flotation and the highest possible profile afterwards in support of the above aims.

In my own organisation, we have a shorthand description for these two stereotypes, (and here I realise the difficulties I am going to cause the interpreters), the non dynastic type we call 'an eager beaver', the dynastic type we call 'a reluctant debutante'

So much for stereotypes, how do European exit mechanisms measure up. Well in part, that is what we shall be hearing about during the rest of the day but, in concluding, I would only offer two comments:

1. The stock exchanges have for the most part, especially in the case of the Unlisted Securities Market, set out to meet the needs of the eager beaver. His needs meet the economic profile desired by conventional stock exchanges - lots of pubicity, heavy trading in shares leading to good commission and 'turn' income, excitement for bids and deals etc.

2. No real effort has yet been made to develop a European wide exit mechanism to assist the dynastically minded reluctant debutante. He is looking for an exit mechanism which will enable him to make a gradual transition to a more public world. It may be that a European wide over the counter market should be developed to fill this gap.

Venture Capital Markets for the Regeneration of Industry
J.M. Gibb (Editor)
Elsevier Science Publishers B.V. (North-Holland)

THE VENTURE CAPITAL INVESTOR'S VIEW

J.P. de Blocq van Kuffeler
Director
Brown, Shipley & Co. Limited

Summary

There has been a rapid development and expansion of secondary level share markets during the past three years, particularly in London, with the development of the Unlisted Securities Market and the Over-the-Counter Market. Some 220 companies' shares are now traded on the USM and some £230 million of capital has been raised for these companies. There are now 24 market makers participating in the OTC market which trades shares in some 70 companies.

The institutional investor in London has considerable sums available for net new investment and the attitude and investment criteria of the investing institutions are of considerable importance to these markets.

Institutional investors regard the USM and OTC markets as an opportunity for investment in new industries and younger companies which provide opportunities for substantial capital growth which might not otherwise be available in first tier markets. The level of dividends paid is therefore less important and in certain circumstances, such as greenfield projects, no dividends need to be paid in the initial years. The raising of further capital by means of further placings of equity or rights issues is encouraged and seen as a positive development.

There is current concern at the small number of shares available in certain companies as this leads to high prices as a result of scarcity value. These high prices lead to unrealistic expectations and consequently highly volatile share prices. The effective market in the shares can be very small as most shares are held by firm holders, and few shares are available for trading.

Nevertheless, it is hoped that this is a temporary phenomenon which will be overcome by subsequent further issues of capital and the move by companies to a full Stock Exchange listing.

1. INTRODUCTION

The active secondary level share markets in Europe have developed only recently for the purposes of financing new industries and for the purpose of providing second and third stage financing for younger companies. In the United Kingdom, the market was first seriously pioneered by the predecessors of Granvilles who started the OTC Market which stimulated the London Stock Exchange to consider promoting the finance for companies under Rule 163. Rule 163's original purpose was only to allow occasional bargains to take place in certain selected shares such as football clubs. The Stock Exchange therefore actively marketed this as a secondary level share market until November 1980. It was felt at this stage that the market was too under regulated and that a more formalised structure was required which would give some protection to investors and would allow the market to attract the younger entrepreneurial businessman to raise capital without the onerous requirements and costs relating to a full Stock Exchange listing.

From these beginnings the Unlisted Securities Market (the USM) was borne and since 1980 some 220 companies have obtained a listing on the USM and have jointly raised £230 million. The total market capital is now approaching £2.1 billion. By any measure, this must be rated a considerable success.

In parallel, the Over-the-Counter Market has developed what is best described as a telephone market. There is no board of prices nor an established trading floor. Over the past eighteen months, the number of market makers has increased from 2 to 24 and the number of companies traded from 30 to 70. Unlike the USM there is no overall regulatory body, which is a cause of some concern.

The importance of the institutional investor, as opposed to the private investor, is of considerable influence in London. The institutional investors which comprise primarily the pension funds, life assurance companies and unit trusts, make up by far the largest proportion of investors in the London market. The private investor, investing his own portfolio, has declined in importance to play a much less important a role. In examining the considerations of the investor I am therefore concentrating on the views of the institutional investor.

The institutional investor in London has considerable sums available for investment. During the current year it is likely that some £14 billion will be available for net new investment by the pension fund and life assurance companies alone. The USM therefore forms only a small part of the institutional investor strategy. Overall it accounts for much less than 5 percent of total institutional investment. This should be seen in the context of the size of the market which is very small in comparison to the total net new funds available for investment (say £100 million per annum versus £14 billion per annum) and the restrictions which are placed upon institutional investors. Unit trusts are restricted to holding not more than 25 percent of their portfolio in unlisted shares, and charities do not generally hold any shares that do not have a full Stock Exchange listing. The pension funds are restricted by the instructions of the Trustees to the Fund Managers.

There are therefore restrictions on the investment funds available but, nevertheless, the supply of institutional investment currently exceeds the demand by companies for issues of share capital on the USM and OTC markets. The views of the investors can probably be divided into three categories:

- The Positive Features which encourage investment by institutions in USM and OTC stocks.
- Negative Features which highlight the risks inherent in such investment.
- Points for the Future which indicate certain important developments.

Each of these is now considered in turn.

2. POSITIVE FEATURES

First, the USM and OTC markets provide an opportunity for investment in new industries which, at the present time, are smaller and younger, but which will in the course of time replace those mature industries for which growth has become restricted. These new industries are best illustrated by electronics, computer, security and financial services companies. Some of those which have recently obtained a listing on the secondary market are as follows:

Acorn Computers
Technology for Business
CPU Computers
Bio-Mechanics

Scusa
A & G Security
Derek Bryant Group

These new industries have a considerably faster rate of growth than the mature industries and it is hoped that in the investors' portfolio there will be companies which will grow to the size of say RACAL or Beecham or Philips in the years to come.

The access to investment in new technology is a second important investor consideration. Particular examples might be as follows:

Selec TV - Cable Television
Renishaw Holdings - Electronic Instrumentation
Real Time Control - Supermarket check-out Bar Codes

There is a third category of company which sees a secondary market as more appropriate than a first tier market. Certain examples could be as follows:

- Aspinall Holdings - Casino Operator
- Miss World - Annual Beauty Contest
- Pineapple Dance Studios - Dance Studio

In summary, the positive features amount to an opportunity to participate in the prospect of a greater capital gain than might otherwise be possible in the first tier markets, but without the restrictions that are placed on a first stage venture capital investment with no market. The USM provides a particularly good, well regulated market with proper control over companies issuing shares to the public.

3. NEGATIVE FEATURES

It is a natural consequence, that if an investment policy is pursued which concentrates on younger, less mature companies with a view to a capital gain, the investment will involve a higher risk. The USM has spawned a number of notable successes as well as failures. Nevertheless, of the 220 or so companies which have obtained the facility for their shares to be dealt in over the last 3 years, only five companies have suffered serious financial difficulties:

Hesketh Motor Cycles - Receiver Appointed
I.O. Technology - Receiver Appointed

American Communications Industries	- Receiver Appointed
Euroflame	- Shares Suspended Dept. of Trade Enquiry
Chemical Methods	- Shares bought in again from the public

This represents a failure rate of some 2 1/4 percent which, under the circumstances is an acceptable level of risk for an investor.

There are a number of "greenfield" project companies which have come to the USM. In October, 1983 there were ten such companies:

- Nimslo International
- Cornell Holdings
- Airship Industries
- Bio-Isolates
- Immediate Business Systems
- Greenwich Cable Communications
- Biomechanics International
- Selec TV
- Swindon Private Hospital
- Metal Sciences

Such greenfield project investment is necessarily of a higher risk nature and in general terms has much less appeal to the institutional and private investor. This greenfields sector amounts to only 4½ percent of USM companies and it is unlikely that this proportion will increase. For investors they are an interesting exception to the normal rule.

One of the most serious concerns of the investor concerns the lack of size in the market. In order to encourage entrepreneurs to come to a secondary market, the USM requires only that 10 percent of a company's equity shares are placed in outside investors' hands. This results in only a small number of shares being available to the general public. This has had the effect of pushing the share prices up to unrealistically high levels, due to the scarcity value. These high prices cause unrealistic expectations from companies and consequently when results are announced, the fall in share prices is sharp and considerable. These high share prices have produced an artificially highly rated market in certain sectors and the Bank of England took the unprecedented step in July, 1983 of drawing attention in its Quarterly Bulletin to the high valuations placed on companies on the USM and the sometimes excessive volatility of its share prices.

A further consequence of the high prices is the distraction this has caused to the managers who are principal shareholders; the "paper millionaire" syndrome. Once the entrepreneurs wealth is quantified at a high level and highlighted in newspaper articles this can cause a major distraction. He may wish to improve his personal position and family pressures increase for him to work less hard. He acquires a Rolls Royce and works less hours. This paper millionaire syndrome is a frequently stated concern of institutional investors.

The relatively small number of shares available in the market has caused a further consequence which is of concern to investors. The shares, particularly when a Placing, as opposed to an Offer-for-Sale takes place, tend to be held in firm hands by investors who do not wish to sell, usually for some years. There are therefore few shares available to be traded in the market. Effectively, regular trading in the shares in any size becomes impossible and share prices stagnate and do not move. This has become a fairly regular feature of quite a number of shares of the USM. Trading in the shares only takes place in any size around the time of the results or other important announcements.

4. POINTS FOR THE FUTURE

The important step which investors would like to encourage is that the secondary markets should only be a temporary market for companies and should be seen as a stepping stone to a full listing on one of the major stock exchanges.

The USM was described in the original proposals as a market which would encourage companies to progress to a full listing on the London Stock Exchange. It is encouraging to see that 12 companies out of the 220 have already taken this step:

- Intasun
- Star Computer
- Carlton Communications
- Jackson Exploration
- Anglo-Nordic
- Trust Securities
- Goal Petroleum
- Markheath Securities
- Oceanics
- Bespak
- Goal Relations
- A & G Security

The investor will then have a shareholding in a more mature company with larger amounts of equity shares available in the market. For example, the London Stock Exchange requires 25% of a company's shares to be held in the hands of the general public as opposed to 10% for the USM. This removes some of the concerns in relation to the USM.

At this stage it is important to consider investors and investors' attitudes towards dividends. The principal reason for considering investment in a secondary market is to obtain a greater capital gain through investment in new industries with significant higher risks.

The level of dividend is not an important criteria for the secondary market institutional investor. It is quite acceptable to have a stated period when no dividends will be paid at all and this is the case with the 10 greenfield companies on the USM. The level of dividend must of course depend upon the type of company and in a more mature company a dividend level in the region of 5 percent to 7 percent on the issue price would be normal. It would be expected that this dividend would be twice covered by earnings.

Investors regard rights issues or further issues of shares as an encouraging feature; provided the companies are profitable and will put the proceeds to good use. The investor would regard this as part of a positive pattern of growth and assists the investors in providing a wider market in the shares. In general terms, it is not advisable to have a rights issue within 1½ years of the original issue unless an acquisition is being made. Thereafter however, a rights issue is likely to be not unwelcome.

When coming to the USM for the first time, companies are generally encouraged to raise new capital for the companies rather than allowing existing shareholders to sell out in the initial sale of shares. The provision of new capital is likely to assist the company in its growth, whereas the sale of shares by the founder in any size will tend to cause a relaxation of his entrepreneurial drive. Investors therefore encourage the issue of new capital rather than sale of shares by existing shareholders.

The growth of the secondary markets in London, being particularly the OTC and USM markets has been a very encouraging feature over the last three years. It has undoubtedly encouraged investors who have sufficient funds available to satisfy these markets and has encouraged smaller companies to consider these for second and third stage financing. More importantly it has encouraged and publicised the role of the entrepreneur through the many press articles that appear on a daily basis. It is a noted feature that this has encouraged many potential entrepreneurs to actually become entrepreneurs.

Venture Capital Markets for the Regeneration of Industry
J.M. Gibb (Editor)
Elsevier Science Publishers B.V. (North-Holland)

THE AMERICAN OVER-THE-COUNTER MARKETS

A. E. Young

Professor of Finance,

School of Management, Syracuse University

Summary

This will be an analysis of over-the-counter versus exchange markets in America because, especially in today's technologically advanced environment, the two basic alternative trading systems of the past are inexorably intertwined. We first look at some of the basic differences between exchange and over-the-counter markets and note the historical metamorphosis which over-the-counter trading has undergone. While as little as half a century ago over-the-counter trading in America was virtually ignored when the basic pieces of legislation regulating the securities markets were drafted, at the present time over-the-counter trading in large company shares constitutes a significant force in the securities industry.However, over-the-counter trading in small company shares remains as little used and forgotten a market segment as in the days of the initial passage of the basic Securities Acts. After this introduction, some of the major forces and elements in the securities industry over the recent past are analyzed. Finally, the proposal for a national market system is developed and the likely position of the over-the-counter market in such a system is considered.

1. INTRODUCTION

It is first necessary to say that the term "over-the-counter" in reference to the securities markets of which we are now speaking is clearly a misnomer. A more proper term would be "over-the-telephone". For in the case of such markets, as opposed to the other kind of secondary market trading mechanisim-the exchange market (where trading takes place at a centralized location on each exchange trading floor), all business is transacted over the telephone or through other means of electronic communications.

A further significant distinction between exchange and over-the-counter (OTC) markets is in the type of trading which occurs. American exchange markets are characterized by a continuous two-way auction process, whereby agents of buyers bid against each other while agents of sellers act similarly. Alternatively, while there is now some movement away from this for large company shares, American OTC markets have historically utilized a negotiated trading procedure in which principals deal among themselves and brokers, in disposing or acquiring stocks for investors, may deal with their customer on either an agency or a principal basis.

When the basic pieces of legislation in the securities field were passed, the Securities Act of 1933 and the Securities Exchange Act of 1934, no mention was made of the OTC market. Only exchange listed securities and the exchange markets were referred to. At the present time, however, OTC trading in large company shares constitutes a significant force in the securities industry and the self-regulatory organ of the OTC market, the National Association of Securities Dealers (NASD), represents as powerful a force as the primary self-regulatory agency in the exchange segment, the New York Stock Exchange (NYSE). Nevertheless, the OTC market for small company shares remains today as illiquid and forgotten as in the days of the initial passage of the basic securities acts.

An understanding of the distinction between exchange and OTC markets in America is particularly relevant at the present time as the securities industry grapples with the Congressional mandated national market system (NMS) for securities trading. Such a system is to include elements of both exchange and OTC markets, and the nature of the trading process which eventually evolves will doubtless be a product of both economic exigencies and political pressures between the two types of trading systems and among the various component forces of each.

2. RECENT HISTORY OF AMERICAN OVER-THE-COUNTER VIS-A-VIS EXCHANGE TRADING

The Securities Acts Amendments of 1964 extended to almost all large and relatively large OTC firms the same continuous disclosure and insider trading requirements which heretofore had pertained solely to exchange listed securities.[1] From the point of view of those OTC firms affected by this legislation much of the advantage of avoidance of exchange listing thus evaporated. The result was an increase in exchange listings (particularly on the (NYSE) and on the American Stock Exchange (AMEX)) and a concomitant reduction in the number of large and relatively large firms whose shares were exclusively traded OTC. The OTC market thus became the habitat of small firms and those larger firms whose off-exchange trading was affected by one or more of the significant market related economic and regulatory or self-regulatory forces of the day. We now turn to a consideration of some of the more important of these forces.

a. The Elimination of Fixed Minimum Exchange Commission Rates

From the initial organization of the NYSE and other U.S. exchange markets, fixed minimum brokerage commission rates prevailed. Rates were based upon the round lot (normally 100 shares) system. Under this procedure the minimum brokerage commission on the trading of a 10,000 share (100 round lots) block of common stock was precisely 100 times the charge for a trade involving 100 common shares (1 round lot). However, to the brokerage firm executing the transaction, the costs involved in consummating a trade involving 10,000 shares is normally far less than 100 times their costs in arranging a 100 share transaction. Thus large block trades became extremely attractive to the brokerage community, a fact which was clear to their growing institutional customers. This placed considerable leverage in the hands of institutions and resulted in the development of a complex system of institutionally directed commission give-ups, whereby an institution was able to designate that a portion of its exchange generated commissions be shared with a brokerage firm not executing the trade but which had provided it with other services.

With respect to the OTC market, however, fixed minimum exchange commissions resulted in the capture of an often considerable segment of institutional trading. Weeden and Company and some other non-NYSE member firms (exchange members were, until relatively recently, prohibited from the practice) began taking positions and making OTC markets in NYSE listed securities for the purpose of trading as a principal on a net (no commission) basis with institutions. The bid-asked spread on this trading often provided both a handsome profit to such firms and a superior net price to the institution than could be obtained on the NYSE. The name coined for such trading[2] was the third market (as opposed to the exchange and traditional OTC markets) and its effect was a reshifting, back to an OTC basis of some of the trading which had been lost to the exchange market as the result of the passage of the Securities Acts Amendments of 1964. Such a reshifting occurred primarily in institutionally favored large company shares.

However, beginning May 1, 1975 as the result of Securities and Exchange Commission (SEC) action, all fixed minimum commissions ended and an era of negotiated rates for all securities trading commenced. This resulted in a drying up of much third market activity, an additional reshifting of business in large company shares back to the exchange markets and a reconstitution of OTC trading as transactions predominantly in the shares of relatively small firms and those large firms for which special OTC markets (such as those described below) were developed.[3]

b. <u>The Growth of Institutional Stockholding and Trading</u>

Over the post-World War II period there has been a continuous and dramatic increase in the extent of U.S. institutional holding and trading of common stock. Of course, the mirror image of this trend has been a corresponding decline in the security holding and trading of individual investors. Of additional consideration in this milieu, particularly as it affects OTC trading and the demand for the equities of smaller companies, is the fact that institutional portfolio turnover is typically at a far more rapid pace than for individuals. Thus, depending upon the estimate one looks at, institutional equity shareholding may now run as high as 40% of the available supply of such securities which are publicly held. More relevant for its effect on the securities markets is the proportion of total trading activity accounted for by institutions, which according to some estimates, amounts to about 50%.

In order to understand the current impact of institutions upon the securities markets one must couple the above considerations with a knowledge of the kind of equity securities generally favored by institutional investors. As the result of their risk-bearing predelections, portfolio concerns and legal constraints, institutional investors generally evidence a far greater demand for the equities of large versus small companies, as opposed to the kind of companies preferred by individual investors. While all investors, institutional as well as individual, demand a trade-off between risk and return, for the most part institutional investors occupy a far lower portion of the risk-return indifference curve than do individual investors. This leads the vast preponderance of institutional investors to prefer the equities of large, generally less risky (lower BETA) firms to those of smaller enterprises.[4] Operating in the same direction are the portfolio concerns of institutional investors. Their vast size, that of the security positions they must take in order to generate a meaningful impact upon their overall portfolio returns, and their need to maintain liquidity, all militate against the holding of the shares of small firms. Finally, federal and state legislation, regulatory bodies, and their own charters often prohibit many institutional investors from placing any significant portion of their portfolios in the equities of small firms.[5]

Thus the trend in the proportion of institutional vis-à-vis individual stockholding and trading, as well as the relative preference of each for large versus small company shares, has lowered the overall demand for the equities of small firms and perhaps increased their cost of capital. These trends have also likely had the impact of shifting a portion of overall trading activity away from the OTC markets for small company shares toward the NYSE where the shares of large firms reside.

c. The Relaxation of the Prohibition Against Over-The-Counter Activity in Listed Shares by Exchange Member Firms

One of the means by which the NYSE sought to restrict OTC competition in its listed shares was by prohibiting its membership from engaging in off-board trading.[6] The effect of the restriction was to limit third market activity to non-NYSE member firms. However, under proding by the SEC, possible Congressional action, and threatened legal attack on antitrust grounds, the prohibition against off-board trading by exchange member firms has been relaxed somewhat.[7]

For a growing number of securities, exchange member firms are now allowed to transact business away from the exchange floor. This means that such firms can execute their customer's orders for exchange listed stocks by doing such things as matching these orders in their back offices, funneling them through an alternate market such as a centralized computer matching installation, or taking positions themselves and engaging in principal transactions with their customers. Each of these activities would withdraw volume from the exchange market and expand the OTC market. For a time many thought that the effect of these activities would be considerable, as Merrill Lynch, the nation's largest securities house, as well as other major wire house retail firms, indicated their intentions to engage in them. Recently, however, those firms have at least temporarily withdrawn from the experiment and returned to the exchange market for almost all of their trading in listed shares.[8]

d. The Rescission of the Rule Restricting Exchange Membership to Persons or Firms Engaged Primarily in the Securities Business

Another major change in recent years which affected the balance between exchange and OTC markets was the rescission of the limitation of NYSE membership to persons or firms engaged primarily in the securities business.[9] This rule effectively prevented institutional investors (primarily mutual funds, pension funds, and insurance companies) from circumventing the fixed minimum commission schedule, prevalent on the NYSE prior to May 1, 1975, by becoming exchange members themselves or establishing a broker-dealer affiliate to become a member, for the purpose of buying and selling securities for their own portfolios. By eliminating this rule, which embodied the so-called "primary purpose" restriction, the road was clear for the recent wave of mergers in the securities industry which has extended the department store concept to the realm of financial institutions as entities as diverse as life insurance companies and national retail outlets married with brokerage houses. While the primary effect of this rule was largely felt in the fixed commission era,its rescission seems to have further strengthened the power, resources and activity of the NYSE.

e. The NASDAQ System

The National Association of Securities Dealers Automated Quotations (NASDAQ) is a computerized quotations system operated by the NASD. Through this system approximately 2,700 of the most active OTC securities are traded.

NASDAQ has been in operation since 1971. It displays continuously updated bid and asked quotations on cathode ray terminals (CRT) located in subscribers offices.[10] There are three levels of operation, designated as Levels I, II and III. Market makers have exclusive use of Level III terminals which consist of a CRT screen and a keyboard. Through the keyboard a market maker can enter, change or cancel any bid or asked quote for any stock in which he makes a market. All current bid and asked quotes entered by market makers in any NASDAQ security are shown on the CRT screens. At the end of 1979, the average security in the NASDAQ system had 8.2 market makers.

Level II terminals are used by brokers and dealers who do not act as market makers. These terminals provide the same information as Level III terminals, except they do not permit the inputting of bid and asked quotes. However, any NASDAQ subscriber with a Level II terminal can readily determine the market maker, in any NASDAQ quoted stock, with the highest bid and lowest asked quote.

Level I terminals are used by the salespeople of brokerage firms. They show only a "representative" bid and asked quote in each NASDAQ quoted stock. Their purpose is to provide both salesperson and customer with an approximate notion of the price at which a security can be bought or sold.

When a brokerage firm receives a customer's order to trade a stock that is quoted in the NASDAQ system it checks the Level II or III screen to determine the market maker with the best bid or asked quote at that time. A telephone call by the broker to the market maker with the best quote can then provide the customer with his best possible execution.

By and large the NASDAQ system has been a considerable success and has probably aided the efficiency of the OTC market by providing smaller bid-asked spreads and better executions for investors.

f. Other Computerized Trading Facilities

In addition to NASDAQ, a number of other computerized trading facilities exist. One of these is known as the Cincinnati Stock Exchange (CSE) or sometimes as the National Securities Trading System (NSTS).

NSTS began in June 1978 and is a fully automated electronic trading system that enables CSE members to enter orders for themselves or their customers without leaving their offices. Such orders are stored in a computer which automatically matches buy and sell orders. The computer is programmed so as to assign priority to orders based on the price and time of entry, with public orders receiving priority over those of members.

Although encouraged by the SEC which saw NSTS as a source of valuable competition to the other exchange markets, the new computerized system has captured a very small share of total exchange trading volume. NSTS average daily trading volume generally ranges from 100,000 to 300,000 shares, while 100 million share trading days are now the norm on the NYSE. Moreover, in July of this year the largest participant in NSTS, Merrill Lynch, withdrew its patronage from the system, thus likely further reducing its relative share of total trading volume.

Another computerized trading facility is known as Instinet. This system is similar to NSTS in terms of its matching orders on an automated basis, but different in that participants can access the system directly without the need to route orders through brokers. Participants pay a membership and a trade fee to the system. Current participants are almost exclusively institutions which trade large blocks of shares and have the resources the fees demand. Instinet promises at least as good an execution as on an exchange and at lower transaction costs. Thus it appears to be gaining both participants and trading volume. Even so, Instinet's trading volume at the present time is very small compared to NYSE volume, seldom exceeding 400,000 shares and institutional investors frequently complain that executions on the system are too slow.

A rather recent electronically based trading system, which unlike NSTS and Instinet is not in competition with the traditional exchange markets, but rather represents a supporting facility of these markets, is known as the Intermarket Trading System (ITS). This is a cooperative venture, between the NYSE and five other exchanges, of an electronic linkage of their respective trading floors for purposes of providing investors in designated stocks with access to that trading floor which gives them the best possible execution. By using the system, traders on one exchange floor can send orders to other exchanges if prices appear better there.

ITS became operational in April, 1978 and has been growing in the number of securities in the system and the volume of shares traded. By November, 1980, ITS was facilitating 4.2% of total share volume and 6.6% of the total number of trades in the 871 stocks then in the system.[11] Moreover, a NYSE study found that in 1981 ITS saved investors $40 million by helping them get better executions.[12] Additional savings may result from a recent SEC mandated electronic linkage between ITS and competing OTC market makers.[13]

Although fully automated securities markets which link all competing forces are technologically feasible at the present time, it should be remembered that automation, in itself, will not create competition or provide better executions for investors. Market makers in numbers must be willing to take positions and risk their capital if real competition is to develop. In addition, there are always the conflicting goals of competition versus depth for securities markets. Should competition result in excessive fragmentation of trading among alternative markets, the depth of each market may be dangerously impaired. We will look below at the issue of conflicting goals for securities markets.

g. The Position of the SEC in Fostering Competition Versus Market Depth

The Securities Exchange Act of 1934 states that the "securities markets are an important national asset which must be preserved and strengthened".[14] This is to be accomplished by the SEC securing for these markets five qualities as follows:

a. economically efficient executions of ... transactions;
b. fair competition among (brokers, dealers, and markets);
c. the availability to brokers, dealers, and investors of information with respect to quotations (and transactions);

d. the practicability of brokers executing investor's orders in the best market; and

e. an opportunity, consistent with efficiency and best executions, for investors' orders to be executed without the participation of a dealer.[15]

Through the years the practical effect of the above criteria for SEC action has frequently centered upon the choice between the potentially conflicting goals of fostering competition between alternate markets versus the creation of maximum depth and liquidity in any particular market. Often when these conflicting objectives presented themselves in reference to the issues which were to be decided concerning the structure of the securities markets, the SEC has opted for the creation of competition, even at the sacrifice of depth in the predominant market place.

In an era, such as the present, of substantial and rising volume in securities markets, this choice would appear to be highly justified. However, much of the increase in volume in recent years can be attributable to the activities of institutional investors. Thus the liquidity of the securities of large companies would seem to be well assured. But for the shares of smaller firms market fragmentation and the concentration of increased market maker interest in large company securities may constitute a genuine threat to their continued liquidity. In essence, as the SEC continues to encourage market maker competition for the highly lucrative institutional trade, interest in smaller company securities may wane. And while SEC policies may well have improved the market for large company securities they seem to have done little to enhance the liquidity of small company shares.

3. THE PROPOSAL FOR A NATIONAL MARKET SYSTEM

In June, 1975, Congress enacted the Securities Acts Amendments of 1975.[16] This legislation, among other things, adopted the SEC proposal for a NMS and gave the SEC broad powers to implement the proposal.

However, while it is clear that by a NMS Congress intended a centralized electronic linkage of the nation's various securities markets, the form this linkage was to take was not spelled out in the Act. In effect, the SEC was left to direct the development and character of the NMS. And the basic thrust of the SEC has been to attempt to construct the kind of linkage of the various market segments that would enable customers to receive the best available execution of their orders (at least for the securities of large firms) on the most favorable market place. The SEC has tried to achieve this by encouraging market makers and specialists to compete.

The SEC has identified six major elements of the NMS as follows:[17]

a. A system for consolidated public reporting of completed transactions (a consolidated tape);

b. A system for the composite collection and display of bid and asked quotations (a composite quotation system);

c. A system for linking the various securities markets by the transmittal, from one market to another, of orders to buy and sell securities and reports of completed transactions (market linkage system);

d. The elimination of restrictions on the ability of exchange members to engage in OTC transactions in listed securities (off-board trading rules);

e. Nationwide protection for limit orders against inferior execution[18] in another market; and

f. Rules for determining the securities that are considered qualified for trading on the NMS.

To date, the progress in these six areas might best be described as variable. Since April 30, 1976, a consolidated tape has been in full operation and the SEC has had some success in the development of a composite quotation system. There has been some progress in the development of ITS and its linkage to the OTC market. There has also been some relaxation of the exchange restrictions against off-board trading by member firms; however, the complete elimination of off-board trading rules for all listed securities has yet to come about. Little or no progress has been made in developing and implementing a system for the nationwide protection of limit orders against inferior execution in another market. Finally, the SEC has developed a set of rules for determining the securities that are considered qualified for trading on the NMS.

4. THE AMERICAN OVER-THE-COUNTER MARKETS AND THEIR FUTURE

The future of the American OTC markets as well as the future shape of the NMS, of which OTC trading will no doubt be an integral part, depends upon an array of political and economic forces and their interplay, such as has been developed in this paper. The relative strengths of the various OTC institutions, as well as their adaptability to the relevant future economic forces, will likely dictate the position of OTC trading in the future NMS.

OTC trading now takes place in an extremely broad spectrum of securities, including government and corporate bonds, and shares of all classes of corporations. For corporate shares five separate segments of OTC trading can be identified at the present time.[19] First there are 30 active stocks of large OTC firms in a new experimental system known as the Computer Assisted Execution System (CAES). CAES is different from traditional OTC trading in that it represents an execution system in which OTC trading takes place on an auction basis. Next, off-board trading restrictions have been removed to the extent that OTC trading by NYSE member firms now takes place in from 100 to 300 stocks.[20] A third kind of OTC market segment is represented by that type of trading in the approximately 3,000 securities contemplated at the present time for inclusion in the NMS. Next NASDAQ has about 1,000 stocks which are not expected to join the NMS. This brings us to the fifth OTC segment represented by the approximately 25,000 publically owned non-NASDAQ firms. These companies are generally smaller and newer than listed firms or those included in the other four OTC market segments. The market for their shares is inactive and illiquid and can be called as forgotten a market segment today as 50 years ago when Congress ignored these kinds of firms when initially passing the basic Securities Acts.

As to OTC vis-à-vis exchange trading in large company shares, and the relative position of each system in the future NMS, the vitality of the OTC market seems well assured. At the present time third market activity seems to be declining relative to NYSE volume,[21] the major wire houses are withdrawing from back office market making and the NSTS appears to be losing volume.However, the NYSE and AMEX have been suffering a decline in their rate of new listings. In 1982 only 33 companies left NASDAQ for the AMEX as compared to 77 in 1981. And 29 companies left NASDAQ in order to become listed on the NYSE in 1982, down from 25 in 1981. Moreover, so far in 1983 the pace of defections from the OTC market has remained slow. Finally, daily OTC trading volume exceeded NYSE volume for the first time on May 27, 1983. This may be the result of more high-volume issues beginning to forego NYSE listing [22] or perhaps it derives from the activities of competing OTC dealer market makers. But in either case, while computer assisted OTC and NMS trading generally appear on the rise, this activity is restricted to the shares of large firms. Smaller company shares in America are as forgotten a trading vehicle as they were 50 years ago.

Footnotes

1. Securities Acts Amendments of 1964, U.S. Public Law No. 88-467,78 Stat. 565 (Codified at 15 U.S.C. ₱ 77d, 78e, 781-78o, 78o-3, 78p, 78t, 78w, 78ff (1976)), on August 20, 1964.
2. OTC trading in exchange listed stocks where securities industry professional firms take positions and make markets.
3. Additional factors in the decline of the third market were the development of a consolidated tape (as discussed below) and the bankruptcy of Weeden and Company.
4. 4 SEC Institutional Investor Study Report, H.R. Doc. No. 64, 92d Cong., 1st Sess. 1529-828 (1971) and Marvin Rosenberg, "Institutional Investors: Holdings, Price and Liquidity," Financial Analysts Journal, March-April 1974, pp.53-59.
5. Rosenberg, Ibid and Investment Company Act of 1940, United States Statutes at Large, Vol. 54, Part 1, 1939-1941, p. 789, United States Government Printing Office, Washington, D.C.
6. The applicable rule was New York Stock Exchange Rule 394. (New York Stock Exchange, Inc., Constitution and Rules 3669-75(1976) (CCH)).
7. Under Rule 19(c)3 securities which have recently been listed or delisted and then relisted are available for off-board trading by exchange member firms.
8. Tim Carrington, "Merrill Lynch Ends Computer Trading Role", The Wall Street Journal, July 13, 1983, p.2.
9. Rule 318(a) of the New York Stock Exchange was rescinded effective March 25, 1980 ([1980] 2 NYSE Guide (CCH) 3072, 3077).
10. Much of the following description of NASDAQ is taken from Norman S. Poser, "Restructuring the Stock Markets: A Critical Look at the SEC's National Market System," New York University Law Review, Vol. 56, November-December, 1981, pp. 883-958.
11. Ibid, p. 925.
12. The Wall Street Journal, January 28, 1983, p.46.
13. The Computer Assisted Execution System, which is another computerized trading facility of the type now being discussed, is considered below.
14. Securities Exchange Act of 1934, ₱ 11A (a) (1) (A), 15 U.S.C.₱78k - 1 (a) (1) (A) 1976. The following analysis of legislation in the securities field is similar to that of Poser, Op. Cit. p. 906.
15. Securities Exchange Act of 1934, ₱ 11A (a) (1) (C), 15 U.S.C.₱78k-1 (a) (1) (C) (1976).

16. Public Law No. 94-29, 89 Stat. 97 (Amending Securities Exchange Act of 1934, 15 U.S.C. ¶ 78-78kk (1976 and Supp. IV 1980)).
17. This list is patterned after Poser, Op. Cit., p. 916.
18. In this sense, "inferior" represents a price below the current bid or above the current asked quote. In effect, the execution is inferior from the point of view of a person on the other side of the transaction. To a customer who has placed a limit buy order on a specialist's book, however, the chance of obtaining an execution at a lower price is, of course, favorable and in that sense may be regarded as "superior" to the customer's limit price.
19. While there is a considerable overlap of individual securities among these five segments, the five types of OTC trading identified represent, in effect, different trading systems.
20. In the terminology used earlier in this paper, this represents a type of third market activity.
21. Third market trading in NYSE stocks amounted to 7% of total volume in those securities in 1971, but fell to 2% in 1980. (NYSE Fact Book 1981, 26th ed., New York Stock Exchange, 1981).
22. The Wall Street Journal, June 23, 1983, p.1.

Venture Capital Markets for the Regeneration of Industry
J.M. Gibb (Editor)
Elsevier Science Publishers B.V. (North-Holland)

THE LONDON "UNLISTED SECURITIES MARKET"

Robin Stormonth-Darling

Chairman Laing & Cruickshank
(inc. McAnally Montgomery & Co.), Stockbrokers, London.
Chairman, Quotations Committee,
The Council of The Stock Exchange

Summary

In November 1980, the Unlisted Securities Market (USM) was launched. Its purpose was two-fold. The principal purpose was to provide a formal, regulated market designed to meet the needs of those smaller, less mature companies unlikely to apply for listing. It was considered that without such a market and some assurance of marketability for their investment, investors were liable to be less willing to take a stake. Secondly the USM brought under the formal regulatory control of The Stock Exchange those unlisted companies whose securities were being freely traded under the provisions of Rule 163(2) of The Stock Exchange. That Rule permitted occasional bargains, subject to the permission of the Council, in the shares of unlisted public and private companies; it continues to be available for that purpose but on a somewhat more restricted basis than in the past.

During the period November 1980 to September 1983, 211 companies were admitted to the USM and £277 million was raised at the time of their entry.

THE STOCK EXCHANGE UNLISTED SECURITIES MARKET

The Formation of The Unlisted Securities Market

The Unlisted Securities Market (the "USM") was launched on 10th November 1980. The USM grew from a general awareness in the late 1970's that companies were not coming forward for a listing of their securities. In 1978 The Stock Exchange drew companies' attention to the opportunities for dealings in their securities under rule 163(2) and perhaps to raise money by a formal marketing. This was the rule that enabled member firms to deal in the securities of unlisted companies normally on a matched basis. It was suggested that dealings under Rule 163(2) could widen shareholdings and create a limited market in the shares of the company without the company going through the 'rigours' of a listing. The interest generated exceeded all expectations and several companies were floated with the intention of active trading taking place in their securities under Rule 163(2). It soon became apparent that the regulation of these was not consistent with the activity in the market and there was general concern that companies were not required to announce price sensitive information.

In the early months of 1979 the Quotations Committee began to examine the possibilities of creating a regulated market. In December 1979, following consultations with Member Firms, City Institutions, Government Departments and companies who were thought to be likely candidates for an USM, a discussion document was published and comments invited from interested parties. Some 66 commentaries were received and in October 1980 the definitive rules for an Unlisted Securities Market were published. On 10th

November dealings began in the securities of eleven companies. At the same time it was announced that companies whose shares were actively traded under Rule 163(2) would be expected to join the USM if the activity was to continue and that, after one year, Rule 163(2) would revert strictly to occasional matched bargains.

All companies in the USM are required to sign a general undertaking similar in many aspects to the Listing Agreement signed by listed companies.

The USM from its inception to the end of September 1983

On 10th November 1980 there were 11 companies in the USM. By the 31st December 1980, 33 companies had been admitted and this grew to 85 by 31st December 1981 and 149 by 31st December 1982. At the end of September 1983, 211 companies had been admitted. The following table shows how turnover and number of bargains per week have grown:

Table I

Turnover and Number of bargains

Period Covered	Number of Days	Total Value £m	Total Bargains
1981	251	282.2	64,040
1982	253	619.6	131,737
04.01.82 - 26.03.82	60	105.4	21,661
28.03.82 - 25.06.82	61	98.3	19,823
28.06.82 - 24.09.82	64	107.2	19,976
27.09.82 - 31.12.82	68	398.7	70,277

1983

04.01.83 - 31.03.83	63	257.9	63,063
05.04.83 - 24.06.83	61	286.0	61,727
27.06.83 - 30.09.83	69	361.5	76,157
01.07.83	5	24.2	4,239
08.07.83	5	43.6	5,575
15.07.83	5	25.2	6,120
22.07.83	5	23.0	4,146
29.07.83	5	22.9	5,343
05.08.83	5	21.2	6,599
12.08.83	5	36.4	7,928
19.08.83	5	24.1	7,052
26.08.83	5	21.5	4,506
02.09.83	4	18.4	3,986
09.09.83	5	18.1	3,882
16.09.83	5	17.1	3,507
23.09.83	5	32.6	8,289
30.09.83	5	33.0	4,985

The USM has achieved two important objectives. First it has provided a market for the shares of companies whose records are too short for listing. The USM normally requires a three-year trading history, but companies with no trading record may be admissible if funds are required to finance a project or product which has been fully researched and costed. Eleven companies have entered the USM without a trading record. These are significant concessions compared to the listing requirements and have particularly attracted high technology companies which require capital injections at an early stage in their development. These companies might have looked for an alternative to the Stock Exchange's central market in securities had the USM not been in existence. Secondly, companies that had the necessary trading record for a listing were able to consider the USM as an alternative. Many companies in the USM have been attracted to the market because they were not required to have at least 25% of their equity capital in public hands as is required for a listing. The minimum for a company entering the USM was set at 10% and although this will tend to lead to narrow markets and exaggerated price movements in some cases it is nevertheless a starting point from which companies can issue shares for acquisitions or raise further capital without the fear of possible loss of control. It is apparent however that few USM companies have as little as 10% in public hands; around 20% is more normal, with several companies having over half of their equity in public hands. "Public hands" for these purposes means shareholders other than the directors, their associates and families and possibly any substantial shareholders normally identified with or represented on the board.

The USM has attracted a wide variety of types and sizes of businesses. A rough breakdown shows companies from, inter alia, the following sectors:

Table II

Brewing	Finance	Motor Trade
Building	High Technology	Newspapers
Chemical	Hotel & Catering	Oil and Gas
Electrical	Insurance	Paper, Printing and Advertising
Engineering	Investment Companies	Property
	Leisure	

A majority of companies have come from the high technology, fast growth sectors such as electricals, and computer hardware and software. Even so, many less glamorous companies have joined the market. The sizes of companies range from a market capitalisation of approximately £300,000 to £150 million. 118 companies in the USM are however in the range of £1 million to £10 million.

By far the most popular method of entering the USM has been through a placing of shares, and 120 companies have used this method. There have been 27 offers for sale to the general public (a placing - which a broker does mostly amongst his own firm's clients is not permitted where more than £3 million is to be raised or the expected market capitalisation of the company exceeds £15 million). Most of the 64 introductions (sufficient shares already being in public hands) have been of companies whose shares were previously dealt in under Rule 163(2). This has led to a reduction in activity under Rule 163(2), the demands of companies and investors being better satisfied by active regulation and disclosure through the USM.

A total of £324 million has been raised by the sale of shares of USM companies up to 31st December 1982 analysed as follows:-

Table III

Money raised by issue of USM securities

	£,000
On entry - for the Company	171,265
- existing shareholders	105,501
Total raised on entry	276,766
By issues after entry	46,910
Total money raised to 30th September 1983	323,676

The following table shows a breakdown of the money raised on entry to the USM up to quarter ended 30th September 1983:

	Raised for Company £	Raised for Shareholder £
10.11.80 to 31.12.80	6,895,000	2,420,250
01.01.81 to 31.03.81	1,400,000	181,300
01.04.81 to 30.06.81	13,055,470	12,387,945
01.07.81 to 30.09.81	5,793,282	5,800,812
01.10.81 to 31.12.81	21,440,668	6,886,041
Total for 1981	£41,689,420	£25,256,098
01.01.82 to 31.03.82	4,785,000	2,416,234
01.04.82 to 30.06.82	5,565,622	8,607,438
01.07.82 to 30.09.82	15,208,337	10,166,500
01.10.82 to 31.12.82	19,127,188	11,258,160
Total for 1982	£44,686,147	£32,448,332
01.01.83 to 31.03.83	£ 7,285,100	£ 1,058,638
01.04.83 to 30.06.83	33,717,317	32,961,504
01.07.83 to 30.09.83	36,990,892	11,356,212
Total since inception:	£171,264,776	£105,501,034

185 of the 211 companies admitted to the USM continued to have their securities traded in the USM at 30th September 1983. 7 companies have had dealings in their securities suspended, 3 of which are expected to return to the USM after completing large acquisitions. The remaining 4 companies experienced financial problems.

One of the encouraging features of the USM has been that it has developed without detracting from listing. Many of the companies entering the USM regard listing as their ultimate aim and have declared their intention to move on to listing in due course. So far, seven companies have transferred from the USM to listing. Two companies have been acquired under offer since joining the USM. One company in the USM has recently made an offer for a listed company and issued its shares as consideration.

The following summarises the number of companies admitted to the Unlisted Securities Market:-

Table IV

USM Companies

At 30th September 1983	185
Suspended from trading	7
Transferred to listing	13
Acquired under offer	6
Total number of companies admitted by 30th September 1983	211

SESSION IV:
PARALLEL WORKING GROUPS

WORKING GROUP 1
Developing Venture Capital Exit Mechanisms at an EC Level 153
Chairman: H. SCHMIDT
Direktor, Institut für Geld- und Kapitalverkehr,
University of Hamburg, Hamburg (Federal Republic of Germany)
Rapporteur: D.L. ADAMSON
An Investigation of Inquoted Holdings of United Kingdom Financial
Institution, Nuffield College, Oxford (United Kingdom)

WORKING GROUP 2
Improving the Capital Environment Affecting VC Investments 156
Chairman: P. FONTANEAU
Professeur Agrégé des Facultés de Droit, Avocat à la Cour d'Appel de
Paris (France)
Rapporteur: P. WECKEL
Assistant, Université de Strasbourg III, Strasbourg (France)

WORKING GROUP 6 AND 3
Stock Options for Managers in Companies with Growth Potential 161
and
Mobilizing Non-Banking VC Investors on EC Level 161
Chairman: R.G. HODGSON
Managing Director, Granville & Co. Ltd., London (United Kingdom)
Rapporteur: S. NEUMANN
Infobrief Luxembourg S.a.r.l., (Luxembourg)

WORKING GROUP 4
Governmental Schemes Stimulating the Venture Capital Market 164
Chairman: K. NATHUSIUS
IVCP – International Venture Capital Partners S.A. Holdings, London (United Kingdom)
Rapporteur: P. DOURNEL
Expert, Directorate General "Information Market and Innovation", Commission of the European Communities, Brussels (Belgium)

WORKING GROUP 5
EC Infrastructure to Link VC Markets 170
Chairman: C. CLEIFTIE
Deputy Director General, SOFINNOVA, Paris (France)
Rapporteur: R. GUTH
Directorate General "Information Market and Innovation", Commission of the European Communities, Brussels (Belgium)

WORKING GROUP 7
Venture Capital through Collective Investment 174
Chairman: J.D. INCLEDON
Chairman, Hilger Analytical Ltd., London (United Kingdom)
Rapporteur: E. PHILLIPS
Directorate General "Information Markets and Innovation", Commission of the European Communities (Luxembourg)

WORKING GROUP 8
Venture Capital Management 176
Chairman: I.N. MOMTCHILOFF
General Manager, Investors in Industry Group P.L.C., London (United Kingdom)
Rapporteur: J.M. GIBB
Directorate General "Information Market and Innovation", Commission of the European Communities (Luxembourg)

Report of Working Group 1

Chairman : Dr. H. SCHMIDT
Reporter : D. L. ADAMSON

Developing Venture Capital exit mechanisms at an EC level

The working group had the task to take a European,not a national perspective in viewing exit mechanisms. Basically, the group thought that two exit mechanisms warrant special attention. First, the use of stock markets in other Member States, and, second, the sale of small innovative company shares to foreign institutional investors. Both mechanisms may be used alternatively, in sequence or in combination.

The working group recommends that the Commission steps up its efforts aimed at removing barriers to cross border equity financing. Given the time constraints the working group did not try to address all these barriers. The group decided to focus on four issues : general market structures, cross border first public offerings, international investment banking and international investment by financial institutions.

In these four areas the working group puts forward the following recommendations :

1. In view of the expense and attendant practical difficulties the working group sees no need to establish a central European market for small company equity instruments. The now existing markets should be utilised with maximum flexibility and improved to accommodate small innovative companies.

Domestic and foreign high risk companies should be admitted to stock markets and assigned to an appropriate market segment.

Stock exchange entry requirements for these companies should be designed in such a way as not to impose an undue burden on small enterprises. Whenever possible investor protection should be underwritten by existing law rather than by the introduction of new and complex measures.

2. It is recommended to remove any regulations that impede small European companies from making first public offerings of shares in other Member States. The working group recognizes and deplores the broad variety of

restrictive regulations. They range from exchange controls to subtle forms of discrimination affecting foreign issuers. The group would welcome further detailed investigation of these barriers.

Moreover, the working group recommends that new ways of disseminating information on new issues markets should be considered. The formation of the European Venture Capital Association represents a good opportunity for the launch of a Journal devoted to this task. It is hoped that this journal would draw the attention of entrepreneurs to the substantial differences of price-earnings multiples that similar companies command in different national capital markets.

3. To promote a vigourous investment banking sector, the working group endorses the recommendation presented in Session III to make available in all Member States a licensed dealer status as it is currently known in the United Kingdom. These licensed dealers should be allowed to make markets over the counter and carry securities accounts for clients. The development of interactive Videotex may facilitate market making activities. To foster competition in investment banking it is also recommended to encourage European wide activities of investment bankers established in any one of the Member States. The Commission should take the actions required to remove the regulatory barriers that currently inhibit such activities.

4. Ideally, there should be no restrictions on international and unquoted investment by institutions. Having regard to the practical difficulties that would be faced by large financial institutions in making and monitoring international unlisted investments, the working group considered that attention should be paid to the idea of creating specialist intermediary vehicles.

A possible model for such a vehicule would be a closed end investment company whose shares would be listed on one or more national stock exchanges. The assets of this company could be held in quoted and/or unquoted form at the discretion of the management. Tax treatment should be the same as for mutual funds. The market will place a value on the portfolio of assets held by the fund. This will reduce the continuing efforts required in difficult and time consuming valuation of individual unlisted investements.

Such funds should attract institutional backing given that the investment policy would be international small company investment - a role that institution will want to subcontract. The active presence of such specialized subcontractors would greatly contribute to the internationalisation of the European capital markets for small companies by stimulating a competitive cross border search for emerging companies seeking additional equity capital.

Report of Working Group 2

Chairman : P. FONTANEAU

Reporter : P. WECKEL

Improving the capital environment affecting VC investments

The Working Party would first draw attention to that fact that since 1975 the Commission of the European Communities has been proposing changes in the tax treatment of certain forms of income currently assessable to income or corporation tax, leading to a degree of harmonization amongst Member States. Such proposals have related in particular to mergers, relations between parent and subsidiary companies, and the question of double taxation of companies resident for tax purposes in more than one Community Member State. Within the limits defined by those proposals, the Working Group proposes the following measures aimed at improving the operation of the Venture Capital market.

The recommendations seek to produce a twofold result : to coordinate and harmonize the tax status of those present on the Venture Capital market, and by this means to work against the fragmentation of the market and in the future give it a European dimension.

The Working Group proposes the following measures as a means of achieving this result :

1. Changes in the tax treatment of individuals investing in the Venture Capital market.
2. Changes in the tax treatment of innovative companies.
3. Changes in the tax treatment of Venture Capital investment funds.

Such changes should be aimed at increasing similarity between the tax systems of the Community's Member States in the treatment of these three economic agents.

The Working Group is aware that the tax treatment of innovation is no more than one element in the overall tax treatment of the three economic agents in question. Tax, particularly income tax and corporation tax, remains the prerogative of Member States. Nevertheless, the Working Group would hope to see the Venture Capital market given a good start by reducing the tax burden as far as possible in the various Member States.

In view of the international nature of innovation and of its importance to growth and employment in Europe, a basic Community policy aimed at stimulating the process of innovation should be considered.

The Working Group consequently proposes that a European code for the tax treatment of innovation should be drawn up. Such a code would be instrumental in restoring an edge to European businesses against their American and Japanese competitors.

The Working Group is aware that changes in the tax treatment of innovation are essential to a healthy start for the Venture Capital market. It is, however, stressed that tax incentives alone will not lead to a rapid growth in the market, and calls for further aids to the firms and individuals involved in the Venture Capital market.

P. FONTANEAU

Minutes of the meeting of Working Party n° 2

The Chairman praised the Commission's efforts since 1975 to harmonize the rates of company tax. He emphasized that any proposals which the Commission might be moved to introduce in order to promote innovation should be based on the actions which it had already undertaken or completed.

The Chairman proposed four points for discussion, arising from the Wednesday afternoon session on the effects of taxation on innovation :

1) If the proposal met with the approval of the Member States, Mr HENRIKSEN had envisaged the setting up of a European investment fund or funds for venture capital which would benefit from tax advantages ;

2) In his paper, Mr INCLEDON had noted that there was no such thing as a common venture capital market ;

3) Income tax had a negative effect on the growth of venture capital. In this area , the Member States had to a large extent preserved their autonomy in taxation matters, but that should not bar proposals on various specific points ;

4) It would be unrealistic to believe that tax incentives would be sufficient in themselves to stimulate venture capital activity.

As far as Germany was concerned, one of those present at the meeting felt that tax incentives were vital because investors needed safer profit expectations and certain guarantees. He suggested therefore that investors should be offered the benefit of substantial tax reductions in the first year and that their profits be subject to a low rate of taxation in subsequent years.

Some of those present pointed out, however, that these reductions in tax levels would have the effect of transferring to the general public the main burden of investment risk. Tax reductions meant that the general public became one of the investor's main partners, but it was to be hoped that it would remain a minority partner.

On the other hand, reference was made to the failure of amortization companies in Germany. When the investor's main incentive was tax concessions, the effect was simply to increase investments in businesses which were not viable.

The view was expressed that the tax authorities should keep their generosity within reasonable limits and maintain a certain balance between the different economic entities.

Mr KAPLAN stated that he was in complete agreement with this reasoning but thought that the example given by the speaker to support his argument, namely the excessively high quotation price for certain shares which would be caused by the Business Expansion Scheme in the United Kingdom, was not a very appropriate choice insofar as this result was inevitable and one of the advantages of the scheme.

The Chairman declared that he was in favour of a system of investment deduction since a reduction in the tax on dividends would be of no advantage during the first few years when no profit was earned.

For his part, Mr WIRK considered that the effectiveness of each tax incentive should be evaluated as part of a given taxation system : it could not be treated in isolation. He considered that in Germany the barrier was of secondary importance.

During the discussion, there seemed to be a consensus of opinion on the statement that the marginal rate for taxing the highest income levels was too high and liable to quell the propensity to save. However, two reservations were expressed. It was pointed out that during the first few years of the investment , the level of taxation could not in fact be excessive since no profit was earned. Secondly, Mr WIRK considered that it was less important to query the tax burden falling to this category of taxpayer than to change the graduated scale of taxation, which was too steep.

Mr WIRK considered that tax concessions should be concentrated mainly on the innovative businesses themselves, especially during the initial profit-making phase. He suggested that tax-free investment reserves be set up for this purpose.

One member of the Working Party proposed that, along with the setting up of the European Innovation Loan, tax concessions should be granted to financial intermediaries in respect of the proportion of investments which they made in shareholders' equity.

The Chairman remarked - and the speaker agreed with him - that such a deduction would in effect free these institutions from the risk which was the very aim of their activities.

The Chairman recalled that the setting up of national investment funds and a European fund to attract capital to the Community had been suggested. He pointed out the advantages of a multinational fund for the countries which had instituted an exchange control system.

The Working Party considered that it would be preferable to have several private funds at national level and did not propose the creation of an international fund. Nevertheless, a link should be established between the various funds. If investors were to find it advantageous to expand their activities to neighbouring countries, they would have to benefit from tax concessions similar to those granted in their own countries. It was suggested that this should be done within the framework of the double taxation agreements.

The Chairman asked the meeting whether it considered it necessary to propose harmonization of taxation rates applying to venture capital within the Community. Those present considered that the diversity of taxation systems and the reluctance of the Member States to limit their autonomy in this field suggested that this objective was unlikely to be attained in the foreseeable future.

This point of view was not, however, unanimous. It was felt, on the contrary, that the Member States would lose an opportunity to further progress in Europe in a key area. Full advantage had to be taken of the novelty and topicality of the venture capital problem.

The Chairman suggested that the Working Party should put the following proposals to the Commission :
both individual investors and venture capital companies should benefit from tax concessions.

However, such measures were incorporated in taxation systems which had to be considered as a whole. It was therefore to be hoped that the governments of the Community countries would reduce the tax burden on the highest incomes.

Finally, the same system of taxation for venture capital should be applied throughout the Community.

Report

Working Group 6 : 'Stock options for managers in companies with growth potential'

&

Working Group 3 : 'Mobilizing non-banking VC investors on EC level'

Chairman : R.G. HODGSON
Reporter : S. NEUMANN

A) Stocks options (U.S. Examples)

The group in general agreed that stock options for managers are an essential tool for the venture capital community. Primarily an incentive for the manager to participate in the company's growth, stock options have to be paid under general practice. This provides for additional incentive and may have some taxation aspects. To combat the high mobility of management (presidents in the U.S. change in an average time of 1 1/2 year), options are building up on a yearly basis. For unquoted companies the valuation of shares is difficult. In one case, it was experimented in averaging the profit on a three year basis. Taxation of gains out of stock options is a very difficult problem in the U.K. In other European countries the problem is less known and will have to be worked through by tax experts on a country by country basis.

The recommendations made by the group :

- The EC Commission should initiate a study on the tax treatment of stock options for managers in EC Member Countries and the US , and should also cover the intellectual case for S.O., the merits, the economic impact, and the barriers to implementation of the stock options approach ;

a) The EC Commission's harmonizing work in company taxation should include management renumeration by stock options & pension rights and take into account the political/social/economic case ;

b) The importance of stock options as a tool for the venture capital community requires a harmonized (tax) treatment of this instrument in the EC to facilitate international operations ;

c) Stocks options should be considered not only for start ups or by-outs but also for follow-on stages of company finance to be taken into account in any fiscal regulations ;

d) The terminology 'stock options' are marked by bad public relations and should be replaced by a more positive term, possibly by EUROPEAN PARTICIPATION RIGHTS as proposed by Prof. SCHMIDT ;

In addition to stock options, the group also discussed management renumeration by pension rights which are low in US quotations and - in the aspect of pension portability - depend on individual arrangements in Europe.

Above all the intellectual case for effectiveness of stock options had to be presented as an essential part of small firm growth. The 'Politics of Envy' would otherwise make reform impossible.

B) Mobilizing VC investors

The group at first defined 'non-banking VC investors' and decided to drop the term 'non-banking'. The major investment groups being discussed during the session, covered :

- pension funds & insurance companies
- industrial funds (i.e. industrial companies)
- academic institutions
- unit trusts & collective investors
- private investors.

The governments and depending nationalised industries were excluded from consideration since they are subject of working group 4. Academic investors which already participate in VC funds in Europe are considered to participate mainly for establishing close-link relationships for technology transfer. To mobilize VC investors, the following recommendations have been worked out :

1. Any stimulation of institutional VC investors must be related to the rate of possible growth of the venture management potential in Europe to avoid negative developments ;

2. Before proposing measures to overcome lagal or statutory barriers which prevent institutions investing in VC. The EC Commission should set up a positive/negative inventory of rules and their impact in the EC ; there could also need to be consideration of barriers arising from the organisational structure of investing institutions ;

3. The EC Commission should support the creation of VC partnerships in a European dimension to built up a dynamic European VC market ($1-2 bn investment/year as a target) ; the Commission should therefore examine barriers to transitional partnerships and arrangements.
Institutional investors, primarily pension funds & insurances, should be allowed encouraged/forced to invest a certain percentage of annual income in venture capital ;

4. Industry should be motivated to use the 'technology window' provided by VC in extending the R&D by volume & efficiency. Industry may also assist in targeting suitable industrial areas for VC investments to create major European companies ;

5. EC Commission is asked to support the development of the VC infrastructure to reduce the risks for people coming up with funds ;

6. University should contribute to this VC infrastructure by entrepreneurial education and in bridging the communication gap between technology & manpower offer & demand ;

To avoid negative effects out of the lack of professional venture management in Europe, any actions to mobilize institutional investors should have their priorities & timescale.

Report of the Working Group 4

Chairman : K. NATHUSIUS
Reporter : P. DOURNEL

GOVERNMENTAL SCHEMES STIMULATING THE VENTURE CAPITAL MARKET

This paper will give a thematic report of the debates in order to have the clearest possible overall view. But the chairman and reporter would first like to thank the members of the group for their very active participation and the interesting positions expressed.

I STATE OF THE ART

Amongst the different measures taken by the Member States of the European Communities, one could distinguish three main categories :

- tax relief options
- direct capital supply
- guarantee schemes.

A. TAX RELIEF OPTIONS

Tax measures are in fact aimed at developing investment in general and thus can benefit venture capital financed programmes. One of the most needed, i.e. loss carry over, is happily present nearly everywhere. Loss carry back is more seldom applied, but it seems that most Member States look interested by this option for some programmes (1).

There are also specific tax measures for venture capital, mostly linked to an innovative aspect. For instance, the German case of "Verlustausfallgarantie des Wagnisfinanzierungsgesellschaft", the French statute for the "Sociétés financières d'innovation" or even the Belgian "Fonds Communs de Placement" (2). There tax measures are either aimed directly at venture capitalist's financial structure consolidation or indirectly through measures favouring private investments in venture capital funds.

B. DIRECT CAPITAL SUPPLY

Some Member States have adopted capital supply schemes to support venture capital. One of the most striking and recent examples is the Irish "National Enterprise Agency" which will be exposed below. State's actions in this field can be manifold, and vary from direct shareholding in some sectors, like in Greece, to supporting the creation from a Venture Capital Society distributing public or semi-public funds (Germany: Wfg, France: SFI,...) (2).

However, we must be aware of the fact that these measures are rather limited both in scale and impact, for they haven't yet reached "critical mass".

C. GUARANTEE SCHEMES

This is a very well developed area of government action. Though the practice of guarantee is already on old tradition for loans, it has recently, - in 1980 - been extended to equity capital: the first were the Germans with the "Verlustausfallgarantie der Wfg, the Dutch with the PPM scheme, followed by the French SOFARIS.

The traditional concept of loan guarantee was amended in order to support innovation, mostly in small and medium sized companies, like in United Kingdom with the British Government small Businesses Bank Loans Guarantee Scheme (2).

II EXPERIENCE AND POSITIONS

In order to clarify the debates, it was decided to try and answer some questions with the help of participants' experience.

A. Which kind of a role can a government play in venture capital?

a) Irish example

The National Enterprise Agency, which was set up in October, is a very original creation. The role of this governmental body is to be a venture capital source for early stages of company foundation, and , once the risks of product development, market introduction and growth problems have been reduced, it will sell its stake on a secondary market.

The originality of NEA is to employ outside experts to deal with venture capital problems with which normal civil servants could not cope. Their remunerations will be 20 % of the fund's capital gains plus managing fees. This is indeed a very original structure which might be a model for other governments.

b) Canadian example

The Canadian example is also interesting because a kind of an answer to a question which arose during last years symposia: what could be the role of military governments?

The Canadians, since they decided to increase their military potential, are using public and military procurments and R - D contracts given to young enterprises as a means to support venture capital.

This was necessary because of the obvious lack of seed corn capital.

B. ENVIRONMENT PROBLEMS : WHICH ACTIONS?

The most evocated topic was venture capital environment, i.e. taxation policies, venture capital managers formation,....

a) Taxation policies

Maybe a major if not the major - inhibitant to a real development of venture capital in continental Europe. Though this problem is manifold, at least these points have to be mentioned:

- Income tax on individuals reduce significantly their saving potential and thus contributes to the situation of rare and expensive money. Furthermore, the few available personal disponibilities are then invested in traditionaly convived low risk sectors. This is obvious: if you have little to invest, you cannot even think of diversification.

- Corporate tax: the rather large range of taxation rates and basis calculation in Member States is surely an obstacle to both high venture capital rentability and trans- or multinational operations.

- Capital gain taxes also have a negative effect, for venture capital investors are obliged to look for higher rentability to compensate potential risks. And high rentability is becoming a rare quality.

On an ethic aspect, the working group was not sure that offering special fiscal arrangements was a good thing. This concept of inequality might, in the long run, be more dangerous than profitable , for it may draw to venture capital firms needing in fact other kinds of finance, and it also seems dangerous to discriminate against traditional growth, which is nowadays responsible of the most of the added value creation.

b) Perception of the entrepreneur's role

This is already an old problem rather typical of our continent. If, in the United States, failures are admitted as a normal part of the risk game, it is not the case in Europe, where it is still considered as infamy and often leads to jail or long term financial consequences - if not both.

It is rather an educational problem which will not be solved unless taken in an early stage of development, which, also means that it might take at least one generation to have a better perception of the entrepreneur's role..

c) <u>General facilities offered to entrepreneurs</u>

This can be a good place for Member States' action. These general conditions can be understood in two ways:

- Creation of a favourable economic environment: better management of public funds and debits, inflation and unemployment policies...

- Creation of favourable structures, like "innovation centres" or "interface centres", supply of real estate with, industrial vocation at low cost,... This last governmental action is already being persued in Member States like Ireland, United Kingdom, France...(2).

d) <u>Managers specialized education</u>

This is obviously a considerable lack in our educational system. But, here, a solution can be rather simple and easy.to implement. Maybe, a simple extension to the education activities of existing associations could be an adequate answer.

Here again, the actions undertaken under the transnational plan will certainly be positive.

e) <u>Motivate the entrepreneurs</u>

Improving executives mobility would obviously be a good thing if linked with support to those wishing to create a company. This positive effect could even be doubled: company creation and substitution employment of young university graduates.

III <u>RECOMMENDATIONS</u>

1. Stimulate private initiative, i.e. stimulate investors from the private sector.

2. The stimulus should not be drained by the sole existing venture capital companies.

3. Create an entrepreneurial climate which will help changing mentalities.

4. Help to educate venture capital managers.

5. Help to develop a venture capital infrastructure.

Footnotes :

(1) See reports EUR 8820 and 8821 on this topic

(2) See report EUR 8819

Report of Working Group 5

Chairman : C. CLEIFTIE

Reporter : R. GUTH

EC infrastructure to link VC markets

In carrying outits allotted task, the working followed three simple principles :

1. Rather than trying to submit recommendations in due and proper form, it seemed to us more sensible simply to submit reports to the European Communities at the various stages in our deliberations, by way of food for their own thoughts.

2. One of the traditional stumbling blocks in the kind of exercise that we are carrying out at the moment is the desire for originality at any price, a desire which most often manifests itself in proposals for setting up new systems, procedures or bodies designed to carry out new tasks. In view of the natural tendency to run down the number of institutions, the working party thought, on the contrary - and this could be considered as its first recommendation - that it did not seem appropriate to innovate systematically for the sake of it, but that the existing institutions were quite capable of supervising the setting up of a Community infrastructure for liaison between venture capital markets.

3. The main features of any practical steps instigated by the European Community should be :

- simplicity of conception and modus operandi,
- widespread circulation among the relevant sections of the public through the organization of better marketing among primary recipients, particularly small, newly-established businesses which suffer most when lines of communication are too long.

- concentration on setting up an infrastructure and the appropriate basic conditions, whilst generating a climate favourable to the opening up of venture capital markets. The members of the working party did not think it desirable that the European authorities should act more than necessary as a substitute for market forces. In so saying, I have just put forward a second recommendation which, although not specifically orientated towards the subject discussed by our committee, is nonetheless well worth mentioning.

One can imagine various ways in which liaison between the different venture capital markets might work. In view of the terms of reference of this symposium and the credentials of the members of the working party, we have, of course, emphasized the financial aspect. Money may not be the only problem involved but without it there would be no venture capital markets !!

The working party considers that :

1. As a matter of utmost urgency, ways and means should be found to facilitate the effective free circulation of capital within the Community. Although this objective is laid down in the Treaties and despite the efforts which have already been made, the European authorities should strive with even greater urgency to abolish the many and varied national barriers which still exist. By way of illustration, I will just quote two typical examples.

In Italy, there is a compulsory interest-free deposit amounting to 50% of the purchase price of foreign securities or securities bought abroad.

There are tax discriminations against investors, depending on the legal nature of their status or nationality, whether they are private individual or public body, national or foreign.

2. The Community ought to take a leaf out of the book of the European Venture Capital Association (EVCA) and continue to work along the lines governing the setting up of this liaison body, which is unique of its kind. The Community ought also to ensure that it makes optimum use of all the opportunities offered by the EVCA as a liaison body between venture capital markets in order, among other things, to derive maximum benefit from the various incentives introduced nationally and to act as a driving force at Community level.

These preliminary standpoints should be rapidly supplemented by the adoption of long-term financial measures, of which the European Innovation Loan constitutes an important first step. In this context, reference has often been made to the activities of the EIB. Consequently the EIB ought also to turn its attention to venture capital companies and consider them as worth talking to with a view to their becoming financial partners.

The working party suggests that the EVCA ought to help endorse the credentials of the venture capital profession and could give it the stamp of respectability vis-à-vis the financial community as a whole and more particularly vis-à-vis the EIB, thereby allowing its members to take advantage of its position as a financial intermediary.

Working Party n° 5 is of the opinion that this is a step which could very rapidly be instituted, in particular by the drawing up of a code of ethics with which the EVCA would ensure compliance.

Concerning parallel capital markets the working party would consider it unreasonable to try to create a single market at Community level. The companies whose shares would be quoted on this market are basically local or at most national in character and the European level is not appropriate for dealings in their securities.

The Community dimension will only be appropriate for shortening contacts between different exchanges and the various parallel markets will be able to profit from it ipso facto.

It does not therefore seem advisable to envisage the creation of separate European links for parallel capital markets alone.

Finally, in conclusion, Working Party n° 5 would like to draw the attention of the European Community to two rather more delicate and yet important matters :

- firstly, the need to improve venture capital investment techniques and the degree of professionalism required of venture capitalists in order to acquire the complex expertise which they will need if they are ambitious enough to consider the Common Market as a whole to be one single market. In this case, too, the EVCA will play the role of pioneer, and should receive ample backing from the European authorities ;

- Secondly, it seemed to us that these same institutions have not yet given sufficient attention to the very real problem of the discrepancy between the time it takes for a particular branch of technology to become fully developed and the constraints of ROI imposed by venture capitalists. This problem, which is experienced every day by entrepreneurs, would seem to merit further research in order to try to reconcile the apparently contradictory demands of the two sides.

Report of Working Group 7

Chairman : J. D. INCLEDON

Reporter : E. PHILLIPS

Venture capital through collective investment

The group saw a number of factors in Europe which make life difficult for new companies as compared with their counterparts in North America. One participant quantified this by saying that the difficulties experienced in the United States are multiplied ten times in the European Community, simply because the Community comprises ten different countries. What he was referring to were the different tax systems, different accounting practices, different languages, different inflation rates to contend with and different currencies which are met in moving from one European Community country to another.

In Europe many companies have to grapple with these problems very early in their life, because individual national markets are so small that even in its first year a company may find itself trying to export. By contrast, in the United States, there are many more companies which may operate for years without ever needing to export outside North America.

There is also a relative lack of experience in Europe, as compared with the United States. It was mentioned in Group 7, as an example, that many entrepreneurs in Europe seem to need help from venture capital organisations in drawing up business plans, whereas it is almost second nature to the entrepreneur in the United States. The group had doubts whether many venture capital organizations in Europe had the expertise to provide the back-up which some entrepreneurs need.

Looking at the situation from the point of view of the investor based in a European Community country, the group noted that such investors may be reluctant to invest outside their own country because they are worried about encountering problems (such as exchange controls) when they want to bring their money back again.

The group also noted a higher level of sophistication among American investors in general, compared with their counterparts in Europe.

Because of all these factors, the group felt that venture capital organisations in the United States were better developed and more experienced than organisations in Europe. As a result, just as some American companies have captured significant shares of the European market for their products, the United States is also drawing venture capital away from Europe. Of course this serves still further to reinforce the strengths of the American venture capital organizations at the expense of their European equivalents.

These considerations led the group to its first recommendation :

> 'Recognizing the relative lack of experience compared with American venture capital organizations, we should look for ways of strengthening the intermediary organizations in Europe so as to ensure that they can compete more effectively'.

Measures specifically mentioned by the group were tax regulations in favour of these organizations, and the abolition of impediments to the free flow of capital across national boundaries.

The group's second recommendation was intended as a direct approach to the perceived lack of experience among venture capital organizations and entrepreneurs in Europe :

> 'There should be selective assistance to aid the intermediary organizations, and the managers of companies taking venture capital, in acquiring the techniques essential to success in their fields'.

Finally, the group felt that venture capital markets would benefit if it could be made easier to realize investments, particularly over short timescales of two to three years ; in other words, there is a need for better exit mechanisms. Another way of expressing this view is to say that until there are exchanges in all the member states (along the lines of the London Unlisted Securities Market) which facilitate investment in venture capital funds, there will remain difficulties in getting money back in the short term. The final recommendation was therefore :

> 'There is a need for a strengthening of the machinery for realizing venture capital investments at an early stage'.

Report of Working Group 8

Chairman : I. MOMTCHILOFF

Reporter : J.M. GIBB

Venture capital management

The working group set out to define in practical terms what venture capital management is about and to identify some of the major policy options open to those embarking on it. Moreover, attention was drawn to certain difficulties encountered by VC managers which could be alleviated through official action at national or Community level.

The group tackled the subject under the following headings :

1. What structures?

2. a) How to find suitable projects
   b) Criteria for investment decisons

3. a) Monitoring investments
   b) When to get out.

1. WHAT STRUCTURES?

Time-scale of a VC operation : fairly long term; at least about 10 years.

Owners : can be individuals;
VC companies;
institutions.

Sectors in which to invest : two major options :

a) wide spectrum of sectors (hence statistical spreading of risks),

or,

b) specialization (hence acquisition of more detailed knowledge, leading potentially to better calculation of risks).

There was a feeling that option a) has a slight edge on option b).

Stage of financing : The financing of start-ups is attractive in terms of growth potential, but riskier than the financing of ventures at later stages of development, for which there is a strong demand. A VC enterprise's portfolio should be diversified in this respect.

What kind of people? A VC enterprise should be run by a team including people : with experience of business managment;
skilled in accountancy;
with financial expertise.

Example of specialized VC unit :

one business management expert) handling about
one financial expert) 5 investments

Example of non-specialized VC unit :

one business management expert)
one financial expert) handling about
+ advisory panel) 15 investments
+ consultants)
+ network of contacts)

Why invest abroad?

To operate in a larger market and to obtain a diversification effect, but advice is required on legal matters, patent protection, taxation etc.

What incentives for the members of a VC team?

One possibility is to arrange directly for the members of the team to have a share of capital gains obtained. This may prove difficult if the VC team is part of an institutional system.

Another possibility is to provide them with stock options. Unfortunately few countries possess an adequate legal framework for this.

Free movement of capital

The free movement of capital, essential if international operations are to be envisaged, is still not a complete reality within the European Community, because of the exchange controls applied by some Member States, and other regulations, such as those pertaining to the nationality of company directors.

International cooperation

Although, as hinted above, it is advantageous to operate in an international context, establishing a solid position in a foreign market is no easy matter. This points to the advisability of transnational syndication. Perhaps the newly-founded European Venture Capital Association could help towards this.

Decisional structure

The basic option is between a hierarchical and a collegiate structure. In the former case, ultimate responsibility for decisions rests with one person. In the second, responsibility is shared, decisions being taken, in the case of some organizations, by a formal voting procedure. A slight preference was expressed for the latter system.

2. a) HOW TO FIND SUITABLE PROJECTS :

- through the technical press;
- through universities;
- through other VC managers;
- through members of the advisory panel (if there is one);
- through industrial buyers;
- through advisers, accountants, consultants, etc.;
- through bank managers;
- through attendance at conferences and fairs;
- through data bases.

2. b) CRITERIA FOR INVESTMENT DECISONS

It must be possible to answer the following questions positively :

- Is the management of the venture adequate?
- Is there a business plan available?
- Has the plan been evaluated from the commercial, industrial and financial point of view and found to be satisfactory?
- Is there an exploitable proprietary or commercial advantage?
- Has the management a personal financial commitment?

3. a) MONITORING INVESTMENTS

Once an investment has been made, it should be monitored :

- by obtaining and scrutinising progress reports;
- by ensuring that the business plan is updated whenever necessary;
- possibly by having a seat on the board;
- by providing actual help to the management.

3. b) WHEN TO GET OUT

No hard and fast rule, obviously, but before growth starts tailing off, i.e. fairly early.

CONCLUSIONS AND RECOMMENDATIONS

Legislative steps should be taken to improve access of managers to stock options.

Totally free movement of capital is necessary within the European Community if the full benefits of transnational VC cooperation are to be reaped.

More courses should be organized on VC management.

Data bases on Community-wide business opportunities should be further developed.

SESSION V:
REPORTING BACK SESSION

Subjects for Future Meetings 183
D. WATSON
Directorate General "Information Market and Innovation",
Commission of the European Communities, Brussels (Belgium)

Summing-Up 187
I.N. MOMTCHILOFF
General Manager, Investors in Industry Group P.L.C.,
London (United Kingdom)

SUBJECTS FOR FUTURE MEETINGS

DENNYS WATSON

Head of Task Force, Industrial Innovation
Commission of the European Communities

You will remember that this is the fourth in an annual series of symposia on various aspects of the financing of innovation, which we initiated in 1980, following the report by Professor Piatier on obstacles to innovation. Four years ago, we had very few other events competing with ours, in which the main thrust was promotion of venture capital; today, I am delighted but somewhat alarmed to see that this has become a very popular topic for seminars and conferences : delighted, because this means that we have perhaps achieved our first aim of sensitizing authorities and institutions at various levels as to the potential contribution that this can make to industrial innovation, but alarmed at the question of whether there is anything useful left to say and discuss on the matter. After hearing the expert contributions and discussions of these last three days, however, it does seem that there are still many topics which provoke lively interest, and the record attendance at this symposium shows that we seem to be doing something useful : perhaps one task we do usefully fulfil is to provide a meeting-place on neutral ground for the activists at national level to discuss their experiences, exchange views, and even set up deals! It has been suggested that we might try and provide a more structured basis for this last activity, and we are giving this some thought.

We certainly cannot afford to be complacent. The formal framework of this meeting must be attractive, and we cannot rely on a kind of "brand loyalty" to ensure that people like yourselves come back for more next year; our "product" must respond to market needs, and we have the familiar problem of trying to assess what these needs will be about one year ahead of today. So, once again, I am going to ask you to help us with our market research. To those of you who were here last year, the method will be familiar. You will each find in front of you a "score sheet", which was produced very early this morning, after listening both to the formal presentations during the first two days, and sampling the discussions in each of the parallel working groups : the score sheet, which, due to our time limits, could only be produced in one language, lists the themes which, in my subjective judgement, may merit further exploration at future meetings.

In looking at these, I would ask you to bear in mind that our justification for running these symposia is the encouragement of industrial innovation, which is a broad subject. We cannot hope to satisfy everyone, both the generalists who come to listen and learn, and the specialists who come to speak their mind and try to gain some added value from the exchanges. One complication this year results from the welcome creation of the European Venture Capital Association, because they have provisionally decided to organize in 1984 at least one "external" event, open to non-members : and such an event may perhaps provide a better framework for certain themes which are related to the techniques of venture management. This is one reason for providing a column headed "separate interest", to allow for separate items which would not be justified for inclusion in a more general meeting. Otherwise, would you please score each item as being, in your opinion, of high, medium, or low interest? The aim of this exercise is to confirm or modify my views, and to allow room for you to put in your own additional ideas under "other suggestions" : when I was going round the various working groups in turn, I may have been absent when your particular idea was raised, and thus missed including it.

I am now going to go through the suggested themes on the score sheet, which are not listed in any order of priority or value :

1. The EVCA - aims, activities, progress made. Who they are, what they are doing, where they are heading.

2. Attracting managers to NTBFs and venture management, and motivating their performance - stock options, uses and constraints.

3. Case studies - 'how it was done' (including failures) by entrepreneurs and creators of new funds.

4. Exploiting results of publicly-financed R&D via spin-offs - financial and other aspects; this could perhaps cover university research, or defence-related R&D, and look at legal and institutional problems as well as financial aspects.

5. Investment opportunities and growth potential in one or more selected new technology fields : for instance one might select fields within new information technologies, bringing in industrial firms involved in ESPRIT, potential users, and venture capitalists active in the field.

6. Techniques of venture management :

   a) The flow of proposals, stimulation, control and filtration - costs and risks at successive phases of the selection process

b) The 'rounds of finance' concept - alternative financial packages at different phases of growth

c) The role and influence of unit trust (mutual fund) portfolio managers on marketability of NTBF shares

7. Any other suggestion? For instance, presentations of this morning have included reference to existing barriers to transborder investments.

I have not included the Commission's "review of progress" as this is now a regular feature, following a suggestion last year. In the "proceedings" of last year's symposium, you may have seen that we published the results of last year's score sheet : so you can see that we take your opinions seriously. I am going to thank you in advance for you help in providing us with this feedback, and look forward to analysing the results.

As I am the last speaker on the programme from the Commission, I would also like to thank you all very much for coming to the meeting, and for for your excellent contributions to the discussions : this particularly applies to the chairmen and rapporteurs of the various working groups, who I know had to put in a lot of extra work. Thank you for giving us the feeling that our efforts have been worthwhile, and we hope to see you again at future meetings.

Summing-up by Mr. I. N. MOMTCHILOFF,

General Manager, Investors in Industry Group PLC, London

I am now to summarise this symposium, but I will avoid that task, because it is almost impossible. However I would like to leave you with just one or two thoughts of mine.

Mme Lebas tried to convince us - passionately, I could almost say, - that it is the system that counts. There is no question in my mind that the development of a secondary market is an essential contribution to the venture capital system.

I strongly support regulations and standards in markets, but in my view, if venture capital activities are to be encouraged, an essential component of any system is a sensibly regulated and sensibly pitched secondary market. It is necessary to the fellow who actually risks his future in starting a company.

After all, during the long periods in which we in the United Kingdom had no access to a secondary market, anyone starting up on his own or within a team, only had two ways in which to make money out of his venture.

The first one was to build a company to such a size and stability and excellence that it could go to the main market and receive a public quotation. That is a daunting target and, for that matter, an ever-moving one, because a few years ago, you could enter the main market if your profits were a quarter of a million pounds, but a few years later, that went up to a million, then a million and a half. Part of that is inflation, but only part of it. Relatively few companies out of the hundreds that are started can aspire to that.

The other way he could make money was to sell out, but many people starting companies do not really have that as an objective. They start companies because they want to found companies.

The existence of the secondary market provides another dimension. It means that these people's chances of both securing access to the public's money and realising a part of their own personal investment (perhaps they can begin to think in terms of affording a car, or a second car, or a Rolls-Royce, if this is what they want) have been dramatically improved in the United Kingdom. After all, if you cannot give incentives to people to try and build up business, then we are all wasting our time, because it is they who are creating wealth. They have to make money; those who finance them have to make money; in fact, everybody in the system has to have an incentive to take the risks that are involved. Therefore, if anything blocks up the system, then it is something that Governments, the Commission, indeed all of us have to work at removing.

The second point I would like to make is one that I have made before, but I do believe it to be terribly important: there is a greater need for development capital in Europe than there is for high-flown venture capital. That sort of investment provides stability and good earning potential. It should not be neglected, because if too many groups start up with ambitions to move only among the stars, then many groups will fail, and I would hate to see this fantastic development of private company equity financing falling into disrepute because of unrealistic ambitions.

This could be the beginning of another little dark age. It happens in America. I can remember seeing in Minneapolis, not many years ago, a portion of a dealing floor with three blank screens. I asked what they were and I was told: "That used to be our Nasdac*section. The market is dead. The days of P.E.'s in double figures are over".

I expect the American market will take a turn down some time. I expect the same will happen also to the U.S.M.

---

* NASDAQ = National Association of Securities Dealers Automated Quotations

The last thought I would like to leave with you has to do with the transborder element. Everybody knows that our chances of attacking the European market as a whole with a product or a service are made very difficult by a whole range of obstacles: non-tariff barriers, different attitudes from country to country, etc. It is unfortunately true that the first place someone looks at if he is trying to establish a modern company is the United States. I do not mean that we should neglect the United States, because it is indeed the biggest single market in the world, but what a pity it is that we Europeans do not have a large market of our own.

At the moment, there is a trend towards even more protectionism. Every country wishes to be seen to be active in fashionable, high technology sectors and tends to want to have its own little robotics company, for instance, to be guarded jealously. That is a fatal mistake.

Now I believe that the development of a strong venture capital industry may be of help here. Perhaps by getting various institutions involved in venture capital and making them understand that they are dealing in an international market place, we will show that it is to the Member States' advantage to work together.

If you can get people to commit large amounts of risk capital, that will affect Governments thinking, it will affect institutional thinking, it will affect industrial thinking. It won't be tomorrow but I have real hope that this is going to be one of the things that for at least those industries which should form our future, we will make more of the Common market than we have with the dying ones.

Zusammenfassung der Vorträge 193

Arbeitsgruppen 1, 2, 6–3, 4, 5, 7, 8 205

Zusammenfassung der Symposiumsergebnisse 237
I.N. MOMTCHILOFF
General Manager, Investors in Industry Group P.L.C., London (United Kingdom)

RENTENFONDS ALS RISIKOKAPITAL-INVESTOREN

D.J. PROSSER
CIN Industrial Investments

Zusammenfassung

Rentenfonds sind neutral in bezug auf die steuerliche Seite von Einnahmen und den Kapitalertrag. Hierdurch ist eine grössere Flexibilität bei der Strukturierung eines Angebotes möglich. Die Rentenfonds sind aufgrund ihrer langfristigen Verbindlichkeit nicht unbedingt darauf angewiesen, kurzfristige Transaktionen zur Realisierung von Gewinnen bei erfolgversprechenden Anlagen durchzuführen.

Unser zwar geringes Engagement in den USA verschaffte einen Ueberblick über den derzeitigen Technologiemarkt und einen Ueberblick über die Strukturierung von Anlagemöglichkeiten. Der amerikanische Risikokapitalmarkt, der schon erheblich länger besteht, ist weitaus umfangreicher als der britische Markt. Für internationale Risikokapitalfonds dürfte es schwierig sein, in Europa Fuss zu fassen. Aufgrund sprachlicher und gesetzlicher Schwierigkeiten sowie aufgrund der unterschiedlichen Rechnungswesen werden Investitionen in kleine, nicht börsengängige Anlagen wohl vorzugsweise auf lokaler Ebene durchgeführt. Zwar wird es einzelne Ausnahmen geben, doch im allgemeinen wird einem auf einer breit gestreuten Grundlage operierenden Fonds ein "die Aktivität förderndes" Element fehlen, wenn nicht eine Vertretung an Ort und Stelle eingerichtet wird. In den meisten Fällen dürfte dies für ausländische Fonds zu kostspielig sein.

CIN Industrial Investments investiert Risikokapital sowohl für die Weiterentwicklung von Unternehmen als auch für einzelne Projekte und für Unternehmensgründungen. Bisher wurden etwa 180 Millionen Pfund investiert, die Geschäftsführung besteht aus 15 Mitgliedern. 1983 wurden 26 Millionen Pfund investiert und Gewinne in Höhe von 13 Millionen Pfund erzielt.

VERSICHERER ALS RISIKOKAPITALGEBER AUS NIEDERLAENDISCHER SICHT

D.S. VAN HOUT
Direktor für Investitionen und Unternehmensfinanzen
Ennia N.V.

Zusammenfassung

Risikokapital gilt zwar als Mittel zur Lösung von strukturellen Problemen in der Industrie der EG, aber Angebot und Nachfrage klaffen offenbar weit auseinander.

Ausserdem darf die Leistungsfähigkeit potentieller Geldgeber nicht überschätzt werden. Wenn sie der Industrie auch neuen Aufschwung geben, so bietet Risikokapital doch nicht Anreiz genug, um die traditionellen Kapitalmarktteilnehmer zu grossen Investitionen in diesem Bereich anzuregen.

Eine Prüfung der niederländischen Lage macht die Merkmale des niederländischen Versicherungsgeschäfts sichtbar. Die Hauptschwierigkeiten sind :

- der Widerspruch zwischen Maximierung von Gewinnbeteiligung und dem hohen Risiko einer Beteiligungsfinanzierung durch Anleihen;
- unterentwickelte Aktienmärkte;
- Erfahrung und Fachwissen der Risikokapitalgeber.

Eine Analyse der niederländischen Situation zeigt, dass grosse Mengen an neuem Risikokapital notwendig sind, um die Beschäftigung auf ein ausreichendes und akzeptables Niveau zu bringen, und dass in einzelnen Industriezweigen wohl ein versteckter Bedarf besteht. Allerdings müssen sowohl auf der Angebots- als auch der Nachfrageseite zahlreiche Hindernisse beseitigt werden; so sind zum Beispiel Möglichkeiten zur Steuerbefreiung und Starthilfen für junge Unternehmer von grosser Bedeutung.

Die Haltung der (niederländischen) Versicherer gegenüber Risikokapital spiegelt trotz einer bislang geringen Entwicklung dieses neuen Finanzierungsinstrumentes ihre soziale, aber auch ihre unternehmerische Verantwortung wider.

INNOVATIONSBESTEUERUNG UND -FINANZIERUNG : VERGLEICH DER BESTEUERUNGSMASSNAHMEN AUF EG-EBENE

Pierre FONTANEAU

Professor der rechts- und wirtschaftswissenschaftlichen Fakultät
Anwalt bei der "Cour d'Appel" von Paris

Zusammenfassung

Im Bereich der Innovationsfinanzierung spielt die Besteuerung eine wesentliche Rolle. Steueranreize gibt es in sämtlichen Mitgliedstaaten der Europäischen Gemeinschaft.

Im Hinblick auf einen Ausbau des Risikokapitalmarkts haben die Länder Europas Massnahmen zur Risikominderung bei Risikokapitalinvestitionen und zur Steigerung ihrer Rentabilität ergriffen.

Zur Erhöhung der Kapitalausstattung innovatorischer Unternehmen wurden Steueranreize für den Erwerb neuer Unternehmensanteile geschaffen und besondere Vorkehrungen zur Förderung der Selbstfinanzierungsmöglichkeiten der Unternehmen getroffen.

Darüber hinaus sind spezifische Massnahmen im Bereich der Forschnung und der Tätigkeiten im Vorfeld der Innovation ergriffen worden, mit denen die Rentabilität erhöht werden soll.

Allerdings ist zu erwarten, dass sich die ausschliesslich innovationsgebundenen Steueranreize im Falle zu hoher Besteuerung der Einkünfte von Unternehmen und natürlichen Personen, die diese Innovatoren besonders hart trifft, als unzureichend erweisen.

Aus diesen Erwägungen und angesichts der Bedeutung der Innovation für das Wachstum der Europäischen Wirtschaftsgemeinschaft sollte deshalb eine dem gesamten Innovationsprozess Rechnungtragende Steuerpolitik entwickelt werden.

Eine solche Innovationssteuerordnung müsste auf Gemeinschaftsebene koordiniert werden, um es den europäischen Unternehmen zu ermöglichen, ihre Wettbewerbsfähigkeit gegenüber ihren wichtigsten amerikanischen und japanischen Konkurrenten zurückzugewinnen.

BESTEUERUNG KOLLEKTIVER UND INSTITUTIONELLER INVESTOREN

D. O'HOGAN
Partner, Arthur Young & Company,
Wirtschaftsprüfer,
Portobello House, Dublin 8

Zusammenfassung

Gegenstand des Referats von Herrn O'Hogan war die Besteuerung von institutionellen bzw. kollektiven Risikokapitalanlegern unter besonderer Berücksichtigung der neutralen Rolle des Besteuerungssystems bei der Beurteilung der Zweckmässigkeit von Investitionen.

BESTEUERUNG DES INDIVIDUELLEN INVESTORS

CORNELIS A.M. RASENBERG
Generaldirektor, Steuerabteilung,
Amsterdam-Rotterdam Bank N.V. (Niederlande)

Zusammenfassung

Die Beschaffenheit des Risikokapitalmarkts erfordert vom individuellen Anleger Investitionen mit hohem Risiko für eine relativ lange Zeitspanne. Seine laufenden Einkünfte aus derartigen Anlagen sind dabei fast immer in voller Höhe zu den üblichen Steuersätzen versteuerbar, und nur in den wenigsten Fällen sind Kapitalverluste von den gewöhnlichen Einkünften steuerabzugsfähig, wogegen sich die Besteuerung von Kapitalerträgen von Land zu Land wesentlich unterscheidet. Inwiefern die üblichen Realsätze oder ermässigte Steuersätze zur Anwendung gelangen, hängt unter anderem davon ab, ob die Gewinne als Geschäftseinkünfte oder sonstige Einkünfte gelten. Steueranreize mit dem Ziel der Herabsetzung des Risikokapitalanteils nach Steuer bei einer Risikokapitalinvestition (steuerliche Absetzbarkeit oder Steuergutschrift) gehören zu den wirksamen Mitteln zur Förderung des Risikokapitalaufkommens. Durch die bestehenden Steueranreize für Beteiligungskapitalinvestitionen werden Investitionen in ausländischen Unternehmen eher benachteiligt.

Viele Staaten haben einseitig eine steuerliche Vorzugsbehandlung von Kollektivinvestitioninstrumenten eingeführt, jedoch in unterschiedlicher Form. Eingeführt werden müssten deshalb gemeinschaftsweit einheitliche Rechtsvorschriften für Risikokapitalgesellschaften, um so die Doppelbesteuerung von Unternehmensgewinnen und die übrigen Kollektivinvestitionen im innovatorischen Bereich hemmenden steuerlichen und sonstigen Vorschriften zu beseitigen.

DER EINFLUSS VON STEUERAENDERUNGEN IN DEN USA AUF VENTURE-CAPITAL-INVESTITIONEN UND INNOVATION

P.T. KAPLAN
Weil, Gotsmal and Manges
New York

Zusammenfassung

Obwohl die Vereinigten Staaten bisher allgemein in sehr grosszügiger Weise Steueranreize für Risikokapitalinvestitionen und Innovation gewährt haben, lässt sich daraus alleine keine Wechselbeziehung zwischen diesen Anreizen und dem hohen Innovationsstand in den Vereinigten Staaten der Nachkriegsjahre ableiten; zu einem solchen Schluss gelangt man nur durch eine Analyse der Auswirkungen der einschlägigen Steueränderungen. In den Vereinigten Staaten hat es eine Vielzahl derartiger Aenderungen gegeben, jedoch liegen bisher keine ausreichenden Erkenntnisse vor, die es den Wirtschaftswissenschaftlern ermöglichen könnten, entsprechende Zusammenhänge zu quantifizieren. Weniger wissenschaftlich betrachtet scheinen bestimmte Steueränderungen, insbesondere auf dem Gebiet der Kapitalertragssteuern, zu einem Wandel im Investitionsgebaren geführt zu haben, auch wenn sonstige Veränderungen im Investitionsgebaren nicht im Zusammenhang mit gleichzeitig in Kraft getretenen Veränderungen in der Besteuerung gebracht werden können. Sieht man von Statistiken ab, so lässt sich die Bedeutung von Steueranreizen für Innovationen in den Vereinigten Staaten in bestimmten Fällen aus gewissen Anlagemöglichkeiten erklären, in deren Rahmen der individuelle Investor F & E-Aufwendungen steuerlich absetzen kann, so dass sich die effektiven Kosten seiner Investition um bis zu 55 % herabsetzen lassen. Da sich diese in den Vereinigten Staaten praktizierte Steuerabzugsfähigkeit nicht auf einen bestimmten geographischen Bereich beschränkt, könnten Investitionsmöglichkeiten in Europa geschaffen werden, bei denen sich für amerikanische Investoren ähnliche Steuervorteile ergeben.

SPEZIELLE BÖRSENSEGMENTE FÜR ANTEILE AN KLEINEN UNTERNEHMEN

Situation und Perspektive

Professor Dr. H. SCHMIDT
Geschäftsführender Direktor des Instituts für
Geld-und Kapitalverkehr an der Universität Hamburg

Kurzfassung

In den letzten Jahrzehnten stellte man sich die ideale Börse als einen einheitlich organisierten Markt ausschliesslich für solche Gesellschaften vor, deren breit gestreute Aktien sich als solide Anlage anboten und die hohen Publizitätsanforderungen erfüllten. Wie aber Entstehen und Erfolg von speziellen Börsensegmenten für kleine und mittlere Unternehmen in verschiedenen Ländern Europas deutlich gezeigt haben, lässt sich über reduzierte Zulassungsanforderungen und mit speziellen Handelsverfahren durchaus ein börslicher Markt für solche Anteile schaffen, deren Umlauf höchstens eineige Millionen Mark beträgt und die folglich auch nur wenige Anleger halten.

Der neue Trend, Gesellschaften zur Börse zuzulassen, die man hierfür früher als zu jung, zu klein und zu riskant ansah, erstreckt sich bisher nur auf Unternehmen, die bereits einem bestimmten gehobenen Qualitätsstandard entsprechen. Grundsätzliche und pragmatische Erwägungen verlangen jedoch auch die öffentliche Emission und den börslichen oder ausserbörslichen Handel von Anteilen an jungen Unternehmen, die diesen Standard noch nicht erreicht haben. Dieser Weg zur externen Eigenfinanzierung junger und innovativer Unternehmen ist eine wichtige Alternative und Ergänzung zur Privatplazierung und zur Finanzierung über Venture Capital Companies. Bewertungsproblem, Kontrollproblem und Ausstiegsproblem lassen sich leichter lösen, wenn solche jungen Unternehmen Zugang zum Grundsegment als dem untersten Segment in der Hierarchie des Effektenmarktes erhalten. Trotz des hohen Risikos der Anteile an diesen Gesellschaften sprechen selbst Anlegerschutzerwägungen nicht dagegen, das Wachstum innovativer Unternehmen und dessen günstige gesamtwirtschaftliche Effekte auf diese Weise zu fördern.

Um die Eigenfinanzierung junger Unternehmen gerade auch über das Grundsegment zu fördern, bieten sich eine Reihe von Massnahmen an. Hier genannt seien lediglich die Einführung eines standardisierten Genusscheins und eines Licensed-Dealer-Status in allen Mitgliedsländern, steuerliche Anreize für eine tendergestützte Ermittlung des Emissionskurses bei öffentlichen Erstemissionen, Aufhebung von Anlagebeschränkungen für institutionelle Anleger und Abbau von steuerlichen Handelshemmnissen, insbesondere durch völligen Verzicht auf die Besteuerung von Kursgewinnen beim Verkauf von Anteilen an kleinen Unternehmen.

ZUGANG MITTLERER UNTERNEHMEN ZU DEN EUROPAEISCHEN KAPITALMAERKTEN

Y. FLORNOY
Syndikus der Börse von Paris

Zusammenfassung

Auch heute noch sind die Klein- und Mittelbetriebe von wesentlicher Bedeutung für die Volkswirtschaft der Europäischen Gemeinschaft. Ob es sich um die Anzahl der Unternehmen oder die Zahl der von ihnen beschäftigten Arbeitskräfte im Verhältnis zum gesamten Personalbestand sämtlicher Unternehmen und zur Gesamtheit der arbeitenden Bevölkerung handelt, wir wissen, dass sie die wahre Grundlage unseres Wirtschaftssystems darstellen.

Da sie aus diesem Grunde in den Genuss zahlreicher öffentlicher Beihilfen der verschiedensten Art gelangen, zeigten die Klein- und Mittelunternehmen bisher nur geringes Interesse an einer Zulassung zu den Börsenmärkten. Gewiss sind die Hindernisse, die ihrer Einführung an der Börse im Wege stehen, noch bedeutend. Die Klein- und Mittelbetriebe beginnen jedoch, sich der Vorteile bewusst zu werden, die ihnen aus einer solchen Einführung entstehen könnten.

Das Experiment des französischen "Sekundärmarkts", das auf dem besten Weg ist, ein grosser Erfolg zu werden, erbringt heute den Beweis für das zunehmende Interesse der mittleren Unternehmen an ihrer Einführung an den Börsenmärkten.

EUROPAEISCHER SEKUNDAERMARKT - STELLUNGNAHME DES UNTERNEHMERS

Robin G. HODGSON
Geschäftsführer, Granville & Co. Limited, London

Zusammenfassung

Die psychologische Einstellung des Unternehmers bestimmt seine Ansicht über die verschiedenen bestehenden Ausstiegmechanismen. Die Unternehmer können in zwei Kategorien unterteilt werden - familiendynastische und nicht-familiendynastische Unternehmer. Die europäischen Börsenmärkte haben sich auf die Bedürfnisse der letzteren konzentriert; den Bedüfnissen der ersten wurde nur wenig Aufmerksamkeit geschenkt.

STELLUNGNAHME DES RISIKOKAPITAL-INVESTORS

J.P. DE BLOCQ VAN KUFFELER
Direktor
Brown, Shipley & Co. Limited

Zusammenfassung

In den letzten drei Jahren hat eine schnelle Entwicklung und Ausdehnung der Sekundärmärkte stattgefunden, insbesondere in London, wo sich der "Unlisted Securities Market" und der "Over-the-Counter Market" erheblich entwickelten. Zur Zeit werden auf dem "Unlisted Securities Market" die Aktien von 220 Gesellschaften gehandelt; für diese Gesellschaften wurde Kapital in Höhe von etwa 230 Millionen Pfund Sterling aufgebracht. Am Over-the-Counter Market", an dem Aktien von etwa 70 Gesellschaften gehandelt werden, beteiligen sich gegenwärtig 24 Kursfestsetzer.

Der institutionelle Investor in London verfügt über beträchtliche Summen für neue Nettoinvestitionen, und die Haltung und Investitionskriterien der investierenden Institutionen sind für diese Märkte von beträchtlicher Bedeutung.

Die institutionellen Investoren betrachten den "Unlisted Securities Market" und den "Over-the-Counter Market" als eine Möglichkeit zur Investition in neuen Industriezweigen und in jungen Unternehmen, die die Chance zur Erzielung eines substantiellen Kapitalzuwachses bieten, der auf dem Effektenmarkt nicht möglich wäre. Aus diesem Grund sind die gezahlten Dividenden nicht so hoch, und unter gewissen Umständen wie z.B. den "greenfield"-Projekten brauchen in den ersten Jahren keine Dividenden gezahlt zu werden. Das Aufnehmen von zusätzlichem Kapital durch weitere Anlage von Eigenkapital oder Bezugsrechtangebote wird gefördert und als positive Entwicklung betrachtet.

Zur Zeit herrscht Besorgnis angesichts der geringen Anzahl der zur Verfügung stehenden Aktien gewisser Gesellschaften, da dies auf Grund des Seltenheitswerts zu hohen Aktienpreisen führt. Diese wiederum rufen unrealistische Erwartungen hervor und bewirken folglich stark schwankende Aktienkurse. Der effektive Aktienmarkt kann sehr klein sein, da sich die meisten Aktien fest in der Hand von Investoren befinden und nur wenige Aktien für den Handel zur Verfügung stehen.

Man hofft jedoch, dass dies nur ein vorübergehendes Phänomen ist, das durch weitere Kapitalerhöhungen und den Uebergang der Unternehmen zu einer vollständigen Börsennotierung überwunden werden wird.

DIE AMERIKANISCHEN FREIVERKEHRSMAERKTE (OVER-THE-COUNTER MARKETS)

A. E. YOUNG
Professor der Finanzwissenschaft
School of Management, Syracuse University

Zusammenfassung

In der folgenden Analyse werden die Freiverkehrsmärkte (over-the-counter markets) und die Wertpapierbörsen in Amerika einander gegenübergestellt, denn diese beiden grundlegenden alternativen Handelssysteme der Vergangenheit sind insbesondere durch die hochentwickelte Technologie der heutigen Zeit untrennbar miteinander verknüpft. Zunächst werden einige fundamentale Unterschiede zwischen Wertpapier- und Freiverkehrsmarkt aufgezeigt, und der geschichtliche Wandel des Freiverkehrsmarktes wird dargelegt. Während der Freiverkehrsmarkt in Amerika noch vor einem halben Jahrhundert, als die grundlegenden Gesetze zur Regelung der Wertpapiermärkte enstanden, praktisch unbeachtet blieb, ist der Freiverkehrshandel mit Anteilen an Grossunternehmen heute ein entscheidender Faktor in der Wertpapierbranche. Hingegen ist der Freiverkehrshandel mit Anteilen an Kleinunternehmen ein Marktbereich, der nach wie vor so selten in Anspruch genommen und so sehr vernachlässigt wird wie zur Zeit der ersten Verabschiedung der grundlegenden Wertpapiergesetze. Nach dieser Einführung wird dann die Entwicklung einiger wesentlicher Kräfte und Elemente der Werpapierbranche im Laufe der jüngeren Vergangenheit analysiert. Schliesslich wird der Vorschlag eines Marktsystems auf Staatsebene dargelegt und der voraussichtliche Stellenwert des Freiverkehrmarktes in einem solchen System erörtert.

DER LONDONER FREIVERKEHRSMARKT ("UNLISTED SECURITIES MARKET")

Robin STORMONTH-DARLING
Vorsitzender der Börsenmaklerfirma Laing & Cruickshank
(inc. McAnally Montgomery & Co.), London
Vorsitzender des Börsenzulassungsausschusses,
The Council of The Stock Exchange (Börsenrat)

Zusammenfassung

Im November 1980 wurde der Freiverkehrsmarkt (Unlisted Securities Market - USM) eingeführt. Dabei wurden zwei Ziele verfolgt. In erster Linie galt es, einen offiziellen, geregelten Markt zu schaffen, der den Bedürfnissen der kleineren, weniger starken Unternehmen, die wohl kaum einen Antrag auf Zulassung zur amtlichen Börsennotierung stellen würden, gerecht werden sollte. Es wurde davon ausgegangen, dass die Investoren, solange ein solcher Markt nicht vorhanden und die Börsenfähigkeit ihrer Investitionen nicht einigermassen sichergestellt sei, wahrscheinlich in geringerem Masse bereit wären, Anlagerisiken auf sich zu nehmen. Zweitens wurden durch den Freiverkehrmarkt die nicht an der Börse zugelassenen Gesellschaften, deren Wertpapiere entsprechend der Vorschrift 163 (2) der Börsenordnung unterworfen. Die genannte Vorschrift machte - vorbehaltlich der Genehmigung der Börsenrates - gelegentlich Börsengeschäfte mit den Aktien nicht zugelassener Aktiengesellschaften (public companies) und Gesellschaften mit beschränkter Haftung (private companies) möglich; sie kann auch weiterhin zu diesem Zweck als Rechtsgrundlage dienen, jedoch auf einer etwas beschränkteren Basis als in der Vergangenheit.

Von November 1980 bis September 1983 wurden 211 Gesellschaften zum Freiverkehrsmarkt (USM) zugelassen und ein Gesamtbetrag von 277 Mio UKL wurde bei ihrer Zulassung aufgebracht.

BERICHT DER ARBEITSGRUPPE NR. I

Vorsitzender : H. SCHMIDT
Berichterstatter : D.L. ADAMSON

ERSCHLIESSUNG VON AUSSTIEGSMOEGLICHKEITEN FUER RISIKOKAPITALANLEGER AUF EG-EBENE

Die Arbeitsgruppe hatte die Aufgabe, Ausstiegmöglichkeiten aus europäischer und nicht nur innenstaatlicher Sicht zu untersuchen. Die Gruppe ist der Ansicht, dass insbesondere zwei dieser Ausstiegsmöglichkeiten besondere Aufmerksamkeit beizumessen ist. Erstens der Rückgriff auf Aktienmärkte in anderen Mitgliedstaaten und zweitens der Verkauf von Anteilen an kleinen innovativen Gesellschaften an ausländische institutionelle Investoren. Beide Möglichkeiten können wahlweise, und zwar nacheinander oder gemeinsam angewandt werden.

Die Arbeitsgruppe empfiehlt, dass die Kommission ihre Bemühungen zur Beseitigung von Behinderungen auf dem Gebiet der grenzüberschreitenden Beteiligungsfinanzierung verstärkt. Aus Zeitmangel wurde nicht versucht, alle diese Hindernisse ausführlich zu behandeln. Die Arbeitsgruppe beschränkte sich auf vier Punkte: die allgemeine Marktstruktur, grenzüberschreitende Börsenneueinführungen, internationale Investitionen durch Investment-Banken und internationale Investitionen durch sonstige Finanzinstitutionen.

Die Arbeitsgruppe legt für diese vier Punkte folgende Empfehlungen vor:

1. Angesichts der Kosten und der sonstigen praktischen Schwierigkeiten hält es die Arbeitsgruppe nicht für erforderlich, einen zentralen europäischen Markt für Beteiligungsfinanzierungs-Instrumente kleiner Gesellschaften zu schaffen. Die derzeit bestehenden Börsen sollten so flexibel wie möglich eingesetzt und im Hinblick auf die Aufnahme von kleinen innovativen Gesellschaften verbessert werden.

Besonders riskante in- und ausländische Gesellschaften sollten an den Aktienbörsen zugelassen und dem entsprechenden Marktgebiet zugeordnet werden.

Die Bedingungen für die Zulassung dieser Gesellschaften an der Börse sollten so ausgelegt sein, dass für kleine Unternehmen keine unangemessenen Belastungen entstehen. Der Anlegerschutz sollte wann immer möglich durch bestehende Gesetze und nicht durch die Einführung von neuen, umfangreichen Massnahmen garantiert werden.

2. Es wird empfohlen, alle Bestimmungen zu beseitigen, die kleine europäische Unternehmen daran hindern, Aktien in anderen Mitgliedstaaten an der Börse einzuführen. Die Arbeitsgruppe bedauert die grosse Zahl der derzeit bestehenden restriktiven Bestimmungen.

Dazu gehören Devisenkontrollen und subtile Formen der Diskriminierung ausländischer Emittenten. Die Arbeitsgruppe würde eine nähere Untersuchung dieser Behinderungen begrüssen.

Die Arbeitsgruppe empfielt ausserdem, neue Wege für die Verbreitung von Informationen über neue Ausgabemärkte in Betracht zu ziehen. Durch die Gründung der European Venture Capital Association (Europäischer Risikokapitalverband) bietet sich eine gute Gelegenheit für die Herausgabe einer entsprechenden Fachzeitung. Man hofft, dass diese Zeitschrift die Aufmerksamkeit der Unternehmer auf die beträchtlichen Unterschiede bei den Kurs-Gewinn-Verhältnissen lenken wird, die vergleichbare Gesellschaften auf Kapitalmärkten in verschiedenen Ländern erzielen.

3. Zur Förderung eines starken Investmentbanken-Sektors unterstützt die Arbeitsgruppe die auf der 3. Sitzung vorgebrachte Empfehlung, dass in allen Mitgliedstaaten ein Statut für zugelassene Effektenhändler anzubieten sei, wie es gegenwärtig im Vereinigten Königreich bereits geschieht. Diese zugelassenen Händler sollten die Möglichkeit haben, Geschäfte ausserbörslich abzuwickeln und Wertpapierkonten im Kundenauftrag zu verwalten. Die Beeinflussung des Marktgeschehens wird möglicherweise durch die Entwicklung von Videotex-Systemen mit Dialogbetrieb erleichtert. Im Hinblick auf eine stärkere Wettbewerbsfähigkeit der Investmentbanken wird ausserdem empfohlen, europaweite Aktivitäten dieser Banken zu fördern, unabhängig davon, in welchem Mitgliedstaat sie ansässig sind. Die Kommission sollte die erforderlichen Massnahmen zur Abschaffung der Ausführungsbestimmungen ergreifen, die gegenwärtig derartige Aktivitäten behindern.

4. Im Idealfall dürfte es keine Beschränkungen für durch sonstige Finanzinstitutionen getätigte internationale, nicht notierte Anlagen geben. In Anbetracht der praktischen Schwierigkeiten, auf die die grossen Finanzinstitutionen bei der Realisierung und Ueberwachung von internationalen, nicht börsengängigen Anlagen stossen, ist die Arbeitsgruppe der Ansicht, dass die Ueberlegung, spezielle Mittler einzusetzen, Beachtung finden sollte.

Ein Beispiel für einen derartigen Mittler könnte ein geschlossener Anlagefonds sein, dessen Anteile an Börsen eines bzw. mehrerer Mitgliedstaaten notiert würden.

Die Aktiva dieser Gesellschaft könnten je nach Ermessen der Geschäftsführung, börsengängig und/oder nicht börsengängig sein. Steuerlich sollten diese Gesellschaften ebenso wie sonstige Kapitalanlagegesellschaften behandelt werden. Die Börse bewertet das Portefeuille sämtlicher, von dem Fonds gehaltenen Aktiva, wodurch die schwierige und zeitaufwendige Bewertung von individuellen, nicht notierten Anlagen erleichtert wird.

Diesen Fonds sollte institutionelle Unterstützung gewährt werden unter der Voraussetzung, dass ihre Unternehmenspolitik auf die Investitionsfinanzierung kleiner internationaler Unternehmen ausgerichtet ist - eine Aufgabe, die diese Institutionen an Bevollmächtigte übertragen. Die Aktivitäten solcher spezieller Bevollmächtigter würde entscheidend zur Internationalisierung der europäischen Kapitalmärkte für kleine Unternehmen beitragen; dieser Beitrag käme insbesondere durch eine verstärkte und wettbewerbsfähige grenzüberschreitende Suche nach zusätzlichem Beteiligungskapital für neu zu gründende Gesellschaften zum Ausdruck.

BERICHT DER ARBEITSGRUPPE NR. 2

Vorsitzender : P. FONTANEAU
Berichterstatter : P. WECKEL

VERBESSERUNG DES DIE RISIKOKAPITAL-INVESTITIONEN BEEINFLUSSENDEN STEUERLICHEN UMFELDS

Der Vorsitzende erinnert daran, dass sich die Kommission seit 1975 für eine Harmonisierung der Bemessungsgrundlage der Körperschaftsteuer eingesetzt hat. Er unterstreicht, dass sich die Vorschläge, die die Kommission in Zusammenhang mit der Innovation machen könnte, auf die bereits durchgeführten bzw. realisierten Arbeiten stützen sollten.

Aus der Sitzung von Mittwochnachmittag, auf der sich die Teilnehmer mit Entwicklungen steuerlicher Art auf die Innovation befassten, greift der Vorsitzende vier Diskussionspunkte auf :

1. Bei entsprechender Zustimmung der Mitgliestaaten zieht Herr HENRIKSEN die Errichtung eines bzw. mehrerer europäischer Investitionsfonds im Bereich des Risikokapitals in Betracht, für die Steuervorteile gelten müssten;

2. Herr INCLEDON stellt in seinem Vortrag fest, dass kein gemeinsamer Risikokapitalmarkt existiert;

3. die Einkommensteuer wirkt sich negativ auf den Einsatz von Risikokapital aus. In diesem Bereich haben die Mitgliedstaaten weitgehend ihre Steuerhoheit bewahrt. Das sollte jedoch nicht daran hindern, Vorschläge zu bestimmten Punkten zu unterbreiten;

4. es wäre sicher illusorisch zu glauben, dass Steueranreize allein genügen würden, um den Einsatz von Risikokapital zu stimulieren.

Was die Bundesrepublik Deutschland betrifft, ist einer der Teilnehmer der Ansicht, dass steuerliche Anreize erfoderlich seien, da der Investor weniger zufallsabhängige Gewinnaussichten und gewisse Garantien benötige. Er regt deshalb an, dass dem Anleger im ersten Jahr hohe Steuerabzüge angeboten werden und dass sein Gewinn in späteren Jahren nur geringfügig zu besteuern sei.

Einige Teilnehmer bemerken hierzu, dass durch diese Steuererleichterungen die Hauptlast des Investitionsrisikos auf die Allgemeinheit übertragen würde. Durch die Steuerermässigungen werde diese ein wichtiger Partner des Investors, sie sollte jedoch eher ein Minderheitspartner bleiben.

Auch das Scheitern der Abschreibungsgesellschaften in Deutschland wird angesprochen. Lässt sich der Anleger hauptsächlich von Steuervorteilen leiten, so erreicht er damit nur, dass verstärkt in nicht existenzfähige Unternehmen investiert wird.

Einige Teilnehmer sind der Ansicht, dass die Steuerbörse ihre Grosszügigkeit bemessen und ein gewisses Gleichgewicht zwischen den Wirtschaftssubjekten aufrechthalten müsse.

Herr KAPLAN stimmt diesen Ueberlegungen voll und ganz zu, hält das Beispiel, das ein Diskussionsteilnehmer zur Unterstützung anführt, nämlich die Ueberbewertung bestimmter Aktionen, die sich aus dem "Business Expansion Scheme" im Vereinigten Könireich ergebe, für falsch gewählt, da dieser Effekt unvermeidlich und somit ein Faktor für die Bedeutung dieses Mechanismus sei.

Der Vorsitzende spricht sich für ein System der Investitionsabschreibungen aus, da eine Steuerermässigung, die sich auf die Dividenden beziehe, in den ersten Jahren, in denen kein Gewinn erzielt werde, keinen Vorteil darstelle.

Herr WIRK ist der Ansicht, dass die Effizienz jeglicher Steuervorteile im Gesamtrahmen des jeweils geltenden Steuersystems zu sehen sei, aus dem sie nicht herausgenommen werden könnten. Seiner Ansicht nach ist das Steuerproblem in Deutschland zweitrangig.

Die Teilnehmer sind sich offenbar darüber einig, dass der Grenzsteuersatz für die Besteuerung von höheren Einkommen zu hoch angesetzt und dass dadurch die Sparneigung gedrosselt werde. Die Teilnehmer bringen jedoch zwei Vorbehalte zum Ausdruck. In den ersten Jahren der Investition sollte das Steuerniveau nicht zu hoch sein, da kein Gewinn erzielt werde. Andererseits geht es für Herrn WIRK weniger um das Problem, die von dieser Gruppe von Steuerpflichtigen zu tragende Steuerlast in Frage zu stellen, sondern eher darum, die zu schnell ansteigende Steuerprogression zu ändern.

Herr WIRK ist der Ansicht, dass Steuererleichterungen vorrangig auf die Innovationsunternehmen selbst, und zwar vor allem in der Phase, in der sich erste Gewinne abzeichnen, zu konzentrieren seien. Zu diesem Zweck schlägt er die Bildung von steuerfreien Investitionsrücklagen vor.

Ein Mitglied der Arbeitsgruppe regt an, dass gleichzeitig mit der Einführung von europäischen Innovationsdarlehen den finanziellen Mittlern Steuervorteile für den Teil der Investitionen gewährt werden, der aus Eigenmitteln bestritten wird.

Der Vorsitzende merkt an - und das betreffende Mitglied der Arbeitsgruppe stimmt ihm zu -, dass ein solcher Steuervorteil die finanziellen Mittler von einem Risiko entbinden werde, das gerade Gegenstand ihrer Geschäftstätigkeit sei.

Der Vorsitzende erinnert an den Vorschlag, Anlagefonds in den Mitgliedstaaten sowie einen europäischen Fonds einzurichten, um Kapital in die Gemeinschaft zu leiten. Er weist auf die Vorteile hin, die ein multinationaler Fonds für die Länder böte, in denen ein Devisenkontrollsystem angewandt werde.

Die Arbeitsgruppe hält die Errichtung mehrerer privater Fonds auf nationaler Ebene für vorteilhafter und spricht sich deshalb nicht für die Gründung eines multinationalen Fonds aus. Dennoch müsste eine Beziehung zwischen den einzelnen Fonds hergestellt werden. Damit ein Investor einen Anreiz hat, in einem Nachbarland eine Geschäftstätigkeit aufzunehmen, wäre es angebracht, ihm ähnliche Steuervorteile wie diejenigen, die ihm in seinem eigenen Land gewährt werden, einzuräumen. Es wird vorgeschlagen, in diesem Zusammenhang die Vereinbarungen über die Doppelbsteuerung heranzuziehen.

Der Vorsitzende befragt die Arbeitsgruppe, ob es notwendig sei, Vorschläge für eine Harmonisierung der Risikokapital-Besteuerungssysteme in der Gemeinschaft zu unterbreiten. Einige Teilnehmer sind der Ansicht, dass dieses Ziel aufgrund der unterschiedlichen Steuersysteme und der zögernden Haltung der Mitgliedstaaten hinsichtlich einer Begrenzung ihrer Steuerhoheit in naher Zukunft wohl nicht zu realisieren sei. Die Meinungen zu diesem Punkt gehen jedoch auseinander. Es wird angemerkt, dass die Mitgliedstaaten vielleicht eine Chance ungenützt liessen, Europa in einem der fortschrittlichsten Bereiche voranzutreiben. Die Neuartigkeit und die Aktualität des Problemkreises Risikokapital sollte genutzt werden.

Der Vorsitzende regt an, dass die Arbeitsgruppe der Kommission folgende Vorschläge unterbreitet:

Für die individuellen Anleger müssten ebenso wie für die Risikokapitalgesellschaften steuerliche Anreize gelten.

Derartige Massnahmen sind aber nur im Gesamtrahmen der jeweiligen Steuersysteme zu sehen. Von daher wäre zu wünschen, dass die Regierungen der Mitgliedstaaten die auf den höheren Einkommen lastenden Steueransätze senken.

Schliesslich sollte in der gesamten Gemeinschaft ein- und dasselbe System zur Besteuerung von Risikokapital angewandt werden.

VORSCHLAEGE DER ARBEITSGRUPPE NR. 2 ZU GUENSTIGEREN STEUERLICHEN BEDINGUNGEN

Zunächst einmal möchte die Arbeitsgruppe daran erinnern, dass die Kommission der Europäischen Gemeinschaften bereits seit 1975 Vorschläge zur Modifizierung und damit auch zur Koordinierung der steuerlichen Behandlung bestimmter Faktoren der Bemessungsgrundlage der Körperschaft- und Einkommensteuer in den einzelnen Mitgliedstaaten unterbreitet hat. Diese Vorschläge bezogen sich insbesondere auf den Begriff der Fusion, auf die Beziehungen zwischen Mutter- und Tochtergesellschaften sowie auf das Problem der Doppelbesteuerung bei Gesellschaften mit Betrieben mit steuerlichem Sitz in mehreren Mitgliedstaaten der Gemeinschaft. Innerhalb dieses vorgegebenen Rahmens schlägt die Arbeitsgruppe folgende Massnahmen vor, die zu einer Verbesserung der Funktionsweise des Risikokapitalmarktes beitragen sollen.

Diese Empfehlungen sollten möglichst zu den zwei folgenden Ergebnissen führen: Koordinierung und Angleichung der steuerlichen Behandlung der Teilnehmer des Risikokapitalmarktes, um so einer Zersplitterung dieses Marktes entgegenzuwirken und ihm in Zukunft eine europäische Dimension zu geben.

Um dieses Ziel zu erreichen, schlägt die Arbeitsgruppe die nachfolgend aufgeführten Massnahmen vor:

1. Modifizierung der steuerlichen Behandlung von individuellen Investoren, die in Risikokapital investieren.

2. Modifizierung der steuerlichen Behandlung von Innovationsgesellschaften.

3. Modifizierung der steuerlichen Behandlung von Investmentfonds, die in Risikokapital investieren.

Diese drei Modifizierungen der steuerlichen Behandlung sollen, wie bereits gesagt, dazu führen, dass die für die drei genannten Wirtschaftssubjekte geltenden Besteuerungssysteme in allen Mitgliedstaaten der Gemeinschaft soweit wie möglich einander angeglichen werden.

Die Arbeitsgruppe ist sich der Tatsache bewusst, dass die steuerliche Behandlung der Innovation nur ein Teil der gesamten steuerlichen Behandlung der genannten Wirtschaftssubjekte sein kann.

Die steuerliche Behandlung und insbesondere die Regelung der Einkommen- und Körperschaftsteuer bleiben das Vorrecht der Mitgliedstaaten. Um jedoch günstigere Voraussetzungen für den Risikokapitalmarkt zu schaffen, ist die Arbeitsgruppe der Ansicht, dass die steuerliche Gesamtbelastung in den einzelnen Mitgliedstaaten soweit wie möglich reduziert werden sollte.

Angesichts des internationalen Aspekts der Innovation und ihrer Bedeutung für das Wirtschaftswachstum und die Beschäftigung in den europäischen Ländern, sollte eine grundlegende Gemeinschaftspolitik, deren Ziel die Stimulation des gesamten Innovationprozesses sein müsste, entwickelt werden.

Die Arbeitsgruppe schlägt deshalb vor, eine regelrechte Innovations-Steuergesetzgebung auf europäischer Ebene zu erarbeiten. Diese Innovations-Gesetzgebung könnte die Grundlage für das Wiedererstarken der Wettbewerbsfähigkeit der europäischen Unternehmen gegenüber ihren amerikanischen und japanischen Konkurrenten sein.

Die Arbeitsgruppe ist sich der Tatsache bewusst, dass die Verbesserung der steuerlichen Behandlung der Innovation einen wesentlichen Faktor für die Ankurbelung des Risikokapitalmarktes darstellt. Dennoch möchte die Arbeitsgruppe darauf hinweisen, dass steuerliche Anreize allein für ein schnelles Wachstum dieses Marktes nicht ausreichen werden, und sie ist der Ansicht, dass den verschiedenen Wirtschaftssubjekten, aus dem sich der Risikokapitalmarkt zusammensetzt, weitere Hilfen gewährt werden müssten.

ARBEITSGRUPPE N. 6 : BEZUGSRECHTE FUER LEITENDE ANGESTELLTE VON UNTERNEHMEN MIT WACHSTUMSPOTENTIAL

und

ARBEITSGRUPPE N. 3 : MOBILISIERUNG VON RISIKOKAPITALINVESTOREN AUS DEM NICHT-BANKBEREICH AUF EG-EBENE

Vorsitzender : R.G. HODGSON
Berichterstatter: S. NEUMANN

A) Bezugsrechte (Beispiele aus den USA)

Die Arbeitsgruppe stimmte im allgemeinen darüber überein, dass Bezugsrechte für leitende Angestellte ein wichtiges Instrument für den Risikokapitalmarkt darstellen. Da die Bezugsrechte vor allem ein Anreiz für die leitenden Angestellten sein sollen, am Wachstum der Gesellschaft teilzuhaben, sind sie zu den normalen Konditionen zu erwerben. Hierin liegt ein zusätzlicher Anreiz, wobei die steuerliche Behandlung noch zu klären ist. Um die hohe Fluktuation innerhalb des Managements zu bekämpfen (in den USA wechseln Generaldirektoren im Durchschnitt nach 1 1/2 Jahren den Arbeitsplatz), berechnet sich der Umfang der Bezugsrechte auf einer jährlichen Basis. Bei nicht börsennotierten Unternehmen ist die Bewertung von Aktien schwierig. In einem Fall wurde versucht, einen Durchschnittsgewinn für einen Zeitraum von drei Jahren zu ermitteln. Die Besteuerung von aus Bezugsrechten stammenden Gewinnen ist im Vereinigen Königreich ein schwieriges Problem. In anderen europäischen Ländern ist dieses Problem weniger bekannt und muss noch innerstaatlich von Steurexperten durchgearbeitet werden.

Die Arbeitsgruppe gelangte zu folgenden Empfehlungen:

- Die EG-Kommission sollte eine Studie über die steuerliche Behandlung von Bezugsrechten für leitende Angestellte in den EG-Mitgliedstaaten und den USA erstellen lassen, in der auch die psychologische Seite der Bezugsrechte sowie die Vorteile, die wirtschaftlichen Auswirkungen und die Hindernisse für die Einführung dieser Anreizsysteme enthalten sein sollten.

a) Die Harmonisierungsbemühungen der EG-Kommission auf dem Gebiet der Unternehmensbesteuerung müssten sich auch auf die Vergütung der leitenden Angestellten in Form von Bezugsrechten und Rentenansprüchen erstrecken sowie die politischen/sozialen/wirtschaftlichen Aspekte berücksichtigen.

b) Die Bedeutung der Bezugsrechte als Instrument für den Risikokapitalmarkt erfordert eine harmonisierte (steuerliche) Behandlung in der EG zur Erleichterung von internationalen Transaktionen.

c) Die steuerlichen Bestimmungen für Bezugsrechte sollten sich nicht nur auf Firmengründungen oder "management buy-outs" (die Risikokapitalgesellschaft unterstützt ein erfolgreiches Management-Team, ein von ihm aufgebautes Unternehmen in eigener Regie zu übernehmen) , sondern auch auf die verschiedenen Stadien der Unternehmensfinanzierung beziehen.

d) Das Wort "Bezugsrechte" hat vielleicht eine negative Bedeutung und sollte durch einen positiveren Ausdruck wie z.B. EUROPAEISCHE BETEILIGUNGSRECHTE, wie von Herrn Professor SCHMIDT vorgeschlagen, ersetzt werden.

Die Gruppe diskutiert in Zusammenhang mit der Vergütung der Geschäftsführer nicht nur über Bezugsrechte, sondern auch über Rentenansprüche, die in den USA kaum vorkommen und - unter dem Aspekt der Uebertragbarkeit - in Europa von individuellen Vereinbarungen abhängen.

Die Nützlichkeit der Bezugsrechte ist vor allem auch als wesentlicher Teil des Wachstums kleiner Unternehmen herauszustellen. Eine "Politik des Neides" würde sonst eine Reform möglich machen.

B) <u>Die Mobilisierung von Risikokapitalinvestoren</u>

Die Arbeitsgruppe ging zunächst von Investoren aus dem Nichtbankenbereich aus und entschied dann, "Nichtbanken" fallen zu lassen. Auf der Sitzung wurde im wesentlichen über folgende Investorengruppen diskutiert:

- Rentenfonds und Versicherungsgesellschaften
- Industriefonds (d.h. Industrieunternehmen)
- Akademische Einrichtungen
- Anlagegesellschaften und kollektive Investoren
- private Investoren.

Nicht berücksichtigt wurden Regierungen und verstaatlichte Industrien, über die in der Arbeitsgruppe 4 diskutiert wurde. Es wird angenommen, dass aus dem akademischen Bereich stammende Investoren, die sich bereits an Risikokapitalfonds in Europa beteiligen, dies im wesentlichen tun, um enge Beziehungen für einen möglichen Technologietransfer herzustellen. Folgende Empfehlungen wurden zur Mobilisierung von Risikokapitalinvestoren erarbeitet:

1. Jegliche Stimulation von institutionellen Risikokapitalinvestoren muss in Beziehung zu der möglichen Wachstumsrate des Risikomanagementpotentials in Europa stehen, um negative Entwicklungen zu vermeiden.

2. Bevor Massnahmen zur Ueberwindung der gesetzlichen Hindernisse vorgeschlagen werden, die insbesondere institutionelle Investoren davon abhalten, in Risikokapital zu investiern, sollte die EG-Kommission ein Verzeichnis der positiven und negativen Bestimmungen und ihrer Auswirkungen in der EG/USA aufstellen; es könnte auch erforderlich sein, die Hindernisse zu untersuchen, die sich aus der Organisationstruktur der investierenden Institutionen ergeben.

3. Die EG-Kommission sollte die Schaffung von Risikokapitalbeteiligungen auf europäischer Ebene unterstützen, damit ein dynamischer europäischer Risikokapitalmarkt aufgebaut werden kann (Ziel: Investitionen in Höhe von ein bis zwei Milliarden Dollar pro Jahr); die Kommission sollte deshalb die Hindernisse für Uebergangsbeteiligungen und -vereinbarungen untersuchen.

Institutionelle Investoren, hauptsächlich Rentenfonds und Versicherungsgesellschaften, sollten die Möglichkeit erhalten, ja ermutigt bzw. gezwungen werden, einen bestimmen prozentualen Anteil der Jahreseinnahmen in Risikokapital zu investieren.

4. Die Industrie sollte motiviert werden, die technologischen Möglichkeiten, die mit Hilfe des Risikokapitals erschlossen werden, zu nutzen, um den Umfang und die Effizienz von Forschung und Entwicklung zu erhöhen. Die Industrie sollte auch bei der Bestimmung von für Risikokapital-Investitionen geeigneten Industriegeländen herangezogen werden, damit europäische Grossunternehmen gegründet werden können.

5. Die EG-Kommission ist aufgefordert, die Entwicklung der Risikokapital-Infrastruktur zu unterstützen, um die Risiken für die Personen möglichst gering zu halten, die Fonds errichten wollen.

6. Die Universitäten sollten zu dieser Risikokapital-Infrastruktur durch eine Ausbildung, die unternehmerischen Zwecken gerecht wird, und durch die Ueberbrückung der mangelnden Kommunikation zwischen Technologie und Arbeitskräfteangebot bzw. -nachfrage beitragen.

Um negative Auswirkungen zu vermeiden, die sich aus dem fehlenden professionellen Risikomanagement in Europa ergeben könnten, sollten alle Aktionen zur Mobilisierung von institutionellen Investoren bestimmte vorrangige Aspekte haben und nach einem bestimmten Zeitplan ablaufen.

BERICHT DER ARBEITSGRUPPE NR.4

Vorsitzender: K. NATHUSIUS

Berichterstatter: P. DOURNEL

STAATLICHE MASSNAHMEN ZUR ANREGUNG VON VENTURE CAPITAL-INVESTITIONEN

An der Arbeit der Gruppe beteiligten sich etwa 50 Personen. Im Anschluß an die Debatte haben wir uns entschlossen, einen nach Themen gegliederten Bericht vorzulegen, um den Inhalt der Debatte besser darstellen zu können.

I DIE AKTUELLE SITUATION

Die von den verschiedenen Mitgliedstaaten der Europäischen Gemeinschaften eingeleiteten Maßnahmen können nach drei großen Kategorien untergliedert werden:

- steuerliche Maßnahmen
- direktes Kapitalangebot
- Garantiesysteme

A. Die steuerlichen Maßnahmen

Die meisten Staaten haben Maßnahmen der Steuererleichterung eingeräumt, um Investitionen zu begünstigen. Diese können natürlich auch den Venture Capital-Aktivitäten nützen. Hier läßt sich als Beispiel die Möglichkeit des Verlustvortrags anführen und, sofern sie existiert, die Verrechnung von Verlusten mit rückliegenden Jahresabschlüssen (1).

Darüber hinaus haben manche Staaten besondere steuerliche Maßnahmen für Unternehmensbeteiligungen und Venture Capital eingeführt. Diese Maßnahmen können sowohl die Venture Capital-Gesellschaften betreffen, beispielsweise die von den Sociétés Financières d'Innovation in Frankreich oder die von der Wagnisfinanzierungs-Gesellschaft in der Bundesrepublik Deutschland realisierten Wertsteigerungen ihrer Beteiligungen, als auch Anreize für Einzelpersonen zur Beteiligung an Innovationsfonds (Belgien) oder an Unternehmen (Vereinigtes Königreich) darstellen.

B. Direktes Kapitalangebot

Mehrere Staaten haben Maßnahmen des direkten Kapitalangebots eingeführt, um die Entwicklung eines Venture Capital-Marktes anzuregen. Eines der besonders beeindruckenden Beispiele stellt die National Enterprise Agency dar, die kürzlich von der irischen Regierung gegründet wurde. Die Staaten können in diesem Bereich auf verschiedene Weise tätig werden, von der Übernahme direkter Beteiligungen in bestimmten Wirtschaftssektoren wie beispielsweise in Griechenland bis zur Gründung einer Gesellschaft, die staatliche oder Mischfonds verteilt (Bundesrepublik Deutschland: WFG, Frankreich: SFI, und andere) (2).

Man muß allerdings einräumen, daß diese Maßnahmen sowohl in ihrem Umfang als auch in ihrer Wirkung beschränkt sind, da sie offensichtlich ihre kritische Masse nicht erreichen.

C Garantiefonds

Auch hier haben die verschiedenen Staaten in den letzten Jahren zahlreiche Programme eingesetzt, um Investitionen zu fördern. Diese Programme sind entweder als Hilfen oder Ergänzungen der bereits bestehenden Garantiesysteme zu verstehen oder aber als eine der zahlreichen Interventionen mit besonderer Zielsetzung. Als Beispiel für diese letzte Kategorie läßt sich das holländische PPM Guarantee Scheme oder die Verlustausfallgarantie der deutschen WFG anführen (2).

Andere Staaten errichten nationale Garantie-Mischfonds und ersetzen so die klassischen Garantieorganisationen, um das Restrisiko des Bankiers zu übernehmen (Frankreich: SOFARIS, Vereinigtes Königreich: Government Guarantee Scheme for Small Business Banl Loans, Belgien: Fonds de garantie de l'Etat,...). Es ist zu vermerken, daß letztere häufig auf die Unterstützung von Klein- und Mittelbetriebe ausgerichtet sind (2).

II ERFAHRUNGEN UND REAKTIONEN DER TEILNEHMER

Um der Debatte eine Richtung zu geben, hat man versucht, eine Reihe von Fragen mit Hilfe der Erfahrungen der Teilnehmer zu beantworten.

A. Welche Rolle kann eine Regierung in dem Bereich übernehmen?

a) Das irische Beispiel

Mitte Oktober wurde die National Enterprise Agency gegründet mit der Aufgabe, Venture Capital in den ersten Phasen der Unternehmensgründungen anzubieten. Sobald die Risiken der Technologien und der Markteinführung überwunden sind, wird sie ihre Anteile über den Sekundärmarkt verkaufen.

Die Besonderheit dieses staatlichen Systems liegt in dem Rückgriff auf die technische Kompetenz von Experten außerhalb der öffentlichen Verwaltung um die unzureichende Erfahrung von Beamten im Venture Capital-Bereich auszugleichen. Diese Experten werden zu einem Teil aus den Wertsteigerungen in den Beteiligungsunternehmen honoriert, die von der NEA be bei der Börseneinführung der Aktien erzielt werden. Dieser Teil könnte 20 % der realisierten Wertsteigerung je Projekt betragen. Dazu kommen Honorare für die Managementunterstützung.

Diese Struktur ist sehr einmalig und könnte anderen Regierungen als Modell dienen.

b) <u>Das kanadische Beispiel</u>

Dises Beispiel ist in mehrfacher Hinsicht interessant. Es könnte unter anderem eine Antwort auf eine Frage bringen, die seit dem Symposium von 1982 offengeblieben war, die Möglichkeit einer staatlichen Intervention über öffentliche Anleihen, insbesondere im Rüstungsbereich.

Nachdem Kanada beschlossen hatte, seine Anstrengungen im Bereich der Wehrtechnik zu verstärken, wurden die Anleihen zum größten Teil auf innovative Firmen orientiert, um ihnen gleichzeitig Forschungs- und Entwicklungsverträge und sichere Finanzierungen zu bieten. Diese Koordination hat die Entwicklung eines Venture Capital-Marktes zugelassen, der die üblichen Probleme eines Kapitalmangels in den ersten Phasen von Innovationen kannte.

B <u>Umfeldprobleme</u>

Probleme im Umfeld und im wirtschaftspolitischen Zusammenhang haben den größten Teil der Diskussionen bestimmt. Dieser Begriff des Umfelds umfaßt die folgenden Themen:

a) <u>Steuerpolitik</u>

Sie wird als größtes Hemmnis für die Entwicklung von Venture Capital-Märkten in Kontinentaleuropa angesehen. Man könnte von den Reaktionen ausgehen, welche von den drei Steuerarten mit Auswirkungen im Venture Capital-Bereich hervorgerufen werden:

- Einkommenssteuern: sie mindern im bedeutenden Umfang die Neigung zum Sparen und tragen dadurch zur aktuellen Situation des knappen und teuren Geldes bei. Außerdem haben die Investoren angesichts ihrer geringen Sparmöglichkeiten eher die Tendenz, ihre Mittel in jenen Sektoren anzulegen, die für ihr geringes Risiko bekannt sind, und machen nicht den Versuch, das potentielle Risiko durch Diversifikation zu mindern.

- Gesellschaftssteuern: die extreme Vielfalt der Steuertarife und der Bewertungsgrundlagen der Gesellschaftssteuer in den verschiedenen Mitgliedstaaten bildet offensichtlich ein Hindernis für transnationale Operationen, insbesondere bei hoher Rentabilität.

- Kapitalgewinnsteuern: sie haben in gleicher Weise eine Negativwirkung, da sie den Investor veranlassen, Projekte mit sehr hoher Rentabilität zu suchen, um diese Abzüge wie bisher zu kompensieren. Da die für notwendig erachteten Rentabilitätsraten nur selten erreicht werden, ziehen die Investoren vor, keine Risiken einzugehen.

- Aus ethischer Sicht zeigte sich die Arbeitsgruppe Nr.1 nicht überzeugt von der Annehmbarkeit einer steuerlichen Sonderbehandlung.

Dieses Konzept einer steuerlichen Ungleichbehandlung könnte sich langfristig sogar als gefährlich erweisen, da es Firmen zu Venture Capital zieht, die andere Finanzierungsformen brauchten, was auf Zeit ein neues Problem schaffen würde.

Darüber hinaus scheint es gefährlich, das traditionelle Wachstum zu benachteiligen, das in unseren Tagen den größten Teil der Wertzuwächse erzeugt.

b) Die Rolle des Unternehmers

Dieses Thema kehrt sehr häufig wieder und scheint für unseren

Kontinent typisch zu sein. Tatsächlich führt ein Mißerfolg im Gegensatz zu den USA, wo er als normaler Bestandteil des Geschäftslebens angesehen wird, in Europa zu einem manchmal ehrenrührigen Ruf.

Es handelt sich in der Tat um ein eng mit unserer Kultur und Erziehung verbundenes Problem. Aus diesem Grund läßt es sich nur durch Erziehung und durch Beispiele offenkundigen Erfolgs überwinden, die nach Mißerfolgen eintreten. Es ist aber vollkommen illusorisch zu glauben, daß dieses Problem noch in dieser Generation gelöst werden könnte.

c) Rahmenbedingungen für Unternehmer

In diesem Bereich könnten die Staaten tatsächlich tätig werden. Diese Rahmenbedingungen können zwei Formen annehmen:

- Schaffung eines günstigen wirtschaftlichen Umfelds: besseres Management des Staatshaushalts und der öffentlichen Verschuldung, Politik gegen Inflation und Arbeitslosigkeit...

- Schaffung günstiger Strukturen wie die Innovationszentren, die Gebäude für industrielle Zwecke gegen geringe Kosten zur Verfügung stellen. Letztgenannte staatliche Hilfe wird bereits in einigen Staaten gewährt, so in Irland, dem Vereinigten Königreich und in FRankreich (2).

d) Ausbildung spezialisierter Manager

Ganz offensichtlich gibt es eine sehr bedeutende Lücke in unserem Ausbildungssystem. In diesem Fall aber ist die Lösung des Problems verhältnismäßig einfach: es würde wahrscheinlich genügen, die Aktivitäten von Verbänden auf Konferenzen und Kurse über Venture Capital auszuweiten. Der EG-Plan zur Entwicklung transnationaler Infrastrukturen wird sich in diesem Bereich sicherlich sehr positiv auswirken.

e) Motivation von Unternehmern

Offensichtlich hätten eine Verbesserung in der Mobilität von Führungskräften sowie eine Unterstützung jeder, die ihr eigenes Unternehmen gründen möchten, eine sehr positive Wirkung: Gründung von Unternehmen und Einstellung neuer Führungskräfte anstelle der Unternehmensgründer.

III EMPFEHLUNGEN

1. Private Initiativen müssen weiter angeregt werden.

2. Die existierenden Venture Capital-Gesellschaften dürfen nicht die gesamte Unterstützung für sich in Anspruch nehmen, was einem weiteren Aufbau des Marktes schaden würde.

3. Das wirtschaftliche und soziale Klima muß verbessert werden, um Initiativen zu fördern.

4. Große Anstrengungen um eine Ausbildung von Managern sind notwendig.

5. Es muß eine transnationale Infrastruktur zur Untersützung von Venture Capital geschaffen und entwickelt werden.

Anmerkungen

(1) Siehe die während des Symposiums verteilten Berichte EUR 8820 und 8821.

(2) Siehe Bericht EUR 8819.

BERICHT DER ARBEITSGRUPPE NR. 5

Vorsitzender : C. CLEIFTIE
Berichterstatter : R. GUTH

INFRASTRUKTUR ZUR VERKNUEPFUNG DER RISIKOKAPITALMAERKTE IN DER GEMEINSCHAFT

Bei ihrer Arbeit orientierte sich die Gruppe an drei einfachen Grundsätzen:

1. Es erschien uns sinnvoll, nicht etwa offizielle Empfehlungen auszuarbeiten, sondern vielmehr Ueberlegungen zu einzelnen Aspekten anzustellen und die dabei gewonnenen Erkenntnisse den europäischen Gemeinschaften als Input für ihre eigenen Ueberlegungen anzubieten.

2. Einer der immer wieder zu beobachtenden grundsätzlichen Fehler bei derartigen Bemühungen besteht darin, um jeden Preis originell sein zu wollen, was im allgemein darin zum Ausdruck kommt, dass neue Systeme und Verfahren oder die Einsetzung von Organen mit neuen Aufgaben vorgeschlagen werden. Angesichts der innerhalb der Institutionen zu beobachtenden grundsätzlichen Tendenz, Problemstellungen mehrgleisig lösen zu wollen, ist unsere Gruppe der Ansicht - und dies könnte bereits als erste Empfehlung verstanden werden - dass es wenig sinnvoll erscheint, systematisch Neues zu schaffen. Die bestehenden Institutionen sind vielmehr durchaus in der Lage, für das Enstehen einer Infrastruktur zur Verknüpfung der Risikokapitalmärkte in der Gemeinschaft Sorge zu tragen.

3. Bei allen auf Initiative der europäischen Gemeinschaft in die Wege geleiteten konkreten Massnahmen müssten folgende Folgerungen berücksichtigt werden :

   - Einfachheit von Konzeption und Modus operandi.

- Umfassende Verbreitung bei den Zielgruppen durch besseres Marketing bei ihren wichtigsten Vertretern, insbesondere bei den kleinen und jungen Unternehmen, die am stärksten darunter zu leiden haben, dass die Informationskanäle bisher zu lang sind.

- Konzentration auf die Schaffung einer Infrastruktur und geeigneter Rahmenbedingungen sowie eines Klimas, das die Entwicklung der Risikokapitalmärkte begünstigt. Nach Ansicht der Mitglieder der Gruppen sollten die europäischen Behörden nicht mehr als unbedingt notwendig in das freie Spiel der Marktkräfte eingreifen. Damit spreche ich bereits eine zweite Empfehlung aus, die zwar nicht unmittelbar der Aufgabenstellung unseres Ausschusses zuzuordnen ist, aber dennoch Beachtung verdient.

Für eine Verknüpfung der Risikokapitalmärkte bieten sich verschiedene Mechanismen an. Aufgrund der Zielsetzungen dieses Symposiums und der Qualifikation der Mitglieder unserer Gruppe haben wir uns selbstverständlich auf die finanziellen Aspekte konzentriert. Zwar lässt sich mit dem Thema Geld nicht die ganze Tiefe dieser Problematik erfassen, doch gäbe es andererseits ohne Geld auch keine Risikokapitalmärkte!

Die Gruppe vertritt folgende Ansichten :

1. Zur Erleichterung des freien Kapitalverkehrs innerhalb der Gemeinschaft muss kurzfristig ein geeigneter Mechanismus entwickelt werden. Obwohl dieses Ziel bereits in den Verträgen genannt wurde und entsprechende Anstrengungen unternommen worden sind, sollten die europäischen Behörden mit Nachdruck auf ein Beseitigung der vielfältigen, auch heute noch bestehenden nationalen Barrieren hinwirken. Ich möchte hierzu nur zwei typische Beispiele anführen.

In Italien ist beim Kauf ausländischer Effekten bzw. beim Effektenkauf im Ausland eine zinslose Kaution in Höhe von 50 % der gekauften Effekten zu hinterlegen.

Investoren werden je nach ihrem Rechtstatus und ihrer Nationalität und je nachdem, ob sie juristische Personen des Privatrechts oder des öffentlichen Rechts und ob sie Inländer oder Ausländer sind, steuerlich diskriminiert.

2. Die Gemeinschaft sollte sich am Beispiel der European Venture Capital Association (EVCA) orientieren und auch in Zukunft die Prinzipien anwenden, die zur Schaffung dieses in seiner Art einmaligen Verbandes geführt haben. Zugleich sollte sie die optimale Nutzung aller Möglichkeiten anstreben, die EVCA als Verbindungsmitglied zwischen den Risikokapitalmärkten eröffnen, um unter anderem in grösstmöglichem Umfang von den verschiedensten nationalen Förderungsmassnahmen profitieren und auf Gemeinschaftsebene Entwicklungsanstösse geben zu können.

Diese erste Reihe von Grundhaltungen müsste umgehend durch die Bereitstellung weiterer Mittel vervollständigt werden. Das Europäische Innovationsdarlehen stellt hierbei einen interessanten ersten Schritt dar. In diesem Zusammenhang wurde häufig die Europäische Investitionsbank erwähnt. Die EIB sollte sich ebenfalls mit den Risikokapitalgesellschaften befassen und sie als würdige Finanzpartner betrachten.

Nach Auffassung der Gruppe sollte EVCA dazu beitragen, diesen Berufsstand mit seinem Adelsbrief zu versehen: EVCA könnte ein "Ehrenhaftigkeitsdiplom" gegenüber der Finanzgemeinschaft als Ganzer und insbesondere gegenüber der BEI ausstellen, so dass die einzelnen Mitglieder als Finanzierungsvermittler auftreten könnten.

Nach Ansicht der Gruppe N.5 ist dies eine Massnahme, die schon sehr bald in die Praxis umgesetzt werden könnte, insbesondere durch die Ausarbeitung eines Kodex der Berufspflichten, dessen Einhaltung von EVCA überwacht würde.

Hinsichtlich der Parallelmärkte hielte es die Gruppe nicht für sinnvoll, einen einzigen Markt auf Gemeinschaftsebene schaffen zu wollen. Die hierzu zugelassenen Unternehmen sind im wesentlichen auf örtlicher bzw. nationaler Ebene tätig; ihre Anteile eingnen sich nicht für den Handel auf europäischer Ebene.

Ein ganz Europa umfassender Markt ist nur bei einem Verbund der Wertpapierbörsen sinnvoll; die verschiedenen Parallelmärkte können sich dann ipso facto die europäische Dimension zunutze machen.

Es erscheint deshalb wenig zweckmässig, für den Kapital-Parallelmarkt getrennte europäische Strukturen vorzusehen.

Abschliessend möchte die Gruppe N.5 die Europäische Gemeinschaft auf zwei wichtige Einzelaspekte hinweisen:

- einerseits die Notwendigkeit, die Investitionstechniken für Risikokapital und die professionellen Fähigkeiten der Risikokapitalgeber zu verbessern und ihnen die komplexen Kenntnisse zu vermitteln, die sie benötigen, wenn sie den Gemeinsamen Markt in seiner Gesamtheit als einen einzigen Markt nutzen wollen. Auch hier wird die EVCA Pionieraufgaben übernehmen und dürfte dabei von den europäischen Instanzen nachhaltig unterstützt werden;

- andererseits haben sich diese Institutionen nach unserer Beurteilung bisher noch nicht ausreichend mit dem reellem Problem der Phasenverschiebung zwischen dem zeitlichen Ablauf, innerhalb dessen eine Technologie zur Reife gelangt und der Forderung der Risikokapitalgeber nach Ertrag aus ihrem investierten Kapital auseinandergesetzt. Dieses Problem, das sich den Unternehmen täglich in der Praxis stellt, sollte Gegenstand zusätzlicher Untersuchungen sein, damit es gelingt, zwei offensichtlich widersprüchliche Forderungen miteinander in Einklang zu bringen.

BERICHT DER ARBEITSGRUPPE NR. 7

Vorsitzender : J.D. INCLEDON
Berichterstatter : E. PHILLIPS

RISIKOKAPITAL DURCH KOLLEKTIVE INVESTITIONEN

Die Gruppe wies auf eine Reihe von Faktoren hin, die für neu gegründete Unternehmen in Europa im Vergleich zu nordamerikanischen Unternehmen Probleme aufwerfen können. Ein Teilnehmer ging näher darauf ein und sagte, dass die in den Vereinigten Staaten auftretenden Schwierigkeiten in der Europäischen Gemeinschaft einfach deshalb zehnmal grösser seien, weil die Gemeinschaft aus zehn Ländern bestehe. Er bezog sich dabei auf die unterschiedlichen Steuersysteme, die unterschiedlichen Rechnungswesen, die verschiedenen Sprachen, die unterschiedlichen Inflationsraten, mit denen zu kämpfen sei und auf die verschiedenen Währungen bei einem Wechsel von einem EG-Land in ein anderes.

In Europa haben sich viele Unternehmen schon sehr früh mit diesen Problemen auseinanderzusetzen, da die Märkte in den einzelnen Ländern so klein sind, dass ein Unternehmen schon im ersten Jahr seines Bestehens möglicherweise versuchen muss, zu exportieren. Im Gegensatz dazu gibt es in den Vereinigten Staaten weitaus mehr Unternehmen, die schon seit Jahren bestehen, ohne in Ländern ausserhalb Nordamerikas exportieren zu müssen.

Verglichen mit den Vereinigten Staaten fehlt es in Europa auch an Erfahrungen. In der Gruppe 7 wurde als Beispiel angeführt, dass viele Unternehmer in Europa bei der Realisierung von Geschäftsvorhaben auf die Hilfe von Risikokapital-Vermittlungsgesellschaften angewiesen zu sein scheinen, während dieser Aspekt für den Unternehmer in den Vereinigten Staaten eher zweitrangig sei. Die Gruppe äussert Zweifel darüber, ob viele Vermittlungsgesellschaften in Europa die nötige Sachkenntniss haben, um die von manchen Unternehmen benötigte Unterstützung geben zu können.

In bezug auf die Lage eines in einem Land der Europäischen Gemeinschaft ansässigen Investors wies die Gruppe darauf hin, dass diese Investoren möglicherweise zögern, Investitionen ausserhalb ihres eigenen Landes zu tätigen, da sie befürchten, auf Probleme (wie z.B. Devisenkontrollen) zu stossen, wenn sie ihr Geld in ihr eigenes Land zurückbringen wollen.

Die Gruppe stellte im Vergleich zu europäischen Investoren bei amerikanischen Anlegern im allgemeinen auch eine grössere Aufgeschlossenheit fest.

Die Gruppe ist der Ansicht, dass die Risikokapital-Vermittlungsgesellschaften in den Vereinigten Staaten aufgrund all dieser Faktoren weitaus besser entwickelt sind und über grössere Erfahrungen verfügen als derartige Gesellschaften in Europa. Dies zeigt sich auch daran, dass die Vereinigten Staaten Risikokapital aus Europa abziehen, so wie einige amerikanische Gesellschaften auch bedeutende Anteile des europäischen Marktes für ihre Produkte erobert haben.

Das trägt natürlich ebenfalls dazu bei, die amerikanischen Risikokapital-Vermittlungsgesellschaften weiter auf Kosten der europäischen Vermittlungsgesellschaften zu stärken.

Die Gruppe gelangte aufgrund dieser Ueberlegungen zu ihrer ersten Empfehlung:

> "In Anbetracht der gegenüber amerikanischen Risikokapital-Vermittlungsgesellschaften relativ geringen Erfahrungen sollten Wege zur Stärkung der europäischen Vermittlungsgesellschaften gefunden werden, damit diese in eine effektivere Konkurrenz zu den amerikanischen Gesellschaften treten können."

Die Arbeitsgruppe nannte insbesondere Massnahmen wie steuerrechtliche Bestimmungen zugunsten dieser Vermittlungsgesellschaften und die Abschaffung von Behinderungen in Zusammenhang mit grenzüberschreitenden Kapitalbewegungen.

Die zweite Empfehlung der Gruppe zielt unmittelbar auf die fehlenden Erfahrungen bei den Risikokapital-Vermittlungsgesellschaften und den Unternehmern in Europa ab:

> "Die Vermittlungsgesellschaften und die Manager von Unternehmen, die Risikokapital übernehmen, sollten gezielt dabei unterstützt werden, sich das für eine erfolgreiche Tätigkeit erforderliche Know-how anzueignen."

Schliesslich ist die Gruppe der Ansicht, dass es sich auf die Risikokapitalmärkte günstig auswirken könnte, wenn die Realisierung von Investitionen erleichtert würde, insbesondere über kurze Zeiträume von zwei bis drei Jahren; in anderen Worten, es sind bessere Ausstiegsmöglichkeiten erforderlich. Anders ausgedrückt kann man auch sagen, dass es solange es nicht in allen Mitgliedstaaten Börsen wie den Londoner Freiverkehrsmarkt (London Unlisted Securities Market) gibt, die Investitionen in Risikokapitalfonds begünstigen, schwierig bleiben wird, Geld kurzfristig wiederzubeschaffen. Daraus ergibt sich die letzte Empfehlung:

> "Die Mechanismen zur Realisierung von Risikokapitalinvestitionen sollten sobald wie möglich gestärkt werden."

BERICHT DER ARBEITSGRUPPE NR.8

Vorsitzender : I. MOMTCHILOFF
Berichterstatter : J.M. GIBB

RISIKOKAPITAL MANAGEMENT

Die Arbeitsgruppe versuchte, eine Definition für Risikokapitalmanagement aufzustellen und einige der Möglichkeiten aufzuzeigen, zwischen denen die Personen wählen können, die in Risikokapital investieren. Ausserdem wurde auf bestimmte Schwierigkeiten hingewiesen, auf die Risikokapitalmanager gestossen sind, die durch offizielle Massnahmen auf der Ebene der Mitgliedstaaten oder der Gemeinschaft vermindert werden könnten.

In Zusammenhang mit diesem Thema behandelte die Arbeitsgruppe folgende Punkte:

1. Strukturen

2. a) Wie lassen sich geeignete Projekte finden?
   b) Kriterien für Investitionsentscheidungen

3. a) Ueberwachung der Investitionen
   b) Zeitpunkt des Ausstiegs.

1. STRUKTUREN

Zeitplan für eine Risikokapital-Transaktion: ziemlich langfristig, wenigstens 10 Jahre.

Anleger: Privatpersonen
Risikokapital-Gesellschaften
Institutionen.

Sektoren, in die investiert werden kann: Im wesentlichen bieten sich zwei Möglichkeiten :

a) breites Spektrum von Sektoren (führt, statistisch gesehen, zu einer Risikostreuung)

oder

b) Spezialisierung (führt zu detaillierteren Kenntnissen und deshalb möglicherweise zu einer besseren Abschätzung des Risikos).

Die Arbeitsgruppe gab Möglichkeit a) den Vorzug gegenüber Möglichkeit b)

Finanzierungsstadium: Unter dem Aspekt des Wachstumspotentials ist die Finanzierung von Firmengründungen reizvoll wenn auch risikoreicher als die Finanzierung von späteren Entwicklungsphasen, nach der im übrigen eine rege Nachfrage besteht. Das Portfolio einer Risikokapital-Gesellschaft sollte entsprechend breit gestreut sein.

Welche Mitarbeiter? Eine Risikokapital-Gesellschaft sollte von einem Team geleitet werden, zu dem folgende Personen zählen: Personen mit Erfahrung in der Geschäftsführung, Personen mit Erfahrung im Rechnungswesen sowie Finanzexperten.

Beispiel für eine spezialisierte Einheit:

eine Person mit Erfahrung in der Geschäftsführung) Abwicklung von etwa
ein Finanzexperte) 15 Investitionsprojekten

Beispiel für eine nicht spezialisierte Einheit:

eine Person mit Erfahrung in der Geschäftsführung) Abwicklung von etwa
ein Finanzexperte) 15 Investitionsprojekten

+ Beratungsgremium)
+ Berater)
+ Kontakte)

Gründe für Investitionen im Ausland:

Die Möglichkeit, auf einem grösseren Markt zu operieren und eine breitere Streuung zu erreichen, wobei jedoch Informationen über gesetzliche Bestimmungen, Patentschutz, Besteuerung usw. erfoderlich sind.

Welche Anreize gibt es für die in einem Team mitarbeitenden Personen?

Eine Möglichkeit könnte darin bestehen, die Mitglieder des Teams anteilmässig an den erzielten Kapitalerträgen zu beteiligen. Dies kann sich als schwierig erweisen, wenn das Team Teil eines institutionellem Systems ist.

Eine weitere Möglichkeit besteht darin, ihnen Bezugsrechte anzubieten. Leider gibt es nur in wenigen Ländern entsprechende gesetzliche Bestimmungen.

Der freie Kapialverkehr

Der freie Kapitalverkehr, der vor allem für internationale Transaktionen von Bedeutung ist, ist innerhalb der Europäischen Gemeinschaft noch nicht vollständig realisiert, da in einigen Mitgliedstaaten Devisenkontrollen und andere einschränkende Vorschriften bestehen, wie zum Beispiel Vorschriften betreffend die Staatsangehörigkeit von Unternehmensleitern.

Die internationale Zusammenarbeit

Auch wenn es, wie oben bereits angedeutet, Vorteile bietet, in einem internationalen Rahmen zu operieren, ist es nicht einfach, auf einem ausländischen Markt eine starke Position zu erlangen. Das lässt die Bildung von übernationalen Konsortien ratsam erscheinen. Vielleicht kann der kürzlich gegründete Europäische Risikokapitalverband (European Venture Capital Association) hierbei Unterstützung leisten.

Die Entscheidungsstruktur

Grundsätzlich besteht die Wahl zwischen einer hierarchischen und einer kollektiven Struktur. Im ersten Fall ist eine Person allein für die Entscheidung verantwortlich. Im zweiten Fall wird die Verantwortung geteilt, Entscheidungen, werden bei einigen Organisationen durch Abstimmungen getroffen. Die Arbeitsgruppe schien dem zweiten System einen leichten Vorzug zu geben.

2. a) <u>WIE LASSEN SICH GEEIGNETE PROJEKTE FINDEN?</u>

- durch technische Fachzeitschriften,
- durch Universitäten,
- durch andere Risikokapitalmanager,
- durch Mitglieder des Beratungsgremiums (wenn vorhanden),
- durch Käufer aus der Industrie,
- durch Berater, Wirtschaftsprüfer, Gutachter usw.,
- durch Bankdirektoren,
- durch den Besuch von Konferenzen und Messen,
- durch Datenbasen.

2. b) <u>KRITERIEN FUER INVESTITIONSENTSCHEIDUNGEN</u>

Folgende Fragen müssen sich positiv beantworten lassen:

- Ist das Risikomanagement angemessen?
- Gibt es einen Projektplan?
- Wurde dieser Plan aus kommerzieller, industrieller und finanzieller Sicht bewertet und zufriedenstellend befunden?
- Gibt es verwertbares Eigentum oder ist ein kommerzieller Nutzen zu erwarten?
- Hat die Geschäftsführung persönliche finanzielle Verpflichtungen übernommen?

3. a) <u>UEBERWACHUNG DER INVESTITIONEN</u>

Wenn eine Investition getätigt wurde, sollten sie überwacht werden:

- durch Anforderung und genaue Prüfung von Fortschrittberichten;
- durch Sicherstellung, dass der Projektplan aktualisiert wird, wann immer
- dies notwendig erscheint;
- möglicherweise durch einen Sitz im Verwaltungsrat;
- durch effektive Unterstützung der Geschäftsführung.

3. b) <u>ZEITPUNKT DES AUSSTIEGS</u>

Es gibt offensichtlich keine feststehende Regel, doch bevor das Wachstum zurückgeht, d.h. ziemlich früh.

SCHLUSSFOLGERUNG UND EMPFEHLUNGEN

Es sollten gesetzgeberische Massnahmen ergriffen werden, die die Möglichkeiten für Manager verbessern, Bezugsrechte zu erwerben.

Innerhalb der Europäischen Gemeinschaft ist der freie Kapitalverkehr unerlässlich, wenn aus der grenzüberschreitenden Risikokapitalkooperation der volle Nutzen gezogen werden soll.

Es sollten mehr Lehrgänge über Risikokapitalmanagement abgehalten werden.

Die Datenbasen, die Informationen über geschäftliche Möglichkeiten in der gesamten Gemeinschaft enthalten, sollten weiter ausgebaut werden.

V. SITZUNG - BERICHTERSTATTUNG : 25.11.83

Zusammenfassung von Herrn I.N. MOMTCHILOFF,
General Manager, Investors in Indsutry Group PLC, London

Meine Aufgabe ist es nun, einen zusammenfassenden Ueberblick über dieses Symposium zu geben; ich werde dies aber nicht tun, da es beinahe unmöglich ist. Ich möchte Ihnen jedoch einige wenige meiner Gedanken darlegen.

Frau Lebas versuchte, uns - ich könnte beinahe sagen : leidenschaftlich - davon zu überzeugen, dass nur das System zählt. Es steht meines Erachtens ausser Frage, dass die Entwicklung eines Sekundärmarktes einen wesentlichen Beitrag für das Risikokapitalsystem darstellen könnte.

Ich unterstütze mit Nachdruck regulierende Vorschriften und Richtlinien für Börsen; wenn jedoch Risikokapitalinvestitionen gefördert werden sollen, so ist meiner Meinung nach ein vernünftig geregelter und vernünftig angelegter Sekundärmarkt ein wesentlicher Bestandteil eines jeden Systems. Das ist für jemand, der tatsächlich seine Zukunft aufs Spiel setzt, wenn er eine Firma gründet, sehr wichtig.

Solange wir im Vereinigten Königreich keinen Zugang zu Sekundärmärkten hatten, hatte jemand, der allein oder gemeinsam mit anderen eine Firma gründen wollte, im Grunde nur zwei Möglichkeiten, aus seinem Risiko Geld zu machen.

Die erste Möglichkeit war die, eine Firma so auszubauen, dass sie gross und gut genug sowie hinreichend wirtschaftlich stabil war, um am Primärmarkt eingeführt zu werden. Das ist eine ermutingende und letzlich auch sich ständig in neuer Weise stellende Aufgabe, denn eine Firma konnte zwar noch vor einigen Jahren am Hauptmarkt aufgenommen werden, wenn ihre Gewinne bei einer Viertelmillion Pfund lagen, einige Jahre später mussten jedoch bereits Gewinne in Höhe von einer Million, dann von eineinhalb Millionen Pfund erzielt werden. Dies ist zum Teil auf die Inflation zurückzuführen, aber eben nur zum Teil. Nur wenige von den Hunderten neugegründeter Unternehmen werden in der Lage sein, dieses Ziel zu erreichen.

Geld liesse sich auch durch Verkauf (die 2. Möglichkeit) verdienen, doch viele Leute, die Firmen gründen, sehen das nicht unbedingt als ihr Ziel an. Sie gründen Firmen, weil sie eben Firmen gründen wollen.

Durch die Existenz von Sekundärmärkten eröffnet sich eine andere Dimension. Dadurch haben sich die Möglichkeiten des in Frage stehenden Personenkreises, Zugang zu dem Geld der Allgemeinheit zu bekommen und einen Teil ihrer eigenen Investitionen zu realisieren (vielleicht können die betreffenden Personen daran denken, ein Auto oder ein zweites Auto oder einen Rolls-Royce zu erwerben, wenn sie dies anstreben) im Vereinigten Königreich erheblich verbessert. Wenn diesem Personenkreis kein Anreiz geboten werden kann, sich an Firmengründungen heranzuwagen, dann verschwenden wir hier alle unsere Zeit, weil es diese Personen sind, die Wohlstand schaffen. Sie müssen Geld verdienen, und diejenigen, die sie finanzieren, müssen auch Geld verdienen. Jeder in diesem System braucht einen Anreiz, um die damit verbundenen Risiken auf sich zu nehmen. Wenn also in diesem System Blockierungen entstehen, dann müssen die Regierungen, die Kommission und wir alle daran mitwirken, die Hindernisse zu beseitigen.

Der zweite Punkt, auf den ich hier eingehen möchte, habe ich bereits erwähnt, und ich halte ihn für äusserst wichtig: in Europa wird mehr Kapital für die Weiterentwicklung von Unternehmen benötigt als für Unternehmungsgründungen. Diese Art der Investition führt zu Stabilität und bietet gute Aussichten auf Gewinn. Dieser Punkt sollte nicht ausser acht gelassen werden, denn wenn zu viele Unternehmer den Ehrgeiz hegen, zu den ganz Grossen zu zählen, dann werden viele von ihnen keinen Erfolg haben; ich würde es sehr bedauern, wenn die so erfolgreiche Entwicklung der Beteiligungsfinanzierung kleiner Unternehmen aufgrund unrealistischer Erwartungen in Verruf käme.

Dies könnte der Beginn einer neuen Krise sein. In Amerika ist es bereits soweit. Ich erinnere mich daran, vor einigen Jahren in Minneapolis in einem Börsenbüro drei leere Bildschirme gesehen zu haben. Ich erkundigte mich näher und erhielt die Antwort: "Das war unsere NASDAQ-Abteilung *. Der Markt ist

---

* NASDAQ = National Association of Securities Dealers Automated Quotations

tot, die Zeiten mit zweistelligen Kurs-Gewinn-Verhältnissen sind vorbei."

Ich nehme an, dass der amerikanische Markt in eine Abwärtsbewegung geraten wird und ich glaube, dass dasselbe auch mit dem Freiverkehrmarkt geschehen wird.

Der letzte Punkt, den ich ansprechen möchte, ist der grenzüberschreitende Aspekt. Wir alle wissen, dass es sehr schwierig ist, auf dem gesamten europäischen Markt ein Produkt oder eine Dienstleistung zu lancieren: Schwierigkeiten bereiten zum Beispiel nichttarifliche Handelshemmnisse, die verschiedenen Verhaltensweisen in den einzelnen Ländern usw. Leider ist es wahr, dass jemand, der versucht, ein modernes Unternehmen aufzubauen, als Standort zunächst einmal die Vereinigten Staaten in Betracht zieht. Ich bin nicht der Ansicht, dass wir die Vereinigten Staaten vernachlässigen sollten, da sie ja tatsächlich den grössten Einzelmarkt in der Welt darstellen, es ist jedoch bedauerlich, dass wir Europäer nicht über einen grossen Markt verfügen.

Zu Zeit wird überall wieder der Ruf nach verstärktem Proktetionismus laut. Jedes Land möchte sich auf modernen, technologisch weit fortgeschrittenen Sektoren engagieren und zum Beispiel sein eigenes kleines Robotik-Unternehmen haben, das argwöhnisch behütet wird. Darin liegt en fataler Fehler.

Ich glaube, dass der Aufbau einer starken Risikokapitalindustrie Abhilfe schaffen könnte. Wenn wir verschiedene, auf dem Risikokapitalmarkt engagierte Institutionen davon überzeugen können, dass sie auf einem internationalen Markt agieren, gelingt es uns vielleicht zu beweisen, dass es für die Mitgliedstaaten nur von Vorteil sein kann, wenn sie zusammenarbeiten.

Wenn man einige Leute überzeugen kann, grosse Beträge von Risikokapital zu investieren, wird sich die Haltung von Regierungen, von Institutionen und der Industrie ändern. Das wird nicht in naher Zukunft zu erreichen sein, doch ich hoffe, dass wir wenigstens für die unsere Zukunft bestimmenden Industrien mehr aus dem Gemeinsamen Markt machen, als wir aus ihm für die untergehenden Industrien gemacht haben.

Résumés des Exposés 243

Groupes de Travail 1, 2, 6–3, 4, 5, 7, 8, 255

Résumés des Conclusions du Symposium 285
I.N. MOMTCHILOFF
General Manager, Investors in Industry Group, P.L.C.,
London (United Kingdom)

LES CAISSES DE RETRAITE EN TANT QU'INVESTISSEURS "A RISQUE"

D.J. PROSSER

CIN Industrial Investments

Le régime fiscal des caisses de retraite est neutre sur le plan des revenus et des plus-values, ce qui donne à l'investisseur une plus grande souplesse dans l'élaboration de ses propositions. Comme les opérations des caisses de retraite sont à long terme, ces caisses ne doivent pas nécessairement vendre leurs titres sur des marchés à court terme pour réaliser les plus-values de leurs investissements.

Bien que peu importants, nos investissements aux Etats-Unis ont été liés aussi bien à l'évolution technologique qu'à l'organisation des opérations. Le marché américain des capitaux à risque est bien plus important et plus ancien que le marché britannique. Les fonds internationaux de capitaux à risque auront du mal à se développer en Europe. En raison des problèmes linguistiques, juridiques et comptables qui se posent, il est préférable que les investissements dans des titres non cotés de petites sociétés soient effectués au niveau local. Bien que des exceptions soient possibles, un fonds reposant sur une base très large et dépourvu d'une succursale locale manquera généralement de professionalisme. Dans la plupart des cas, le coût d'une succursale serait excessif pour un fonds étranger.

La société CIN Industrial Investments considère que les investissements à risque peuvent porter sur des capitaux d'exploitation, le financement de projets et la création d'entreprises. Environ 180 millions de livres sont actuellement investis dans ces domaines et l'équipe de gestion comprend une quizaine de cadres. En 1983, 26 millions de livres ont été investis et des investissements d'un montant de 13 millions de livres ont été réalisés.

LES COMPAGNIES D'ASSURANCES EN TANT QU'INVESTISSEURS DE CAPITAUX A RISQUE

POINT DE VUE NEERLANDAIS

D.S. VAN HOUT

Directeur général de la "Investments and Corporate Finance Ennia N.V."

Résumé

Si les capitaux à risque sont considérés comme une solution aux problèmes structuraux qui se posent dans l'industrie de la CE, il semble qu'il y ait un large fossé entre l'offre et la demande.
En outre, il convient de ne pas surestimer la capacité des bailleurs de fonds potentiels. En dépit de leur contribution à la reconstruction industrielle, l'attrait des investissements à risque est considéré comme insuffisant pour inciter les agents traditionnels du marché des capitaux à investir massivement.

Après avoir analysé la situation existant aux Pays-Bas, l'orateur présente les caractéristiques des compagnies d'assurances néerlandaises. Les principaux problèmes rencontrés sont les suivants :

- la contradiction entre la maximisation des bénéfices distribués et le financement de prêts participatifs à haut risque ;
- le sous-développement des marchés de valeurs mobilières ;
- l'expérience et la connaissance du marché en tant que bailleurs de capitaux à risque.

L'analyse de la situation existant aux Pays-Bas montre qu'un afflux considérable de nouveaux capitaux à risque est nécessaire pour stimuler l'emploi jusqu'à un niveau suffisant et acceptable et qu'il existe une demande cachée dans divers secteurs industriels. Toutefois, tant du côté de l'offre que du côté de la demande, il faut prendre des mesures pour éliminer un grand nombre d'obstacles, parmi lesquelles des instruments d'exonération fiscale et une aide logistique aux jeunes entrepreneurs sont décisifs.

En dépit du sous-développement de ce nouvel instrument de financement, l'attitude des compagnies d'assurances (néerlandaises) à l'égard des capitaux à risque donne la mesure de leur engagement social, mais aussi de leur responsabilité en tant que sociétés.

"LA FISCALITE ET LE FINANCEMENT DE L'INNOVATION" COMPARAISON DES DIFFERENTES DISPOSITIONS EN VIGUEUR DANS LA C.E.E.

P. FONTANEAU
Professeur Agrégé des Facultés de Droit
et de Sciences Economiques
Avocat à la Cour d'Appel de Paris

Résumé :

La fiscalité joue un rôle essentiel dans le financement de l'innovation. Des incitants fiscaux existent dans tous les pays de la Communauté Européenne.

Pour développer le marché des capitaux à risque, les pays européens ont pris des mesures portant sur la réduction du risque attaché au placement et l'amélioration de la rentabilité nette du placement.

Pour accroître le financement des entreprises innovatrices, ont été adoptées des mesures d'incitation aux achats d'actions nouvelles et des dispositions visant à améliorer la capacité d'autofinancement des entreprises.

Pour développer leur rentabilité, des mesures spécifiques concernant la recherche et le stade amont de l'innovation ont été prises.

Toutefois, les incitations ficales limitées à la seule innovation se révèleront insuffisantes si la fiscalité générale sur les revenus des sociétés et des personnes physiques est trop lourde et frappe donc trop durement les innovateurs.

Compte tenu de ces remarques et de l'importance de l'innovation pour la croissance de la Communauté Economique Européenne, une politique fiscale qui englobe l'ensemble du processus d'innovation devra être élaborée.

Ce Code Fiscal de l'Innovation devra être coordonné à l'échelle communautaire pour restaurer la compétitivité des entreprises européennes vis-à-vis de leurs principaux concurrents américains ou japonais.

LE REGIME FISCAL DES INVESTISSEURS INSTITUTIONNELS ET COLLECTIFS

D. O'HOGAN

Partner, Arthur Young & Comapny, Experts comptables,

Portobello House, Dublin 8

Résumé

M. O'HOGAN a évoqué le régime fiscal auquel sont soumis les investisseurs institutionnels/collectifs de capitaux à risque et il a indiqué, en particulier, que le système fiscal n'avait pas d'incidence sur la décision concernant le lieu d'investissement.

TRAITEMENT FISCAL DE L'INVESTISSEUR INDIVIDUEL

CORNELIS A.M. RASENBERG

Directeur du Département Fiscal

de l'Amsterdam-Rotterdam Bank N.V.

(Pays-Bas)

Résumé

La nature du marché des capitaux à risque exige de l'investisseur individuel un investissement présentant un risque élevé pour une période de temps assez longue. Ses revenus courants provenant de cet investissement seront presque toujours soumis entièrement à l'impôt aux taux ordinaires ; dans quelques cas seulement, les moins-values seront déductibles des revenus ordinaires alors que l'imposition des plus-values varie considérablement d'un pays à l'autre. En fonction notamment de la question de savoir si la plus-value est considérée comme un revenu mobilier ou comme un autre revenu, un taux ordinaire ou réduit sera applicable. Les mesures d'incitation fiscale visant à réduire le montant d'un investissement dans des capitaux à risque après déduction de l'impôt (déduction ou crédit d'impôt sur l'investissement) sont des moyens efficaces pour attirer des capitaux à risque. Les mesures d'incitation fiscale en vigueur tendent à faire une discrimination envers les investissements dans des entreprises étrangères. Beaucoup de pays ont institué unilatéralement un régime d'imposition privilégié à l'intention des organismes d'investissement collectif, mais chacun selon des modalités différentes. Il conviendrait d'instaurer une législation communautaire uniforme pour les organismes de capitaux à risque, qui éliminerait la double imposition des bénéfices de sociétés et d'autres obstacles fiscaux ainsi que les entraves réglementaires aux investissements collectifs dans des sociétés innovatrices.

IMPACT DES REFORMES FISCALES SUR LES INVESTISSEMENTS DE CAPITAUX A RISQUE ET SUR L'INNOVATION AUX ETATS-UNIS

P.T. KAPLAN
Weil, Gotshal Manges
New York City

Résumé

Alors que, dans l'ensemble, les Etats-Unis se sont montrés généreux dans l'octroi d'avantages fiscaux pour les investissements de capitaux à risque et pour l'innovation, il n'est pas possible, à partir de ce seul fait, d'établir une corrélation entre ces mesures d'incitation et le haut niveau d'innovation atteint aux Etats-Unis au cours des années de l'après-guerre ; on ne peut tirer cette conclusion qu'en observant les modifications apportées aux impôts en vigueur. Il y a eu beaucoup de modifications de ce genre aux Etats-Unis, mais on ne dispose pas encore de données suffisantes pour quantifier leur impact. Si l'on procède d'une manière moins scientifique, certaines réformes fiscales, notamment l'impôt sur les plus-values, semblent avoir entraîné des modifications de comportement à l'égard des investissements, mais d'autres modifications de comportement à cet égard ne peuvent pas être imputées à des réformes fiscales récentes. En laissant de côté les statistiques, on peut déterminer l'importance des mesures d'incitation fiscale pour l'innovation aux Etats-Unis, en observant, dans des cas spécifiques, certaines offres d'investissement, qui font bénéficier l'investisseur individuel de dégrèvements fiscaux au titre de la recherche et du développement, ce qui réduit donc le coût réel de son investissement d'un montant allant jusqu'à 55%. Puisque ces dégrèvements fiscaux ne sont pas limités géographiquement, les projets d'investissement européens pourraient être structurés de manière à faire bénéficier les investisseurs américains des mêmes dégrèvements fiscaux.

SEGMENTS BOURSIERS SPECIAUX POUR LES PARTICIPATIONS DANS DE PETITES ENTREPRISES

Situation et perspectives

Professeur H. SCHMIDT
Directeur de l'"Institut für Geld- und Kapitalverkehr"
Université de Hamburg

Résumé

Durant les dernières décennies, la bourse idéale était considérée comme un marché à structure homogène, réservé aux sociétés dont les actions, dispersées parmi un large public, constituaient un placement sûr et qui satisfaisaient à de sévères exigences de publicité. Or, comme l'ont clairement démontré l'apparition et le succès de segments boursiers spéciaux pour les petites et moyennes entreprises dans divers pays européens, il est parfaitement possible, en réduisant les exigences d'admission et en recourant à des méthodes commerciales particulières, de créer un marché boursier pour les participations dont le montant en circulation s'élève tout au plus a quelques millions de marks et qui sont donc détenues par un petit nombre d'investisseurs.

La tendance nouvelle consistant à admettre à la bourse des sociétés qui auraient été jugées précédemment trop jeunes, trop petites et trop peu solides pour cela ne porte actuellement que sur les entreprises qui ont déjà atteint un niveau de qualité élevé. Des raisons de principe et des considérations pragmatiques exigent cependant aussi l'émission publique et l'échange en et hors bourse des participations dans de petites entreprises qui n'ont pas encore atteint un tel niveau de qualité. Ce mode d'autofinancement externe des entreprises jeunes et innovatrices constitue une solution de remplacement et un complément important à l'investissement privé et au financement par des sociétés de capitaux à risque. Les problèmes de l'évaluation, du contrôle et de la sortie trouvent plus facilement une solution lorsque de jeunes entreprises de ce genre ont accès au segment boursier de base, c'est-à-dire au segment le plus bas dans la hiérarchie du marché des titres. Malgré le risque élevé attaché aux participations dans ces sociétés, la défense des investisseurs elle-même ne s'oppose pas à l'utilisation de ces moyens en vue de promouvoir la croissance des entreprises innovatrices et les effets favorables de celle-ci sur l'ensemble de l'économie.

Il existe différentes mesures permettant de favoriser l'autofinancement des jeunes entreprises dans le cadre, précisément, du segment de base notamment l'adoption d'un certificat de participation uniforme et d'un statut de "licensed-dealer" dans tous les pays membres, les incitations fiscales favorisant le recours aux appels d'offres en vue de déterminer les taux d'émission lors des premières émissions publiques, la suppression des dispositions limitant les possibilités d'investissement des investisseurs institutionnels et l'élimination des entraves fiscales aux échanges, grâce en particulier à l'abandon total de la taxation des bénéfices sur les cours de change lors de la vente de participations dans de petites entreprises.

L'ACCES AUX MARCHES EUROPEENS DES SOCIETES DE MOYENNE DIMENSION

Y. FLORNOY

Syndic de la Compagnie des Agents de Change

L'importance des petites et moyennes entreprises dans les économies de la Communauté européenne reste encore aujourd'hui déterminante. Qu'il s'agisse du nombre d'entreprises ou de la main d'oeuvre qu'elles emploient, rapporté à l'effectif global des entreprises et de la main d'oeuvre au travail, nous savons qu'elles forment réellement la trame de notre tissu économique.

Bénéficiant à ce titre de tout un réseau d'aides au développement multiples et variées, les PME se sont peu intéressées jusqu'à présent à leur accès aux marchés boursiers. Certes les obstacles à leur introduction en Bourse restent encore importants. Néanmoins, elles commencent à prendre conscience des avantages qu'elles pourraient en obtenir.

A ce titre, l'expérience en voie de réussite du Second Marché français apporte aujourd'hui une preuve de l'intérêt croissant des sociétés de dimension moyenne pour accéder aux marchés boursiers.

MARCHES SECONDAIRES EUROPEENS DES ACTIONS-

POINT DE VUE DE L'ENTREPRENEUR

ROBIN. G. HODGSON

Directeur de la Granville & Co. Limited, Londres.

Résumé

La nature psychologique de l'entrepreneur détermine son point de vue sur les divers mécanismes de sortie existants. Les entrepreneurs peuvent être divisés grosso modo en deux catégories - les entrepreneurs à vocation "dynastique" et "non dynastique". Les bourses européennes sont concentrées sur les besoins de la dernière catégorie ; les besoins des entrepreneurs dynastiques n'ont guère été pris en considération.

L'OPINION DE L'INVESTISSEUR DE CAPITAUX A RISQUE

J.P. de BLOCQ VAN KUFFELER

Directeur de

Brown, Shipley & Co. Limited

Résumé

On a observé un développement et une expansion rapides des marchés secondaires des actions au cours des trois dernières années, notamment à Londres, avec le développement du marché des valeurs non cotées et du marché hors cote. Quelque 220 actions de sociétés font actuellement l'objet d'opérations sur le marché des valeurs non cotées et près de 230 millions de capitaux ont été récoltés pour ces sociétés. Il y a à présent 24 opérateurs sur le marché hors cote, qui négocient les actions d'environ 70 sociétés.

A Londres, l'investisseur institutionnel dispose de sommes considérables pour effectuer de nouveaux investissements nets ; l'attitude et les critères d'investissements des organismes de placement revêtent une importance considérable pour ces marchés.

Les investisseurs institutionnels considèrent le marché des valeurs non cotées et le marché hors cote comme un instrument d'investissements dans de nouveaux secteurs et dans des sociétés plus jeunes offrant des possibilités de plus-values substantielles qui autrement ne pourraient pas être disponibles grâce aux marchés primaires. Le montant des dividendes versés est est donc moins important et dans certains cas, lorsqu'il s'agit de projets entièrement neufs, aucun dividende ne doit être versé au cours des premières années. La mobilisation de capitaux plus supplémentaires par de nouvelles émissions de titres ou de droits est encouragée et considérée comme un progrès positif.

A l'heure actuelle, d'aucuns se préoccupent du petit nombre d'actions disponibles dans certaines sociétés, car la rareté de titres entraîne des cours élevés. Ces cours élevés donnent lieu à des prévisions irréalistes et, par conséquent, à des cours hautement volatils. Le marché effectif des actions peut être fort restreint car la majorité des actions sont aux mains de détenteurs fidèles et peu d'actions sont disponibles pour le marché.

Néanmoins, il faut espérer qu'il s'agit d'un phénomène temporaire qui disparaîtra avec l'émission ultérieure de nouveaux titres et avec le développement des sociétés permettant une cotation boursière à part entière.

LES MARCHES HORS COTE AMERICAINS

A.E. Young

Professeur de sciences financières,

Ecole de gestion de l'université de Syracuse

Résumé

L'orateur se propose d'analyser les marchés hors cote par rapport aux marchés boursiers aux Etats-Unis, car en particulier dans l'environnement technologique moderne d'aujourd'hui, les deux grands marchés différents du passé sont inexorablement liés. L'orateur passe d'abord en revue quelques différences fondamentales entre les marchés boursiers et les marchés hors cote et ils soulignent la métamorphose historique qu'a subi le marché hors cote. Alors qu'il y a à peine 50 ans, le marché hors cote était pratiquement ignoré aux Etats-Unis lorsque les bases de la législation réglementant les marchés de valeurs ont été jetées, à l'heure actuelle les opérations hors cote portant sur les actions de grandes sociétés constituent une force importante dans le marché des valeurs mobilières. Toutefois, les opérations hors cote portant sur les actions des petites sociétés restent un segment du marché oublié et aussi peu utilisé qu'à l'époque de l'adoption initiale de la législation de base relative aux valeurs mobilières. Après cette introduction, l'orateur analyse certaines des forces et des composantes majeures des marchés des valeurs mobilières de ces dernières années. Pour terminer, il développe la proposition de marché national et il examine la position qu'occuperait probablement le marché hors cote dans un tel système.

LE "MARCHE DES VALEURS NON COTEES" DE LONDRES

Robin Stormonth-Darling

Président de Laing & Cruicksbank

(inc. McAnally Montgomery & Co.), Agent de change, Londres,

Président du Comité des Cotations du Conseil de la Bourse de Londres.

Résumé

En novembre 1980 a été inauguré le marché des valeurs non cotées. Son but était double. D'une part, il visait principalement à fournir un marché formel et réglementé pour répondre aux besoins des petites sociétés peu développées qui ne sont pas susceptibles de faire une demande de cotation de leurs titres. On a estimé qu'en l'absence d'un tel marché et de l'assurance d'une certaine négociabilité de leurs investissements, les investisseurs seraient sans doute moins disposés à s'engager. D'autre part, le marché des valeurs non cotées a placé sous le contrôle réglementaire formel de la Bourse de Londres les sociétés non cotées dont les titres étaient échangés librement en vertu des dispositions de l'article 163 (2) du règlement de la Bourse de Londres. Sous réserve de l'approbation du Conseil de la Bourse de Londres, ce règlement autorise des opérations occasionnelles portant sur les titres de sociétés publiques et privées non cotées; ces dispositions restent applicables à cette fin, mais sur une base quelque peu plus restreinte que par le passé.

Au cours de la période allant de novembre 1980 à septembre 1983, 211 sociétés ont été admises au marché des valeurs non cotées et 277 millions de livres ont été récoltés au moment de leur admission.

Compte rendu du groupe de travail n° 1

Président : Dr. H. SCHMIDT

Rapporteur : D.L. ADAMSON

Développement de mécanismes de sortie au niveau communautaire

Le groupe de travail avait pour tâche d'étudier des mécanismes de sortie dans une perspective non pas nationale, mais européenne. Dans l'ensemble, le groupe estime que deux mécanismes de sortie méritent une attention particulière. Le premier est l'utilisation des marchés de valeurs mobilières dans les autres Etats membres et le deuxième, la vente d'actions de petites sociétés d'innovation à des investisseurs institutionnels étrangers. Les deux mécanismes peuvent être utilisés alternativement, consécutivement ou simultanément.

Le groupe de travail recommande à la Commission d'intensifier ses efforts en vue de supprimer les entraves au financement transfrontalier par voie d'émissions d'actions. Etant donné le temps imparti, le groupe de travail renonce à aborder toutes ces entraves. Il décide de concentrer son attention sur quatre thèmes, à savoir, la structure générale des marchés, les premières émissions publiques transfrontalières, les opérations internationales des banques d'affaires et les investissements internationaux des institutions financières.

Dans ces quatre domaines, le groupe de travail propose les recommandations suivantes :

1. Eu égard au coût et aux difficultés connexes d'ordre pratique, le groupe de travail estime qu'il n'est pas nécessaire d'établir un marché européen central pour les instruments de financement des petites sociétés. Il convient d'utiliser les marchés existant à l'heure actuelle avec un maximum de souplesse et de les améliorer pour permettre aux petites sociétés d'innovation d'y avoir accès.

Les sociétés résidentes et non résidentes à haut risque devraient être admises aux marchés de valeurs mobilières et affectées à un segment approprié du marché.

Les conditions d'admission de ces sociétés aux marchés de valeurs mobilières doivent être fixées de manière à ne pas imposer de charge excessive aux petites sociétés. Si possible, il faut que la protection des investisseurs soit assurée par la législation en vigueur plutôt que par de nouvelles mesures complexes.

2. Il est recommandé que toutes les dispositions réglementaires qui empêchent les petites sociétés européennes d'effectuer une première émission publique d'actions dans d'autres Etats membres soient supprimées. Le groupe de travail reconnaît et déplore la grande variété de dispositions réglementaires restrictives. Elles vont des dispositions relatives au contrôle des changes à des formes subtiles de discrimination touchant les émetteurs non résidents. Le groupe souhaiterait que cesentraves fassent l'objet d'une étude plus détaillée.

En outre, le groupe de travail recommande qu'on envisage de nouveaux modes de diffusion des informations concernant les nouvelles émissions. La création de l'Association européenne des capitaux à risque constitue une bonne occasion pour lancer une publication ad hoc. Le groupe espère que cette publication attirera l'attention des entrepreneurs sur les différences substantielles de coefficients de capitalisation que des entreprises similaires obtiennent sur les différents marchés nationaux des capitaux.

3. Pour assurer l'existence de banques d'affaires dynamiques, le groupe de travail approuve la recommandation présentée lors de la session n° 3 visant à instituer dans tous les Etats membres un statut de "licensed dealer" tel qu'il est connu actuellement au Royaume-Uni. Ces opérateurs seraient autorisés à organiser des marchés hors cote et à détenir des comptes titres pour leurs clients. La mise au point du videotex interactif pourrait faciliter le déroulement des opérations sur ce marché. Pour renforcer la concurrence entre les banques d'affaires, il est également recommandé d'encourager les activités à l'échelle européenne des banques d'affaires établies dans les différents Etats membres. La Commission devrait prendre les mesures nécessaires pour supprimer les entraves réglementaires qui empêchent actuellement ces activités.

4. En théorie, in ne devrait pas y avoir de restrictions aux investissements institutionnels relatifs à des titres non cotés à l'échelle internationale. Eu égard aux difficultés d'ordre pratique auxquelles les grandes institutions financières auraient à faire face pour effectuer et surveiller les investissements internationaux en titres non cotés, le groupe de travail estime qu'il faut creuser l'idée de la création de secteurs intermédiaires spécialisés.

Un modèle de secteur possible serait la société d'investissement fermée dont les actions seraient cotées dans une ou plusieurs bourses nationales. Les avoirs de cette société pourraient être détenus sous forme de titres cotés et/ou non cotés au choix de la direction. Le régime fiscal serait le même que celui des sociétés d'investissement à capital variable. Le marché attribuerait une valeur au portefeuille d'avoirs détenus par le fonds. Ainsi, on réduirait les efforts incessants que requière l'évaluation longue et difficile des différents investissements non cotés.

De tels fonds bénéficieraient d'un appui institutionnel étant donné que la politique d'investissement se situerait à l'échelle internationale dans le domaine des petites sociétés - un rôle que les institutions souhaitent voir sous-traiter. La présence active de ces sous-traitants spécialisés contribuerait grandement à l'internationalisation des marchés des capitaux européens destinés aux petites sociétés en suscitant une concurrence transfrontalière entre les nouvelles sociétés recherchant des capitaux sociaux supplémentaires.

Compte rendu du groupe de travail n° 2

Président : P. FONTANEAU

Rapporteur :: P. WECKEL

Comment améliorer l'environnement fiscal des investissements à risque?

Tout d'abord, le groupe de travail rappelle que, depuis 1975, la Commission des Communautés européennes a fait des propositions pour que le statut fiscal de certains éléments de l'assiette de l'impôt sur les sociétés ou sur le revenu soit modifié et, de ce fait, coordonné dans les différents Etats membres. Ces propositions ont notamment porté sur la notion de fusion, les relations entre sociétés mères et sociétés filiales, le problème de la double imposition des sociétés ayant des établissements fiscaux dans plusieurs Etats de la Communauté. A l'intérieur du cadre ainsi tracé, le groupe de travail se permet de proposer les mesures suivantes, afin d'améliorer le fonctionnement du marché des "Venture Capital".

Ces recommandations s'efforceront d'aboutir au double résultat suivant : coordonner et similariser le statut fiscal des participants au marché des "Venture Capital", et ce, afin de lutter contre sa fragmentation et de lui donner dans le futur une dimension européenne.

Pour parvenir à ce résultat, le groupe de travail propose les mesures suivantes :

1. Modification du statut fiscal de l'investisseur individuel dans le "Venture Capital".
2. Modification du statut fiscal de la société innovatrice.
3. Modification du statut fiscal des fonds de placement dans le "Venture Capital".

Ces trois modifications de statut fiscal devront, comme il a déjà été dit, s'efforcer de rendre aussi similaire que possible, le système fiscal concernant ces trois agents économiques, et ce dans les différents pays de la Communauté.

Le groupe de travail est conscient du fait que le statut fiscal de l'innovation n'est qu'une partie, un sous-ensemble du statut fiscal global des agents économiques précités. Le statut fiscal, et plus spécialement l'impôt sur le revenu et sur les sociétés, demeure la prérogative des Etats membres. Toutefois, afin de faciliter le démarrage du marché du "Venture Capital", le groupe de travail souhaite que la charge fiscale globale soit réduite autant que faire se pourra dans les différents pays de la Communauté.

Compte tenu de l'aspect international de l'innovation et de son importance pour la croissance et l'emploi dans les pays européens, une politique communautaire de fond visant à stimuler l'ensemble du processus d'innovation doit être envisagée.

Le groupe de travail propose donc l'élaboration d'un véritable Code Fiscal de l'Innovation à l'échelle européenne. Ce Code Fiscal de l'Innovation sera l'instrument du renouveau de la compétitivité des entreprises européennes face à leurs concurrentes américaines ou japonaises.

Le groupe de travail est conscient du fait que l'amélioration du statut fiscal de l'innovation est un élément nécessaire pour le démarrage du marché du "Venture Capital". Il insiste toutefois sur le fait que les incitants fiscaux ne seront pas suffisants pour susciter une croissance rapide de ce marché et il souhaite que d'autres aides soient apportées aux différents agents composant le marché du "Venture Capital".

P. FONTANEAU

Le Président rend hommage à l'activité déployée depuis 1975 par la Commission en vue de l'harmonisation de l'assiette de l'impôt sur les sociétés. Il souligne que les propositions qu'elle pourrait être amenée à formuler en faveur de l'innovation devraient prendre pour base ces actions déjà entreprises ou réalisées.

De la séance du mercredi après-midi consacrée à l'impact de la fiscalité sur l'innovation, le Président retient quatre points de discussion :

1) M. HENRIKSEN a envisagé la mise en place, si cette proposition rencontrait l'approbation des Etats membres, d'un fonds,ou de fonds européens d'investissement dans le domaine des capitaux à risque et bénéficiant d'avantages fiscaux ;

2) dans son exposé, M. INCLEDON a constaté l'inexistence d'un marché commun du capital à risque ;

3) l'impôt sur le revenu produit un effet négatif sur le développement du capital à risque. En ce domaine les Etats membres ont largement conservé leur souveraineté fiscale, mais cela ne saurait faire obstacle à des propositions sur des points limités ;

4) il serait excessif de croire que l'incitation fiscale suffirait à elle seule à stimuler les activités de "venture capital".

Pour ce qui concerne l'Allemagne, l'un des participants estime que l'incitation fiscale est une nécessité parce que l'investisseur a besoin d'une perspective moins aléatoire de profit et de certaines garanties. Il suggère par conséquent, que lui soit offerte la possibilité d'une déduction fiscale importante la première année et pour les années ultérieures que son profit soit faiblement imposé.

Certains participants observent toutefois que ces allègements auraient pour effet de transférer à la collectivité publique la charge principale du risque de l'investissement. Par la déduction fiscale, celle-ci devient un partenaire privilégié de l'investisseur, mais il est souhaitable qu'elle reste un partenaire minoritiare.

On évoque, d'autre part, l'échec des sociétés d'amortissement en Allemagne. Lorsque l'avantage fiscal devient la motivation principale de l'investisseur, il n'a d'autre effet que de multiplier l'investissement dans les entreprises non viables.

On exprime dans l'assistance que le Fisc doit mesurer sa générosité et maintenir un certain équilibre entre les agents économiques.

M. KAPLAN se déclare tout à fait en accord avec ce raisonnement, mais pense que l'exemple donné par l'intervenant pour l'appuyer, la surcote de certaines actions qu'entraînerait le "Business Expansion Scheme" au Royaume Uni, est mal choisi, dans la mesure où cet effet est inévitable et contribue à l'intérêt du mécanisme.

Le Président se déclare favorable à un système de déduction de l'investissement parce qu'un allègement portant sur des dividendes ne présente aucun avantage durant les premières années pendant lesquelles aucun bénéfice n'est dégagé.

M. WIRK estime, pour sa part, que l'efficacité de chaque avantage fiscal doit être apprécié en tenant compte du système fiscal dans lequel il s'intègre et dont on ne peut l'isoler. Il considère, qu'en Allemagne l'obstacle fiscal est secondaire.

De la discussion un consensus semble se dégager sur la constatation que le taux marginal d'imposition des revenus les plus élevés est trop important et de nature à limiter la propension à l'épargne. Deux réserves sont cependant exprimées dans l'assistance. On remarque en effet que dans les premières années de l'investissement le niveau de taxation ne saurait être excessif dans la mesure où aucun profit n'est dégagé. D'autre part, il s'agit moins, pour M. WIRK, de remettre en cause la charge fiscale supportée par cette catégorie de contribuable que de modifier la progressivité de l'impôt qui est trop rapide.

Mr. WIRK considère que les allégements fiscaux devraient être concentrés, par priorité, sur les entreprises innovatrices elles-mêmes et surtout dans la phase où elles commencent à faire du profit. A cet effet, il suggère la constitution de réserves d'investissements exonérées d'impôt.

Un membre du groupe de travail propose que la mise en place du prêt européen à l'innovation soit accompagnée d'avantages fiscaux accordés aux intermédiaires financiers pour la part desinvestissements qu'ils réalisent en fonds propres.

Le Président observe -et l'intervenant en convient- qu'une telle déduction aurait pour effet de libérer ces institutions d'un risque qui forme précisemment l'objet de leur activité.

Le Président rappelle que la mise en place de fonds de placement nationaux et d'un fond européen destiné à attirer les capitaux vers la Communauté avait été suggérée. Il montre les avantages qu'un fond multinational présenterait pour les pays ayant mis en place un système de contrôle des changes.

Le groupe estime préférable qu'il y ait plusieurs fonds privés au niveau national et ne propose pas la création d'un fond international; Une liaison entre les différents fonds devrait néanmoins être établie. Pour que l'investisseur ait quelque intérêt à développer son activité dans un pays voisin, il conviendrait qu'il y bénéficiât d'avantages fiscaux semblables à ceux qui lui sont accordés dans son propre pays. La suggestion est faite d'utiliser à cette fin le cadre des conventions sur la double imposition.

Le Président interroge le groupe sur la nécessité de proposer une mise en harmonie des régimes d'imposition du capital à risque dans la Communauté. On estime dans l'assistance que la diversité des systèmes fiscaux et la réticence des Etats à limiter leur souveraineté dans cette matière impliquent que cet objectif n'est pas réalisable dans un avenir prévisible. Ce point de vue n'est pas partagé unanimement. On remarque au contraire que les pays membres manqueraient là une occasion de faire progresser l'Europe dans un domaine de pointe. Il convient de tirer parti de la nouveauté et de l'actualité du problème du capital à risque.

Le Président suggère que le groupe de travail fasse à la Commission les propositions suivantes :

les investisseurs individuels tout comme les sociétés de capital à risque devraient bénéficier d'incitations fiscales.

Mais de telles mesures s'intègrent dans des systèmes fiscaux qu'il importe de prendre en considération dans leur globalité. Ainsi, peut-on souhaiter que les Gouvernements de la Communauté réduiront la charge fiscale grevant les plus hauts revenus.

Enfin, un même régime d'imposition du capital à risque devrait être appliqué dans l'ensemble de la Communauté.

Compte rendu

du groupe de travail n° 6 : "Options sur titre pour les cadres supérieurs des sociétés à potentiel de croissance élevé".

et

du groupe de travail n° 3 : "Mobilisation des investisseurs non bancaires de capitaux à risque au niveau communautaire".

Président : R.G. HODGSON

Rapporteur: S. NEUMANN

A) options sur titre (exemples américains)

Dans l'ensemble, le groupe admet que les options sur titre constituent, pour les cadres supérieurs, un outil essentiel dans les sociétés à risque. Il s'agit d'abord d'une mesure incitant le cadre supérieur à participer à la croissance de la société, car les options doivent généralement être acquises à titre onéreux. Cela augmente l'effet d'incitation et peut avoir certaines incidences fiscales. Pour lutter contre la forte mobilité des cadres (aux Etats-Unis, les directeurs changent en moyenne tous les 18 mois), des options sont accumulées annuellement. Pour les sociétés non cotées, l'évaluation des actions s'avère difficile. Dans un cas, on a tenté de faire la moyenne des bénéfices réalisés sur une période de trois ans. _'imposition des gains résultant des options sur titre est un problème très difficile au Royaume-Uni. Dans les autres pays européens, le problème est moins connu et il devra être étudié par des experts fiscaux dans chaque pays.

Recommandations faites par le groupe :

- la Commission des Communautés européennes devrait demander qu'une étude soit effectuée sur le régime fiscal applicable aux options sur titre pour les cadres supérieurs dans les pays membres des Communautés européennes et aux Etats-Unis, ainsi que sur les arguments qui plaident en faveur de ces options, leurs avantages, leur impact économique et les obstacles qui s'opposent à leur création ;

a) Les travaux d'harmonisation de la Commission des Communautés européennes en matière d'impôts sur les sociétés doivent inclure la rémunération des cadres supérieurs au moyen d'options sur titre et de droits à la pension et prendre en considération les arguments politiques/sociaux/économiques ;

b) L'importance des options sur titre comme outils dans les sociétés à risque exige un traitement (fiscal) harmonisé de cet instrument dans la CE pour faciliter les opérations à l'échelle internationale ;

c) Les options sur titre doivent être prises en compte dans toute réglementation fiscale, non seulement pour la création ou le rachat de sociétés, mais aussi pour les phases ultérieures du financement des sociétés ;

d) L'expression "option sur titre" ne jouissant pas d'une bonne réputation auprès du public, il convient de la remplacer, comme l'a proposé le Prof. SCHMIDT, par une expression plus positive, peut-être par DROIT DE PARTICIPATION EUROPEEN ;

Outre les options sur titre, le groupe aborde également la rémunération des cadres supérieurs au moyen de droits à la pension, qui ne sont pas fort appréciés aux Etats-Unis et qui dépendent en Europe - du point de vue de la portabilité - des accords spécifiques qui ont été conclus.

Les arguments en faveur de l'efficacité des options sur titre tiennent surtout au fait qu'il s'agit d'un élément essentiel de la croissance des petites sociétés. Sinon, la "politique de la carotte" rendra toute réforme impossible.

B) Mobilisation des investisseurs de capitaux à risque

Le groupe définit d'abord ce qu'il entend par "investisseurs non bancaires de capitaux à risque " et décide de supprimer l'adjectif "non bancaire". Les principaux groupes d'investisseurs examinés durant la session sont :

- les fonds de pension et les compagnies d'assurances ;
- les fonds industriels (c.-à-d. les sociétés industrielles ;
- les institutions universitaires ;
- les fonds de placement et les investisseurs collectifs ;
- les investisseurs privés.

Les administrations publiques et les entreprises nationalisées sont exclues de la discussion puisqu'il s'agit du thème du groupe de travail n° 4. On considère que les investisseurs des milieux universitaires qui sont déjà engagés dans des fonds de capitaux à risque en Europe visent essentiellement à établir des liens étroits permettant des transferts de technologie. Pour mobiliser les investisseurs de capitaux à risque, les recommandations suivantes sont élaborées :

1. Toute incitation des investisseurs institutionnels de capitaux à risque doit être liée au taux de croissance possible du potentiel de gestion des sociétés en Europe pour éviter une évolution négative ;

2. Avant de proposer des mesures permettant de surmonter les entraves légales ou statutaires qui empêchent les organismes d'investir dans des capitaux à risque, la Commission des Communautés européennes devrait établir un inventaire positif/négatif des règles et de leur impact dans la Communauté européenne et aux Etats-Unis ; il pourrait également être utile d'examiner les entraves résultant de l'organisasion structurelle des organismes d'investissement ;

3. La Commission des C.E. devrait soutenir la création d'association de capitaux à risque à l'échelle européenne pour développer un marché européen dynamique des capitaux à risque (ayant comme objectif un volume d'investissement de 1 à 2 milliards de dollars par an) ; la Commission devrait donc examiner les entraves qui empêchent la création d'associations et la conclusion d'arrangements transitoires.

Les investisseurs institutionnels, notamment les fonds de pensions et les compagnies d'assurances, doivent être autorisés, encouragés voire forcés à investir un certain pourcentage de leur revenu annuel en capitaux à risque ;

4. L'industrie doit être incitée à utiliser la "vitrine technologique" fournie par les capitaux à risque en développant le volume et l'efficacité de la R&D. L'industrie peut également jouer un rôle en choisissant des domaines industriels appropriés pour effectuer des investissements de capitaux à risque en vue de créer de grandes sociétés européennes ;

5. La Commission des C.E. est invitée à soutenir le développement de l'infrastructure des capitaux à risque pour réduire les risques pris par les

investisseurs ;

6. L'université doit contribuer à la mise en oeuvre de cette infrastructure en formant des cadres supérieurs et en comblant le fossé de la communication entre la technologie et l'offre et la demande de main-d'oeuvre ;

Pour éviter que la pénurie de gestionnaires des capitaux à risque n'ait des effets négatifs en Europe, toute action visant à mobiliser les investisseurs institutionnels doit faire l'objet de priorités et d'un calendrier.

COMPTE RENDU DU GROUPE DE TRAVAIL N. 4

Président : K. NATHUSIUS
Rapporteur : P. DOURNEL

DISPOSITIONS GOUVERNEMENTALES VISANT UNE STIMULATION DES INVESTISSEMENTS A RISQUE

Les travaux de ce groupe se sont déroulés grâce à la participation active de la cinquantaine de personnes qui le composait. Les débats ayant été animés, nous avons choisi de présenter un compte rendu thématique qui permettra de mieux exposer le contenu.

I SITUATION ACTUELLE

Les mesures prises par les différents gouvernements des Etats Membres des Communautés Européennes peuvent être regroupées en trois grandes catégories:

- les mesures fiscales
- l'offre directe de capitaux
- les systèmes de garantie

A. Les mesures fiscales

La plupart des Etats ont pris des mesures d'abattements fiscaux pour favoriser l'investissement. En tant que telles, elles peuvent évidemment bénéficier aux opérations de capital à risque. On peut citer en exemple la possibilité de report des pertes vers des exercices futurs, et, quand elle existe, la possibilité de déduction de ces pertes sur exercices antérieurs (1).

De plus certains Etats ont adopté des mesures fiscales spécifiques aux opérations de prises de participation et de capital à risque. Ces mesures peuvent toucher soit des sociétés de capital à risque, par exemple le traitement des plus values de cession réalisées par les Sociétés Financières d'Innovation en France ou par la Wagnisfinanzierungsgesellschaft en RFA, soit constituer des incitants pour que des particuliers investissent dans des Fonds d'Innovation (Belgique) ou dans des entreprises (Royaume-Uni).

B. L'offre directe de capitaux

Plusieurs Etats ont adopté des mesures d'offres de capitaux afin de stimuler le capital à risque. Un des exemples les plus frappants est la "National Enterprise Agency" créée récemment par le gouvernement Irlandais. L'action des Etats en la matière peut prendre plusieurs formes, allant de la prise directe de participation dans certains secteurs, par exemple en Grèce, à l'appui à la création de société distribuant des fonds d'origine étatique ou mixte (Allemagne: Wfg, France: SFI,.) (2).

Cependant, il faut remarquer que ces mesures restent limitées, tant par leur taille que par leur impact, n'ayant visiblement pas atteint leur marge critique.

C Les fonds de garantie

Ici encore, les différents Etats ont appliqué ces dernières années de nombreux programmes visant à stimuler les efforts d'investissements. Ces programmes peuvent se concevoir soit comme auxiliaires ou supplements d'organismes de garantie pré-existants, soit comme intervenants nombreux à vocation spécifique. Citons, comme exemple de cette dernière catégorie, le "PPM guarantee scheme" néerlandais et la "Verlustausfallgarantie des Wfg" allemand (2).

D'autres Etats mettent en place des fonds de garantie nationaux mixtes, et se substituent ainsi aux organismes de garantie classiques pour prendre en dernier ressort le risque du banquier (France: SOFARIS, Royaume-Uni: Government Guarantee Scheme for Small Business Bank Loans, Belgique: Fonds de garantie de l'Etat,...). Remarquons que ces derniers sont fréquemment axés vers le soutien aux PME (2)

II EXPERIENCES ET REACTIONS DES PARTICIPANTS

Afin de canaliser les débats, il a été décidé de tenter de répondre à une série de questions avec l'aide de l'expérience des participants.

A. Quel peut être le rôle d'un gouvernement en la matière?

a) Exemple irlandais.

La National Enterprise Agency a été fondée mi-octobre, avec pour mission d'offrir des capitaux à risque lors des premiers stades de la création d'entreprises. Une fois les risques technologiques et d'introduction sur le marché maîtrisés, elle vendra ses parts sur le second marché. L'originalité de ce système étatique réside dans l'utilisation des capacités techniques d'experts issus de milieux hors de la fonction publique pour pallier le manque d'expérience en matière de capital à risque des fonctionnaires. Ces experts seront rémunérés grâce à une part des plus values de cession enregistrées par la NEA lors de la réalisation de ses actions. Cette part pourra être de 20 % de la plus value réalisée par projet, à laquelle s'ajoutent des honoraires versés au titre de l'assistance à la gestion.

Cette structure est une création très originale et pourrait servir de modèle à d'autres gouvernements.

b) Exemple canadien

Cet exemple est intéressant à plus d'un titre. Il pourrait entre autre apporter une réponse à une question laissée en suspens lors du symposium de 1982, à savoir les possibilités d'intervention de l'Etat grâce aux appels d'offre publics, notamment en matière de défense.

Le Canada ayant décidé d'augmenter son effort en matière militaire, les appels d'offre se sont en grande partie tournés vers des firmes innovatrices, en leur offrant à la fois des contrats de recherche et développement et des débouchés sûrs. Cette coordination a permis le développement du capital à risque qui connaissait les problèmes habituels de manque de capitaux pour les premiers stades de l'innovation.

B. Poblèmes d'environnement

Les problèmes d'environnement et de contexte économico-politique ont constitué la majeure partie des travaux. Cette notion d'environnement regroupe les thèmes suivants:

a) Politique fiscale

Elle peut être considérée comme l'inhibiteur principal au développement réel du capital à risque en Europe continentale. On pourrait répartir les réactions qu'elle suscite selon les trois types d'impôts pesant sur le capital à risque:

- Impôts sur le revenu: ils réduisent de façon significative la propension à épargner et par là même participent à la situation actuelle d'argent rare et cher. De plus, devant la faiblesse de leur épargne, les investisseurs ont plutôt tendance à placer leurs fonds dans des secteurs réputés pour leur faible risque sans essayer de diminuer le risque potentiel grâce à la diversification.

- Impôts sur les sociétés: l'extrême variabilité des taux et assiettes de l'impôt sur les sociétés dans les différents Etats Membres constitue évidemment un obstacle aux opérations transnationales, potentiellement à haute rentabilité.

- Impôts sur les plus values en capital: ceux-ci ont également un effet négatif dans la mesure où, ils poussent l'investissseur à rechercher des projets à très haute rentabilité pour compenser ces prélèvememts comme jusqu'à présent, les taux de rentabilité estimés nécessaires ne sont que rarement atteints, les investisseurs préfèrent ne pas prendre de risques.

- D'un point de vue éthique, le groupe de travail N. 1 ne s'est pas montré convaincu de l'acceptabilité d'un traitement fiscal privilégié.

Ce concept de traitement fiscal inégalitaire pourrait même s'aviser dangereux à long terme car il attirerait vers le capital à risque des firmes nécessitant d'autres types de financement, ce qui concourrait à terme à créer un problème de nature des opérations.

De plus, il semble dangereux de défavoriser la croissance traditionnelle qui est génératrice de la majorité des plus values dégagées de nos jours.

b) Perception du rôle de l'entrepreneur

C'est en fait un sujet qui revient très fréquemment et semble assez typique de notre continent. En effet, à l'inverse des Etats Unis où l'echec est considéré comme faisant normalement partie du jeu, il apporte en Europe une réputation parfois infamante.

Il s'agit en fait d'un problème lié à notre culture et à notre éducation, et, de ce fait, ne peut être résolu que grâce à l'éducation et à des exemples de succès notoires survenant après les échecs. Mais croire qu'il pourrait être résolu en un laps de temps inférieur à au moins une génération est parfaitement illusoire.

c) Conditions générales offertes aux entrepreneurs

Il pourrait s'agir ici des véritables possibilités d'action des Etats en la matière. Ces conditions générales peuvent être perçues de deux façons:

- Création d'un environnement économique favorable: meilleure gestion du budget de l'Etat et de la dette publique, politique de lutte contre l'inflation et le chômage...

- Création de structures favorables, comme les "innovation centres" mise à la disposition d'immeuble à vocation industrielle à faible coût. Cette dernière action gouvernementale est déjà menée dans certains Etats comme l'Irlande, le Royaume-Uni et la France (2).

d) Formation des gestionnaires spécialisés

C'est à l'évidence une lacune très importante dans notre système éducatif. Mais, pour une fois, on peut considérer que la solution est assez simple: il suffirait probablement d'étendre les activités des associations à des conférences et à des cours sur le capital à risque. L'action du "Plan transnational de développement des infrastructures" sera certainement très positive en la matière.

e) Motivation des entrepreneurs

Il est évident qu'une amélioration de la mobilité des cadres ainsi qu'un soutien à ceux qui souhaitent créer leur propre entreprise auraient un effet très positif: créations d'entreprises et embauche de plusieurs cadres en remplacement des créateurs.

III RECOMMANDATIONS

1. Il faut continuer à stimuler l'initiative privée

2. Les sociétés de capital à risque existantes ne doivent pas drainer l'ensemble des soutiens, ce qui nuit à l'augmentation du nombre des intervenants.

3. Le climat économique et social devrait être élevé pour pousser à l'initiative.

4. Un gros effort de formation de gestionnaires doit être fait.

5. Il faut créer et développer une infrastructure transnationale de soutien au capital à risque.

Notes :

(1) Voir à ce sujet les rapports EUR 8820 et 8821 distribués lors du symposium.

(2) Voir à ce sujet le rapport EUR 8819

Compte rendu du groupe de travail n° 5

Président : C. CLEIFTIE

Rapporteur : R. GUTH

Infrastructure communautaire de liaison entre marchés de capitaux à risque

Les travaux du groupe se déroulèrent en suivant trois principes simples :

1. Plutôt que de vouloir présenter des recommandations en bonne et due forme, il nous a paru plus sage de nous limiter à des étapes de réflexion que nous soumettons aux Communautés européennes en guise "d'input" à leur propre réflexion.

2. Un des écueils traditionnels de l'exercice auquel nous nous livrons en ce moment consiste à vouloir à tout prix faire preuve d'originalité, ce qui se traduit le plus souvent par des propositions de mise en place de nouveaux systèmes, procédés ou organes chargés de tâches nouvelles. Face à la tendance naturelle de démultiplication institutionnelle, le groupe pense bien au contraire, et ce pourrait déjà faire l'objet d'une première recommandation, qu'il ne paraît pas utile de créer systématiquement du neuf, mais que les institutions existantes sont tout à fait à même de présider à la mise en place d'une infrastructure communautaire de liaison entre marchés de capitaux à risque.

3. Toute démarche concrète lancée à l'initiative de la Communauté européenne devrait se singulariser par :

- sa simplicité de conception et de modus operandi,

- sa bonne diffusion auprès du public destinataire en organisant un meilleur marketing auprès des primo destinataires, et notamment auprès des petites et jeunes entreprises qui souffrent le plus de la longueur des canaux d'information.

- sa concentration sur la mise en place d'une infrastructure et sur les conditions cadre adéquates tout en générant un climat propice à l'éclosion des marchés de capitaux à risque . Il n'a pas paru souhaitable aux membres du groupe que les autorités européennes se substituassent plus que nécessaire aux forces du marché. En disant cela, je viens d'énoncer une deuxième recommandation qui bien que non spécifiquement orientée vers le thème de notre commission, n'en conserve pas moins toute sa valeur.

Les mécanismes de liaison des marchés de capitaux à risque peuvent s'envisager sous diverses formes. De par l'orientation de ce symposium et les qualifications des membres du groupe, nous avons bien évidemment privilégié le volet financier. Si le thème de l'argent n'épuise pas l'entièreté de la problématique, sans argent il n'existerait pas de marchés de capitaux à risque !!

Le groupe estime que :

1. Un mécanisme doit être trouvé de toute urgence pour faciliter la libre circulation effective des capitaux au sein de la Communauté. Bien que cet objet figure dans les Traités et malgré les efforts déjà accomplis, les autorités européennes devraient oeuvrer avec insistance à la suppression des diverses et multiples barrières nationales existant encore. En guise d'illustration de ce propos, je me contenterai de citer deux exemples typiques.

En Italie, obligation est faite de déposer une caution sans intérêt représentant 50% des achats de valeurs étrangères ou effectués à l'étranger.

Les discriminations fiscales des investisseurs selon la nature juridique de leur statut ou de leur nationalité, personne privée ou publique, nationale ou étrangère.

2. La Communauté devrait s'inspirer de l'exemple de l'European venture capital association (EVCA) et continuer à oeuvrer selon les mêmes principes qui ont sous-tendu la création de cet organisme de liaison unique en son genre. Elle devrait également veiller à optimiser toutes les potentialités que représentent l'EVCA comme mécanisme de liaison entre marchés de capitaux à risque afin, entre autres, de tirer un profit maximum des diverses mesures incitatives d'origine nationale et jouer un rôle dynamisant au

niveau communautaire.

Cette première série d'attitudes devrait être complétée rapidement par l'adoption d'un prolongement financier dont le prêt européen d'innovation (PEI) constitue un premier pas intéressant. Dans ce contexte, l'action de la BEI a souvent été évoquée. Il en résulte que la BEI devrait se tourner également vers les sociétés de capital à risque en les considérant comme des interlocuteurs dignes de devenir des partenaires financiers.

Le groupe suggère que l'EVCA devrait contribuer à conférer à cette profession ses lettres de noblesse et pourrait délivrer un brevet de respectabilité vis-à-vis de la Communauté financière dans son ensemble et plus particulièrement vis-à-vis de la BEI,ce qui autoriserait ses membres à se prévaloir de la qualité d'intermédiaire financier.

Le groupe N° 5 pense qu'il s'agit là d'une mesure qui pourrait connaître très rapidement un commencement d'exécution par l'élaboration notamment de règles déontologiques dont l'EVCA assurerait le respect.

En ce qui concerne les Marchés parallèles de capitaux, le groupe estimerait déraisonnable de vouloir créer un marché unique à l'échelon de la Communauté. Les sociétés admises à ces cotations particulières ont essentiellement une vocation locale voire nationale, le niveau européen n'est pas adéquat pour la négociation de leurs titres.

La dimension communautaire n'aura de sens qu'au travers de l'interconnexion des bourses de valeurs entre elles et de ce fait les divers marchés parallèles pourront profiter ipso facto de la dimension communautaire.

Il ne semble donc pas opportun d'envisager la création de liens européens séparés propres aux marchés parallèles de capitaux.

Enfin, et pour conclure, la groupe n° 5, attire l'attention de la Communauté européenne sur deux aspects plus pointus quoique importants :

- d'une part, la nécessité d'améliorer les techniques d'investissement de capitaux à risque et le degré de professionnalisme des venture capitalistes pour leur conférer la maîtrise complexe que nécessite l'ambition de considérer le marché commun dans son ensemble comme un marché unique. Ici aussi, l'EVCA jouera un rôle de pionnier qui devrait être largement supporté par les instances européennes ;

- d'autre part, il nous a semblé que ces mêmes institutions n'ont pas encore apporté suffisamment d'attention au réel problème du décalage de phase entre la durée de maturation d'une technologie et les contraintes de ROI imposées par les venture capitalistes. Ce problème vécu au quotidien par les entrepreneurs mériterait des recherches complémentaires pour essayer de concilier aux exigences apparemment contradictoires.

Compte rendu du groupe de travail n° 7

Président : J.D. INCLEDON

Rapporteur : E. PHILLIPS

Placements à risque par les investisseurs collectifs

Le groupe voit un certain nombre de facteurs en Europe, qui rendent la vie difficile aux nouvelles sociétés par rapport à leurs homologues d'Amérique du nord. Un participant quantifie cette difficulté en indiquant que les difficultés rencontrées aux Etats-Unis étaient multipliées par dix dans la Communauté européenne, par le simple fait que la Communauté comprend dix pays différents. En cela, il fait référence aux différents systèmes fiscaux, aux différentes pratiques comptables, aux langues différentes, aux différents taux d'inflation contre lesquels il faut lutter et aux monnaies différentes que l'on rencontre en passant d'un pays à l'autre de la Communauté européenne.

En Europe, beaucoup de sociétés doivent faire face à ces problèmes très tôt dans leur existence, car les différents marchés nationaux sont si étroits qu'il n'est pas rare que des sociétés essayent d'exporter même au cours de leur première année d'existence. En revanche, aux Etats-Unis, il y a beaucoup plus de sociétés qui peuvent exister pendant des années sans jamais éprouver le besoin d'exporter en dehors de l'Amérique du nord.

Il y a aussi un manque d'expérience relatif en Europe, par rapport aux Etats-Unis. A titre d'exemple, des membres du groupe 7 indiquent que beaucoup d'entrepreneurs en Europe semblent avoir besoin de l'aide d'organisations de capitaux à risque pour établir des plans d'activités, alors que chez l'entrepreneur aux Etats-Unis, c'est presque une seconde nature. Le groupe émet des doutes sur le point de savoir si de nombreuses organisations de capitaux à risque en Europe ont l'expertise voulue pour fournir l'assistance dont ont besoin certains entrepreneurs.

En observant la situation du point de vue de l'investisseur établi dans un pays de la Communauté européenne, le groupe fait remarquer que ces investisseurs peuvent se montrer réticents à investir en dehors de leur propre pays, car ils sont préoccupés par les problèmes rencontrés (tels que les contrôles des changes) lorsqu'ils ont l'intention de rapatrier leurs capitaux.

Le groupe a noté également que les investisseurs américains ont plus d'expériences que leurs homologues européens.

Etant donné tous ces facteurs, le groupe estime qu'aux Etats-Unis les organisations de capitaux à risque sont mieux développées et plus expérimentées qu'en Europe. Par conséquent, tout comme certaines sociétés américaines ont conquis des parts importantes du marché européen pour écouler leurs produits, les Etats-Unis sont également en train d'attirer des capitaux à risque d'Europe. Bien sûr, cela vient encore renforcer les capacités des organisations américaines de capitaux à risque aux dépens de leurs homologues européens.

Ces considérations ont amené le groupe à éléborer sa première recommandation :

> "Vu le manque d'expérience relatif des organisations de capitaux à risque par rapport à leurs homologues américains, il convient de rechercher des moyens permettant de renforcer les organisations servant d'intermédiaires en Europe afin qu'elles puissent être plus compétitives".

Le groupe mentionne des mesures spécifiques, notamment des mesures fiscales en faveur de ces organismes et la suppression des entraves à la libre circulation des capitaux par-delà les frontières nationales.

La deuxième recommandation du groupe est destinée à faire face directement au manque d'expérience observé dans les organisations de capitaux à risque et chez les entrepreneurs en Europe :

> "Il convient d'offrir une assistance sélective pour aider les organisations servant d'intermédiaires et les gestionnaires des sociétés dans lesquelles sont investis des capitaux à risque, à acquérir les techniques essentielles au succès dans leurs domaines d'activité".

Enfin, le groupe estime qu'il serait profitable aux marchés des capitaux à risque si les investissements pouvaient être réalisés plus facilement, en particulier sur de courtes périodes de deux à trois ans ; en d'autres termes, il convient d'améliorer les mécanismes de désengagement. Une autre façon d'exprimer cette idée consiste à dire que jusqu'à ce que tous les Etats membres soient dotés de bourses (analogues au marché des valeurs non cotées de Londres) facilitant les placements dans des fonds de capitaux à risque, il continuera à y avoir des difficultés pour récupérer rapidement les fonds investis. C'est pourquoi le groupe propose la recommandation finale suivante :

"Il est nécessaire de renforcer les mécanismes permettant de mobiliser prématurément des investissements en capitaux à risque".

Compte rendu du groupe de travail n° 8

Président : I. MOMTCHILOFF

Rapporteur : J.M. GIBB

Gestion des capitaux à risque

Le groupe de travail se donne pour tâche de définir, en termes pratiques, ce qu'est la gestion de capitaux à risque et de déterminer quelques-unes des grandes options ouvertes à ceux qui s'engagent dans cette voie. L'attention est en outre attirée sur certaines difficultés rencontrées par les gestionnaires de capitaux à risque, qui pourraient être atténuées grâce à des actions des pouvoirs publics au niveau national ou au niveau communautaire.

Voici les points essentiels examinés par le groupe de travail :

1. Structures

2. a) Sélection de projets appropriés

   b) Critères pour la décision d'investir

3. a) Contrôle des investissements

   b) Moment opportun pour se désengager.

1. STRUCTURES

Durée d'une opération sur capitaux à risque : opération à relativement long terme, s'étendant sur au moins 10 ans environ.

Propriétaires : ce peuvent être - des individus,
- des sociétés de capitaux à risque,
- des institutions.

Secteurs d'investissement : deux grandes options :

a) large gamme de secteurs (dont répartition statistique des risques)

ou

b) spécialisation (dont acquisition de connaissances plus approfondies, permettant le cas échéant de mieux calculer les risques).

On estime que l'option a) offre un léger avantage par rapport à l'option b).

Stade de financement : le financement d'entreprises nouvellement créées est séduisant en termes de potentiel de croissance, mais il est plus risqué que le financement à des stades ultérieurs de développement qui fait l'objet d'une forte demande. Le portefeuille d'une société de capitaux à risque devrait être diversifié à cet égard.

Personnel : une société de capitaux à risque devrait être dirigée par une équipe comprenant :
- des personnes ayant l'expérience de la gestion d'entreprise,
- des personnes se connaissant en comptabilité,
- des experts en finances.

Exemple d'unité CR spécialisée :

un expert en gestion d'entreprise)
) gérant environ 5 investissements
un expert financier)

Exemple d'unité CR non spécialisée :

un expert en gestion d'entreprise)
)
un expert financier)
+ comité consultatif) gérant environ 15 investissements
+ expert-conseil)
+ réseau de contacts)

Raison d'être des investissements à l'étranger :

Opérer sur un marché plus vaste et obtenir un effet de diversification, mais il faut être conseillé en matière de droit, de protection des brevets, de fiscalité, etc...

Intéressement des membres d'une équipe de gestion de capitaux à risque :

L'une des possibilités est de prévoir directement pour les membres de l'équipe une participation aux plus-values en capital. Cette solution peut être difficile à mettre en oeuvre si l'équipe fait partie d'un système institutionnel.

Une autre possibilité est d'offrir des options sur titres. Malheureusement, peu de pays possèdent un système juridique acceptant cette solution.

Libre circulation des capitaux

La libre circulation des capitaux, qui est une condition essentielle pour les opérations internationales, n'est pas encore complètement assurée dans la Communauté européenne en raison du contrôle des changes appliqué par certains Etats membres, ainsi que d'autres réglementations telles que celles qui ont trait à la nationalité des administrateurs de sociétés.

Coopération internationale

Bien qu'il soit avantageux, comme cela a été indiqué plus haut, d'opérer dans un contexte international, il n'est pas facile de s'implanter solidement sur un marché étranger. Cela met en lumière l'utilité de la syndication transnationale. La nouvelle European Venture Capital Association pourrait peut-être s'avérer précieuse à cet égard.

Structure de la prise de décision

L'option fondamentale porte sur l'alternative structure hiérachique ou structure collégiale. Dans le premier cas, la responsabilité des décisions appartient en fin de compte à une seule personne. Dans le second cas, la responsabilité est partagée, les décisions étant parfois prises à l'aide d'une procédure de vote formel. Une légère préférence est exprimée pour le dernier système.

2. a) SELECTION DE PROJETS APPROPRIES :

- par la presse spécialisée ;
- par les universités ;
- par d'autres gestionnaires de capitaux à risque ;
- par les membres du comité consultatif (s'il y en a un) ;
- par les acheteurs industriels ;
- par les conseillers, comptables, experts-conseils, etc. ;

- par les banques ;
- par la participation à des conférences ou foires ;
- par des bases de données.

2.b) CRITERES POUR LA DECISION D'INVESTIR

Il faut pouvoir donner une réponse positive aux questions suivantes :

- L'entreprise à financer est-elle bien gérée?
- Un plan d'activité est-il disponible?
- Ce plan a-t-il été évalué du point de vue commercial, industriel et financier, et a-t-il été satisfaisant?
- Existe -t-il un avantage exploitable en matière de propriété industrielle ou sur le plan commercial?
- La direction est-elle personnellement engagée financièrement?.

3.a) CONTROLE DES INVESTISSEMENTS

L'investissement réalisé, il importe de le contrôler :

- en se procurant et en examinant minutieusement les rapports d'activité ;
- en s'assurant que le plan d'activité est mis à jour chaque fois que cela est nécessaire ;
- en siégeant si possible dans le conseil d'administration ;
- en apportant une aide effective à la direction.

3.b) MOMENT OPPORTUN POUR SE DESENGAGER

Il n'existe manifestement aucune règle absolue en la matière, mais ce doit être avant que la croissance ne commence à faiblir, c'est-à-dire à un stade relativement précoce.

CONCLUSIONS ET RECOMMANDATIONS

Des mesures législatives devraient être prises en vue d'améliorer l'accès des gestionnaires aux options sur titres.
Une totale liberté de mouvement des capitaux est nécessaire dans la Communauté européenne si l'on veut tirer pleinement profit des avantages de la coopération transnationale en matière de capitaux à risque.
Il convient d'organiser davantage de cours de gestion de capitaux à risque.
Les bases de données sur les possibilités d'action à l'échelle de la Communauté devraient être développées davantage.

SESSION V - SESSION CONSACREE AUX CONCLUSIONS : 25.11.1983

Résumé de M. I.N. MOMTCHILOFF,

Directeur général de la société "Investors in Industry Group PLC", Londres

Je suis donc chargé de résumer les conclusions de ce symposium, mais c'est une tâche à laquelle je vais me soustraire, car elle est pratiquement impossible. J'aimerais, cependant, vous faire part de quelques observations.

Mme LEBAS a cherché - avec passion serais-je tenté de dire - à nous persuader que c'est le système qui compte. A mon avis, il est hors de doute que le développement d'un marché secondaire constitue une contribution essentielle au système des capitaux à risque.

J'approuve sans réserves la réglementation et la normalisation des marchés mais j'estime que, si l'on veut encourager les activités dans le domaine des capitaux à risque, il est essentiel de disposer d'un marché secondaire qui soit réglementé et organisé judicieusement. En effet, ce marché constitue une nécessité pour celui qui met son avenir en jeu en créant une société.

Après tout, pendant les longues périodes au cours desquelles les Britanniques n'avaient pas accès à un marché secondaire, les personnes ou groupes de personnes désirant lancer une société n'avaient que deux possibilités de rentabiliser leur entreprise.

La première était de créer une société suffisamment grande, stable et performante pour pouvoir être admise à la cote sur le marché principal. C'est là un objectif ambitieux, et même de plus en plus ambitieux : voici quelques années, une société avait accès au marché principal quand ses bénéfices atteignaient un quart de million de livres ; un peu plus tard, il fallait un million, puis un million et demi. Ces augmentations s'expliquent en partie - mais en partie seulement - par l'inflation. Parmi les centaines de sociétés qui sont créées, peu ont des chances d'atteindre cet objectif.

La seconde manière de rentabiliser une entreprise consistait à en vendre la totalité de ses titres, mais quand on constitue une société, on ne poursuit pas souvent cet objectif-là. On constitue une société parce qu'on veut créer une entreprise.

L'existence du marché secondaire ouvre des horizons nouveaux aux créateurs d'entreprises au Royaume-Uni, puisque ceux-ci ont désormais accès à l'argent des investisseurs et peuvent réaliser une partie de leur propre investissement. (Peut-être peuvent-ils commencer à envisager l'achat d'une voiture ou d'une seconde voiture, voire d'une Rolls-Royce, si telle est leur idée). Après tout, si on ne peut encourager les gens à lancer des entreprises, nous perdons tous notre temps, car ce sont ces gens-là qui créent la richesse. Ils doivent gagner de l'argent; ceux qui les financent doivent gagner de l'argent ; en fait, tous ceux qui interviennent dans le système doivent être encouragés à prendre les risques que leur activité implique. Dès lors, si un obstacle entrave le bon fonctionnement du système, les gouvernements, la Commission et nous tous devons oeuvrer pour éliminer cet obstacle.

La seconde observation que j'aimerais faire concerne un problème que j'ai déjà évoqué, mais qui me semble terriblement important : en Europe, les besoins en capitaux d'expansion sont plus grands que les besoins en capitaux à risque poursuivant des objectifs plus ambitieux. Ce sont les capitaux d'expansion qui permettent d'assurer la stabilité et la rentabilité des entreprises. Ce type d'investissement ne doit pas être négligé car, si trop de groupes sont créés avec l'ambition d'atteindre des sommets, les échecs seront légion, et je regretterais que le développement fantastique du financement de sociétés privées perde sa crédibilité à cause des ambitions irréalistes de quelques-uns.

Ce pourrait être là, en quelque sorte, un retour au moyen-âge. C'est ce qui se passe aux Etats-Unis. A la bourse de Minneapolis, j'ai vu, voici quelques années seulement, un emplacement avec trois écrans vides. Quand j'ai demandé de quoi il s'agissait, on m'a répondu : "c'était l'emplacement du "Nasdaq" [1]. Le marché est mort. Les temps où le rendement atteignait 10 % ou plus du cours des titres sont bien révolus."

---

1)"National Association of Securities Dealers' Automated Quotation" = système de cotation pour les valeurs hors cote.

Je pense que le marché américain retombera un jour ou l'autre et qu'il en ira de même pour le marché des valeurs hors cote.

Le dernier point que j'aimerais évoquer concerne le problème des frontières. Chacun sait que nos tentatives de pénétrer le marché européen tout entier avec un produit ou un service se heurtent à tout une série d'obstacles : barrières non-tarifaires, attitudes différentes d'un pays à l'autre, etc. Il est malheureusement vrai que celui qui veut créer une société moderne se tournera d'abord vers les Etats-Unis. Je ne dis pas que nous devrions négliger les Etats-Unis, car ce pays constitue le plus grand marché individuel au monde, mais quel dommage que les Européens n'aient pas leur propre grand marché !

A l'heure actuelle, nous assistons même à un regain de protectionnisme. Chaque pays veut se donner une image de marque en s'ergageant dans les secteurs à la mode, les secteurs à haute technologie, et chacun cherche, par exemple, à garder jalousement sa propre petite société de robotique. Grossière erreur !

Cependant, je pense que le développement d'un solide marché des capitaux à risque pourrait avoir une incidence bénéfique à cet égard. Si nous amenons différentes institutions à s'engager dans le domaine des capitaux à risque et si nous leur faisons comprendre qu'elles interviennent ainsi sur un marché international, nous arriverons peut-être à prouver que les Etats membres ont intérêt à coopérer.

Si on peut amener des investisseurs à mettre en jeu d'importantes quantités de capitaux à risque, l'optique des Etats, des institutions et de l'industrie s'en trouvera modifiée. Ce n'est pas pour demain, mais je vois réellement là un des domaines dans lesquels nous pourrons faire, pour la cause du Marché commun, en investissant dans les industries du futur davantage que nous n'avons pu faire en investissant dans les industries destinées à disparaître.

Riassunti dele Relazioni 291

Gruppi di Lavoro 1, 2, 6–3, 4, 5, 7, 8, 303

Sintesi dei Risultati del Simposio 330
I.N. MOMTCHILOFF
General Manager, Investors in Industry Group, P.L.C.,
London (United Kingdom)

I FONDI PENSIONI IN QUANTO INVESTITORI DI CAPITALI DI RISCHIO

D.J. PROSSER

CIN Industrial Investements

Compendio

I fondi pensioni hanno un comportamento neutrale nei riguardi del reddito e della remunerazione del capitale per quanto concerne l'aspetto fiscale. Cio' consente una maggiore flessibilità nella strutturazione di una proposta. La natura a lungo termine delle casse pensioni significa che queste non devono necessariamente mirare ad una emissione a breve termine per realizzare il profitto sugli investimenti coronati da sussesso.

Il nostro investimento negli U.S.A., per quanto modesto, ha fornito un'apertura sulla tecnologia nonché sulle operazioni di ordine strutturale. Il mercato americano del "venture capital" è notevolmente più vasto e vanta una maggiore tradizione di quello britannico.I fondi di capitali di rischio internazionali incontreranno notevoli difficoltà per espandersi in Europa. I problemi di ordine linguistico, giuridico e contabile stanno a significare che collocamenti in piccoli investimenti non quotati vengono effettuati in modo ottimale a livello locale. Se, ovviamente, da un lato vi saranno delle eccezioni a dei casi singoli, in generale l'elemento "pro-attivo" mancherebbe da un fondo a base ampia senza l'insediamento di un ufficio locale. Nella maggioranza dei casi, cio' comporterebbe spese eccessive per un fondo straniero.

La CIN Industrial Investments considera gli investimenti di capitale di rischio in relazione al capitale di espansione ed alla finanza destinata ai progetti nonché agli "avvii" o "start-up". In questo settore sono investiti circa 180 milioni di sterline e "l'équipe gestionale" conta quindici dirigenti. Nel 1983, sono stati investiti 26 milioni di sterline ed effettuati realizzi pari a 13 milioni di lire sterline.

GLI ISTITUTI DI ASSICURAZIONE COME INVESTITORI

UN PUNTO DI VISTA OLANDESE

D.S. Van HOUT

General Manager Investments and Corporate Finance

ENNIA N.V.

Compendio

Benché l'investimento in titoli azionari sia visto come una soluzione principe dei problemi che incontra l'industria nella Comunità europea, in realtà ampio è il divario tra la domanda e l'offerta di capitale a tal fine.

Inoltre, la capacità di potenziali fornitori di tale capitale non deve essere sopravvalutata. Nonostante il sostanziale contributo che potrebbe dare alla ripresa industriale, l'investimento di capitale di rischio non è ritenuto abbastanza forte da consentire agli operatori del mercato dei capitali di investire in grande stile.

Da un'analisi della situazione nei Paesi Bassi risulta che le maggiori difficoltà incontrate dagli Istituti di assicurazione olandesi in questa attività di investimento sono :

- l'incompatibilità tra la massimizzazione della partecipazione agli utili e il finanziamento di prestiti azionari ad alto rischio ;
- mercati ufficiali poco attivi ;
- esperienza e conoscenza limitate come fornitori di capitali di rischio.

Dall'analisi della situazione olandese emerge la necessità di un consistente afflusso di nuovo capitale di rischio per promuovere l'occupazione a un livello sufficiente e accettabile e per potere individuare e soddisfare le domande potenziali in vari settori dell'industria. Tuttavia, sia dal lato dell'offerta che da quello della domanda, dovranno essere rimossi numerosi ostacoli, i più importanti dei quali sono l'eccessiva pressione tributaria e la neccesaria assistenza monetaria ai giovani imprenditori.

L'attegiamento degli Istituti di assicurazione (olandesi) verso il capitale di rischio, nonostante la scarsa disponibilità di questo nuovo strumento finanziario, riflette le loro responsabilità non solo sociali ma anche giuridiche.

"LA FISCALITA' ED IL FINANZIAMENTO DELL'INNOVAZIONE" CONFRONTO TRA LE DIVERSE DISPOSIZIONI VIGENTI NELLA C.E.E.

P. FONTANEAU
Incaricato delle facoltà di Diritto e Scienze Economiche
Avvocato alla Corte d'Appello di Parigi

Compendio

La fiscalità svolge un ruolo essenziale nel finanziamento dell'innovazione. In tutti i paesi della Comunità europea esistono sistemi di incentivazione fiscale.

Onde sviluppare il mercato dei capitali di rischio, i paesi europei hanno adottato apposite misure inerenti alla riduzione del rischio connesso con il collocamento ed il miglioramento della redditività netta di questo.

Per accrescere il finanziamento delle imprese innovatrici si sono adottati provvedimenti volti ad incentivare l'acquisto di nuove azioni e disposizioni intese a migliorare la capacità di autofinanziamento delle imprese stesse.

Ai fini dello sviluppo della loro redditività, sono state prese misure specifiche concernenti la ricerca nello stadio a monte dell'innovazione.

Tuttavia, gli incentivi fiscali limitati esclusivamente all'innovazione si riveleranno insufficienti se il sistema tributario generale applicato ai redditi delle società e delle persone fisiche è eccessivamente gravoso e colpisce quindi troppo duramente gli innovatori.

Avuto riguardo a queste osservazioni e all'importanza dell'innovazione per la crescita della Comunità Economica europea, sarà necessario elaborare una politica fiscale che conglobi l'intero processo innovativo.

Tale Codice Fiscale dell'innovazione dovrà essere coordinato su scala comunitaria per ripristinare la competitività delle imprese europee nei riguardi dei principali concorrenti americani o giapponesi.

LA TASSAZIONE DEGLI INVESTITORI ISTITUZIONALI COLLETIVI

D. O'HOGAN

Partner, Arthur Young & Company, Chartered Accountants,

Portobello House, Dublin 8.

Compendio

Il Sig. O'HOGAN ha parlato della tassazione del capitalista di rischio istituzionale collettivo e, in particolare, della neutralità del sistema fiscale in sede di definizione degli opportuni settori di investimento.

TRATTAMENTO FISCALE DEL SINGOLO INVESTITORE

CORNELIS A.M. RASENBERG

Direttore generale, servizio fiscale
Amsterdam-Rotterdam Bank N.V.
(Paesi Bassi)

Compendio

La natura stessa del mercato dei "venture capital" (capitali di rischio) obbliga il singolo investitore ad operare un investimento ad alto rischio per un periodo di tempo abbastanza lungo. Il reddito derivantegli da un tale investimento è quasi senza eccezione pienamente soggetto alle normali aliquote fiscali ; soltanto in pochi casi, le perdite di capitale (derivanti da operazioni su titoli) sono detraibili dal reddito ordinario, mentre la tassazione sugli utili da capitale differisce notevolmente da paese a paese. Possono venire applicate aliquote normali o ridotte a seconda, fra l'altro, del fatto se gli utili sono considerati reddito da lavoro o altro. Gli incentivi fiscali volti a ridurre l'ammontare al netto del prelievo fiscale dell'investimento operato sul mercato dei capitali di rischic (detraibilità o abbuono fiscale) sono strumenti efficaci per alimentare il flusso dei capitali di rischio. Gli incentivi fiscali attualmente concessi in caso di investimenti di capitale azionario (equity capital) tendono ad essere discriminatori nei confronti di investimenti in imprese estere. Molti paesi hanno unilateralmente introdotto un trattamento fiscale privilegiato per organismi di investimento collettivi, ma con diverse modalità. Sarebbe opportuno introdurre una legislazione armonizzata a livello comunitario per le organizzazioni che raccolgono capitali di rischio, eliminando la doppia imposizione dei profitti delle società o altri impedimenti fiscali e legislativi agli investimenti collettivi nel campo dell'innovazione.

IMPATTO DEI CAMBIAMENTI FISCALI SUGLI INVESTIMENTI DI CAPITALI DI RISCHIO E SULL'INNOVAZIONE NEGLI STATI UNITI

P.T. KAPLAN

Weil, Gotshal Manges
New York City

Compendio

Anche se è vero che, in generale, gli Stati Uniti hanno accordato generosi incentivi fiscali agli investimenti di capitali di rischio e all'innovazione, non per questo si puo' affermare che esiste una correlazione tra tali incentivazioni e l'alto livello di innovazione raggiunto in detto paese negli anni del dopoguerra: questa conclusione puo' essere tratta solamente dall'osservazione degli effetti provocati dai relativi cambiamenti d'ordine fiscale. Negli Stati Uniti ci sono state numerose modifiche riguardo l'imposizione fiscale, ma i dati non sono ancora sufficienti per consentire agli economisti di quantificare la relazione che intercorre tra un fattore e l'altro. Seguendo un procedimento meno scientifico, sembra che alcuni cambiamenti intervenuti del prelievo fiscale, in particolare di quello dei capitali speculativi, abbiano provocato mutamenti nel comportamento degli investitori; non è pero' possibile mettere in relazione altri mutamenti nella condotta degli investitori con le contemporanee modifiche fiscali. Statistiche a parte, si puo' dedurre l'importanza degli incentivi fiscali per l'innovazione negli Stati Uniti in casi specifici osservando alcune offerte d'investimento che fanno beneficiare delle detrazioni fiscali per la ricerca e lo sviluppo il singolo investitore, riducendo in tal modo il costo effettivo dell'investimento fino al 55%. Poiché tali detrazioni operate negli Stati Uniti non hanno limitazioni geografiche, il sistema di investimenti europeo potrebbe essere strutturato in modo tale da accordare analoghe detrazioni direttamente agli investitori statunitensi.

SEGMENTI DI BORSA SPECIALI PER LE QUOTE DI PARTECIPAZIONE ALLE PICCOLE IMPRESE

Situazione e prospettive

Prof. Dr. H. Schmidt

Direttore amministrativo dell'Istituto per il movimento monetario e finanziario dell'Università di Amburgo

Compendio

Negli ultimi decenni, la borsa era concepita idealmente come un mercato a struttura unitaria riservato esclusivamente alle società le cui azioni a larga diffusione si offrivano come un solido investimento e soddisfacevano elevati requisiti di pubblicità. Tuttavia, come hanno evidenziato il sorgere e il successo di segmenti di borsa specifici per le piccole e medie imprese in diversi paesi europei, è possibile creare, riducendo i requisiti di ammissione e adottando procedure commerciali specifiche, un mercato borsistico per quote di partecipazione che ammontano al massimo ad alcuni milioni di DM e che sono quindi detenute soltanto da pochi investitori.

La nuova tendenza ad ammettere alla quotazione in borsa società che erano considerate finora troppo giovani, troppo piccole e troppo rischiose, si limita per il momento, alle imprese che corrispondono già ad un determinato livello elevato di qualità. Tuttavia, considerazioni di principio e pragmatiche esigono altresi' l'emissione pubblica e la negoziazione in borsa o fuori borsa delle azioni di giovani imprese che non hanno ancora raggiunto il suddetto livello qualitativo. Questo sistema di autofinanziamento esterno delle imprese giovani ed innovative rappresenta un complemento e un'alternativa importante al collocamento privato e al finanziamento tramite società di capitale di rischio (venture capital companies). I problemi di valutazione, di controllo e di recesso possono essere risolti più facilmente se dette giovani imprese sono ammesse al segmento di base quale segmento inferiore nella gerarchi del mercato dei titoli. Nonostante l'elevato rischio inerente alle azioni di tali società, non ci sono ragioni, nemmeno la necessità di tutelare gli investitori, per non incentivare in tal modo la crescita delle imprese innovatrici e i loro effetti positivi per l'intera economia.

Per incentivare, in particolare, le imprese di recente costituzione tramite il segmento di base, esiste tutta una serie di misure. In questo contesto ci limitiamo a menzionare l'introduzione in tutti gli Stati membri di azioni di godimento standardizzate e di un "licensed-dealer-status", incentivazioni fiscali per un accertamento "tender" del corso di nuove emissioni pubbliche, la soppressione dei limiti esistenti per gli investitori istituzionali e l'eliminazione degli ostacoli fiscali agli scambi, in particolare rinunciando completamente alla imposizione delle plusvalenze derivanti dalla vendita di azioni di piccole imprese.

L'ACCESSO AI MERCATI EUROPEI DELLE SOCIETA' DI MEDIE DIMENSIONI

Y. FLORNOY

Sindaco della "Compagnie des Agents de Change"

Compendio

L'importanza delle piccole e medie imprese nelle economie della Comunità europea è ancor oggi determinante. Sia dal punto di vista del numero delle imprese, sia da quello della manodopera da esse impiegata, in rapporto, rispettivamente, al numero complessivo delle imprese e alla manodopera globalmente occupata, le piccole e medie imprese costituiscono in pratica la trama del nostro tessuto economico.

Beneficiando a questo titolo di un'intera rete di aiuti allo sviluppo, molteplici e variati, le PMI hanno finora dimostrato scarso interesse a un accesso al mercato azionario. Indubbiamente restano ancora notevoli gli ostacoli al loro ingresso in borsa. Tuttavia le PMI cominciano a prendere coscienza dei vantaggi che gliene potrebbero derivare.

Sotto questo profilo l'esperienza, che sta conoscendo successo, del Mercato secondario francese costituisce una prova dell'interesse costante delle società di medie dimensioni a un accesso ai mercati azionari.

MERCATI AZIONARI EUROPEI DI LIVELLO SECONDARIO - L'OPINIONE DELL'IMPRENDITORE

Robin G. HODGSON

Managing Director, Granville & Co. Ltd., London.

Compendio

La struttura psicologica dell'imprenditore determina la sua posizione rispetto ai vari meccanismi di disinvestimento esistenti. Gli imprenditori possono essere grosso modo classificati in due tipi : dinastici e non dinastici. I mercati azionari europei si sono concentrati sulle necessità di questi ultimi, mentre le esigenze dei primi hanno ricevuto scarsa considerazione.

IL PUNTO DI VISTA DEGLI INVESTITORI DI CAPITALE DI RISCHIO

J.P. de Blocq van Kuffeler
Direttore
Brown, Shipley & Co. Limited

Compendio

Negli ultimi tre anni sono stati constatati il rapido sviluppo e l'espansione dei mercati azionari di livello secondario, e in particolare a Londra con il crescere del mercato dei titoli non quotati e del mercato dei titoli non trattati in borsa. Sul primo dei due suddetti mercati vengono attualmente trattate azioni di circa 220 società, per le quali sono stati reperiti capitali per circa 230 milioni di sterline. Quanto al secondo, che tratta le azioni di circa 70 società, vi agiscono attualmente 24 operatori.

Gli investitori istituzionali dispongono a Londra di fondi considerevoli per nuovi investimenti netti e il loro atteggiamento, nonché i criteri di investimento da essi seguiti, contano notevolmente per questi mercati.

Gli investitori istituzionali considerano il mercato dei titoli non quotati e il mercato dei titoli non trattati in borsa come un'occasione per investire in nuove industrie e in società di recente costituzione, investimento che offre la possibilità di raccogliere capitali notevoli altrimenti irreperibili sui mercati di livello primario. L'altezza dei dividendi è, di conseguenza, meno elevata e in taluni casi, come nel caso del finanziamento di progetti agricoli, nessun dividendo viene pagato per i primi anni. La ricerca di ulteriori capitali a mezzo di nuovi conferimenti o con l'emissione di nuove azioni è incoraggiata e considerata come uno sviluppo positivo.

Qualche difficoltà è data attualmente dallo scarso numero di azioni disponibili in talune società, che si traduce in corsi elevati delle medesime. I corsi elevati, a loro volta, inducono ad aspettative irrealistiche e, di conseguenza, sono molto instabili. Il mercato reale delle azioni puo' risultare ristrettissimo in quanto la maggior parte delle azioni è detenuta dai proprietari delle imprese e poche azioni restano disponibili per la contrattazione.

Nondimeno si spera che questo sia un fenomeno temporaneo, superabile con successive ulteriori emissioni di azioni e con l'immissione delle azioni societarie a una libera contrattazione in borsa.

I MERCATI RISTRETTI AMERICANI

A.E. YOUNG

Professore di scienze finanziarie,

School of Management, Syracuse University

Compendio

Si tratta di un'analisi dei mercati ristretti rispettc alle borse valori in America. In un paese tecnologicamente avanzato ccme il nostro, i due sistemi commerciali alternativi di base del passato sono oggi intimamente interconnessi. Si prendono innanzitutto in esame alcune differenze fondamentali fra le borse valori e i mercati ristretti, mettendo in rilievo le metamorfosi subite dalle operazioni su questi ultimi. Mentre non più tardi di cinquant'anni fa, quando furono elaborate le componenti essenziali della legislazione che disciplina i mercati dei valori mobiliari, securities le negoziazioni sul mercato ristretto erano praticamente sconosciute in America, le stesse operazioni con azioni di grandi imprese occupano oggi un posto di rilievo sul mercato mobiliare. Le contrattazioni sul mercato ristretto di azioni di piccole società sono tuttavia poco frequenti e di scarso rilievo come ai tempi dell'emanazione della normativa fondamentale sui valori mobiliari. Dopo questi accenni di carattere generale, vengono analizzate alcune delle principali componenti e forze che hanno ultimamente influito sul mercato mobiliare. Viene infine illustrata la proposta di un mercato nazionale, indicando la funzione che il mercato ristretto potrebbe eventualmente espletare nell'ambito di un tale sistema.

"IL MERCATO LONDINESE DEI TITOLI NON QUOTATI IN BORSA"

Robin Stormonth-Darling

Presidente, Laing & Cruickshank
(inc. McAnally Montgomery & Co.) Agenti di borsa, Londra
Presidente della Commissione quotazioni,
Consiglio di Borsa

Compendio

Nel novembre 1980 è stato istituito il Mercato dei titoli non quotati (USM Unlisted Securities Market) con un duplice scopo. Lo scopo principale era quello di creare un mercato regolamentato ufficiale per venire incontro alle esigenze delle società minori e relativamente giovani, con poche probabilità di essere ammesse alla quotazione in borsa. Si riteneva che, senza un simile mercato e alcune garanzie di negoziabilità per gli investimenti, gli investitori sarebbero stati poco inclini a prendere rischi. In secondo luogo, l'USM ha sottoposto al controllo regolare ufficiale della borsa le società non quotate le cui azioni venivano negoziate liberamente in conformità della norma 163 (2) della Borsa. Tale norma consentiva contrattazioni occasionali, soggette all'autorizzazione del Consiglio (Council of the Stock Exchange), delle azioni di società pubbliche e private non quotate; essa è tuttora applicabile a tale scopo ma su una base un po' più ristretta rispetto al passato.

Durante il periodo novembre 1980 - settembre 1983 sono state ammesse all'USM 211 società e alla data di ammissione sono stati raccolti 277 milioni di sterline.

Relazione del Gruppo di Lavoro 1

Presidente : Dr. H. SCHMIDT

Relatore : D.L. ADAMSON

Meccanismi atti a favorire l'investimento di capitali di rischio a livello comunitario

Al gruppo di lavoro è stato assegnato il compito di prospettare quali siano i meccanismi più idonei a stimolare l'investimento di capitale di rischio a livello europeo e non esclusivamente nazionale. In sostanza il gruppo di lavoro ritiene che due siano i meccanismi meritevoli di particolare attenzione. Primo : il ricorso diretto ai mercati azionari negli altri Stati membri; secondo, lo smercio delle azioni delle piccole società innovative a investitori istituzionali stranieri. I due meccanismi possono essere utilizzati sia in alternanza, sia in ordine successivo, sia simultaneamente.

Il gruppo di lavoro invita la Commissione ad aumentare gli sforzi intesi a rimuovere gli ostacoli intracomunitari al finanziamento azionario. Per mancanza di tempo il gruppo di lavoro non si è attardato ad analizzare tutti questi ostacoli, ma ha preferito appuntare la sua attenzione su quattro elementi : la struttura generale del mercato azionario; l'offerta intracomunitaria sul mercato primario, l'investimento internazionale attraverso gli organismi bancari; l'investimento internazionale attraverso le istituzioni finanziarie.

Per i suddetti quattro settori il gruppo di lavoro formula le seguenti raccomandazioni :

1. In considerazione della spesa che comporterebbe e delle difficoltà pratiche di realizzazione il gruppo di lavoro non vede alcuna necessità di istituire un mercato centrale europeo delle azioni delle piccole società. A suo avviso basta ricorrere ai mercati attualmente esistenti, utilizzandoli con un massimo di flessibilità e potenziandoli al fine di favorire le piccole società innovative.

Le società nazionali e straniere costituite per il finanziamento di nuovi iniziative dovrebbero essere ammesse ai mercati azionari, assegnando loro un settore specifico dei medesimi.

I requisiti per l'ammissione in Borsa di queste società dovrebbero essere definiti in modo che esse non siano fonte di oneri insostenibili per le piccole imprese. Nella misura del possibile la tutela dell'investitore dovrebbe essere garantita dalla legislazione esistente senza bisogno di introdurre norme nuove e complesse.

2. Il gruppo di lavoro raccomanda di eliminare le disposizioni legislative che impediscono l'immissione da parte delle piccole società europee delle loro azioni sul mercato primario di altri Stati membri della Comunità. Il gruppo di lavoro constata e deplora l'esistenza di troppe disposizioni legislative di carattere restrittivo, che variano dai controlli sugli scambi alle forme di discriminazione nei confronti degli emittenti stranieri. Il gruppo si dichiara invece favorevole a un approfondito esame particolareggiato di queste disposizioni.

Inoltre il gruppo di lavoro raccomanda lo studio di nuovi sistemi atti a divulgare l'informazione relativa ai nuovi mercati azionari. L'istituzione dell'Associazione europea del capitale di rischio è un'ottima occasione per lanciare un periodico inteso ad attirare l'attenzione degli imprenditori sul vantaggiosissimo rapporto utile/prezzo delle azioni che siffatte società possono immettere sui diversi mercati nazionali di capitale.

3. Il gruppo di lavoro si associa alle raccomandazioni, formulate nella III sessione, di varare in tutti gli Stati membri uno statuto di agente autorizzato , quale esiste attualmente nel Regno Unito, per promuovere un vigoroso settore bancario di investimento. Questi agenti sarabbero autorizzati a operazioni in titoli non quotati in borsa o ad altre operazioni finanziarie per i loro clienti. Lo sviluppo di un videotex interattivo puo' facilitare le contrattazioni. In tutti gli Stati membri dovrebbe essere incoraggiato l'investimento a livello europeo da parte degli istituti bancari, cio' che varrebbe ad incrementare in generale il loro livello d'investimento. La Commissione dovrebbe compiere i passi necessari per rimuovere gli ostacoli normativi che attualmente impacciano questa attività.

4. L'ideale sarebbe che non ci fossero restrizioni all'investimento internazionale o all'investimento in titoli non quotati in Borsa ad opera delle istituzioni finanziarie. Stanti le difficoltà pratiche che le grandi istituzioni finanziarie si troverebbero ad affrontare negli investimenti

internazionali in titoli non quotati e nelle relative operazioni di controllo, il gruppo di lavoro è giunto alla conclusione che non sarebbe male prendere in esame l'eventualità di veicoli intermediari specializzati.

Modello di tali veicoli potrebbe essere una società di investimento "chiuso", le cui azioni fossero quotate in una o più Borse nazionali. I titoli di tale società potrebbero assumere la forma di azioni quotate o non quotate in Borsa, a discrezione della gestione. Il regime fiscale dovrebbe essere analogo a quello riservato ai Fondi comuni di investimento. Sarà il mercato stesso a determinare il valore del portafoglio-azioni detenuto dal Fondo. Cio' ridurrà i continui sforzi necessari per una valutazione lunga e difficile degli investimenti individuali in azioni non quotate.

Tali Fondi non macherebbero di attirare il mondo bancario, cato che la politica di investimento si identificherebbe con l'investimento internazionale in piccole società : un ruolo che l'istituzione desidererà affidare in subappalto. La presenza attiva di subappaltatori specializzati contribuirebbe moltissimo all'internazionalizzazione dei mercati finanziari europei di azioni di piccole società, stimolando la ricerca intracomunitaria di nuovo capitale per le giovani imprese.

Relazione del Gruppo di Lavoro 2

Presidente : P. FONTANEAU

Relatore : P. WECKEL

Agevolazioni fiscali per gli investimenti con capitali di rischio

In primo luogo, il gruppo di lavoro ricorda che, dal 1975, la Commissione delle Comunità europee ha formulato delle proposte volte a modificare lo statuto fiscale di taluni elementi della base imponibile dell'imposta sulle società o sul reddito e, pertanto, a coordinare detto statuto nei vari Stati membri. Tali proposte riguardano, in particolare, il concetto di fusione, le relazioni tra società madri e filiali, il problema della doppia imposizione delle società che hanno domicili fiscali in più Stati della Comunità. Nell'ambito di tale quadro, i gruppo di lavoro si permette di proporre i seguenti provvedimenti nell'intento di migliorare il funzionamento del mercato del "Venture Capital" o capitale di rischio.

Siffatte raccomandazioni sono intese a pervenire al seguente duplice risultato: coordinare e armonizzare lo statuto fiscale dei partecipanti al mercato dei "Venture Capitals", e cio' al fine di combatterne la frammentazione e assegnargli in futuro una dimensione europea.

Onde conseguire detto risultato, il gruppo di lavoro propone le misure seguenti:

1. Modifica dello statuto fiscale dell'investitore individuale nel settore del "Venture Capital"
2. Modifica dello statuto fiscale della società innovatrice
3. Modifica dello statuto fiscale dei fondi di investimento nel "Venture Capital".

Le tre modifiche dello statuto fiscale suddette dovranno, come si è già detto, tendere a rendere il più omogeneo possibile il sistema fiscale inerente a questi tre operatori economici nell'ambito dei diversi paesi della Comunità.

Il gruppo di lavoro è cosciente del fatto che lo statuto fiscale dell'innovazione costituisce soltanto una parte, un sottoinsieme dello statuto fiscale globale dei soggetti economici succitati. Lo statuto fiscale, in special modo l'imposta sul reddito e sulle società, resta prerogativa degli Stati membri. Tuttavia, onde agevolare il "decollo" del mercato del "Venture Capital", il gruppo di lavoro auspica una riduzione dell'onere fiscale globale nei limiti del possibile nei vari paesi della Comunità.

Avuto riguardo all'aspetto internazionale dell'innovazione e alla sua rilevanza ai fini della crescita e dell'occupazione nei paesi europei, occorre mettere a punto una politica comunitaria di fondo intesa a stimolare l'intero processo innovativo.

Il gruppo di lavoro propone pertanto l'elaborazione di un vero "Codice fiscale dell'innovazione" su scala europea. Tale codice costituirà lo strumento di rinnovamento della competitività delle imprese europee di fronte ai concorrenti americani o giapponesi.

Il gruppo di lavoro è conscio del fatto che il perfezionamento dello statuto fiscale dell'innovazione rappesenta un elemento necessario per l'avvio del mercato del "Venture Capital". Esso insiste peraltro sul fatto che gli incentivi fiscali non saranno sufficienti per dar luogo a una crescita rapida di detto mercato e auspica che vengano forniti altri aiuti ai vari operatori che costituiscono detto mercato.

P. FONTANEAU

Il presidente rende omaggio all'attività svolta dalla Commissione fin dal 1975 in vista dell'armonizzazione dell'imponibile sugli utili delle società. Ricorda che eventuali proposte della Commissione in materia di innovazione dovrebbero prendere le mosse delle iniziative già intraprese o concretizzate.

Riferendosi alla riunione di mercoledi' pomeriggio, dedicata all'impatto fiscale sull'innovazione, il presidente prende in considerazione i seguenti quattro punti e apre la discussione.

1) Il sig. HENRIKSEN ha esaminato la possibilità di istituire, in caso di parere favorevole degli Stati membri, un fondo o dei fondi europei di investimento nel settore dei capitali di rischio che dovrebbero fruire di sgravi fiscali.

2) Nel suo intervento, il sig. INGLEDON ha constatato la mancanza di un mercato comune dei capitali di rischio.

3) L'imposta sul reddito influisce negativamente sullo sviluppo dei capitali di rischio. In questo settore, gli Stati membri hanno in gran parte conservato la loro sovranità fiscale, ma cio' non costituirebbe un ostacolo a proposte precise su punti circoscritti.

4) Sarebbe ingenuo credere che gli incentivi fiscali bastino da soli a stimolare le attività dei capitali di rischio.

Per quel che riguarda la Germania, a detta di uno dei partecipanti gli incentivi fiscali sono necessari per offrire all'investitore una prospettiva più sicura di profitto sulla base di determinate garanzie. Si suggerisce quindi di dare all'investitore la possibilità di godere il primo anno di un consistente sgravio fiscale e di vedere i suoi profitti assoggettati a una modesta imposizione gli anni successivi.

Alcuni partecipanti fanno tuttavia osservare che effetto di tali sgravi sarebbe quello di imporre alla collettività l'onere principale dei rischi collegati all'investimento. Grazie alla detrazione fiscale, la collettività diventa "partner" privilegiato dell'investitore, ma appare auspicabile che resti "partner" minoritario.

Non va d'altronde dimenticato il fallimento, in Germania, delle società di ammortamento. Quando sono i vantaggi fiscali a rappresentare la motivazione principale dell'investitore, unica conseguenza è la moltiplicazione degli investimenti in imprese non suscettibili di sviluppo.

Si fa rilevare che il fisco dovrebbe saper misurare la sua generosità e mantenere una certa equidistanza fra gli agenti economici.

Il sig. KAPLAN dichiara di condividere "in toto" l'argomentazione, ma crede che l'esempio presentato a sostegno della propria tesi dall'intervenuto, vale a dire l'eccessiva quotazione di alcune azioni quale conseguenza del "Business Expansion Scheme" nel Regno Unito, è scelto male nella misura in cui tale effetto è inevitabile e contribuisce a rendere interessante il meccanismo in questione.

Il presidente si dichiara favorevole a un sistema di detrazione dell'investimento, in quanto uno sgravio applicabile ai dividendi non presenta alcun vantaggio durante i primi anni quando non si ricavano ancora degli utili.

Il sig. WIRK è del parere che l'efficacia di ogni sgravio fiscale vada valutata nell'ambito del relativo sistema fiscale, trattandosi di due realtà inscindibili. In Germania, gli impedimenti di carattere fiscale appaiono secondari.

I partecipanti alla discussione sembrano concordare sul fatto che il tasso marginale di imposta sui redditi più elevati è eccessivo e di natura tale da limitare la propensione al risparmio. Dall'uditorio vengono tuttavia fatte valere due riserve. Si fa rilevare che, durante i primi anni dell'investimento, il livello di imposizione fiscale non puo' essere eccessivo in quanto non si ricava ancora alcun utile. Non si tratta tanto, a detta del sig. WIRK, di rimettere in discussione gli oneri fiscali che gravano su questa categoria di contribuenti, quanto di modificare la progressività eccessivamente rapida dell'imposta.

Secondo il sig. WIRK, gli sgravi fiscali dovrebbero andare con priorità a favore delle imprese innovatrici, soprattutto quando cominciano a produrre degli utili. A tale scopo, suggerisce la costituzione di riserve di investimenti che possono godere di esonero fiscale.

Un membro del gruppo di lavoro propone che il lancio di un prestito europeo per l'innovazione sia accompagnato da sgravi fiscali accordati agli intermediari finanziari per quella quota di investimenti che realizzano con fondi propri.

L'oratore condivide il rilievo del presidente, secondo cui una tale deduzione avrebbe come effetto quello di liberare tali istituzioni dal rischio che è il vero oggetto della loro attività.

Il presidente ricorda che era stata proposta l'introduzione di fondi di investimento nazionali e di un fondo europeo destinato ad attirare i capitali verso la Comunità, illustra quindi i vantaggi di un fondo multinazionale per i paesi che abbiano introdotto un sistema di controllo dei cambi.

Secondo il gruppo, sarebbe preferibile che esistessero più fondi privati a livello nazionale, respingendo la proposta relativa alla creazione di un fondo internazionale. Dovrebbe essere comunque stabilito un collegamento fra i vari fondi. Per invogliare gli investitori a sviluppare l'attività in un paese limitrofo, sarebbe opportuno che beneficiassero di agevolazioni tributarie simili a quelle loro concesse nel proprio paese. Si suggerisce di far leva, a tal fine, sulle convenzioni che regolano la doppia imposizione.

Il presidente interroga il gruppo sulla necessità di proporre un'armonizzazione dei regimi fiscali in materia di capitali di rischio nella Comunità. I partecipanti sono del parere che la varietà dei sistemi fiscali e la reticenza degli Stati membri a limitare la loro sovranità nel settore fanno si' che l'obiettivo in questione non appaia realizzabile in un prossimo avvenire.

Tale posizione al riguardo non è unanime. Si fa invece rilevare che, in tal modo, i paesi membri perderebbero l'occasione di far avanzare l'Europa in un settore di punta. Sarebbe quindi opportuno aprofittare della novità e dell'attualità del problema costituito dai capitali di rischio.

Il presidente suggerisce al gruppo di lavoro di sottoporre alla Commissione le seguenti proposte.

I singoli investitori e le società operanti con capitali di rischio dovrebbero beneficiare di incentivi fiscali.

Tali misure sono pero' correlate a sistemi fiscali che vanno considerati nella loro globalità. E' quindi auspicabile che i governi della Comunità europea riducano la pressione fiscale che grava sui redditi più elevati.

Ai capitali di rischio dovrebbe essere infine applicato lo stesso regime fiscale in tutta la Comunità.

Relazione

Gruppo di lavoro 6 : " Opzione su nuove azioni per i dirigenti delle società con potenziale di crescita"

&

Gruppo di lavoro 3 : " Mobilitazione degli investitori non bancari di capitale di rischio a livello comunitario"

Presidente: R.G. HODGSON

Relatore : S. NEUMANN

A) <u>Opzione su nuove azioni</u> (esempi U.S.A.)

In generale, il gruppo conviene che l'opzione su nuove azioni per i dirigenti costituisce uno strumento essenziale per le società di capitali di rischio. Essendo innanzitutto un incentivo per i dirigenti a partecipare alla crescita della società, le opzioni devono essere pagate secondo la prassi corrente. Cio' costituisce un incentivo supplementare e puo' avere delle implicazioni fiscali. Per frenare l'elevata mobilità della dirigenza (negli Stati Uniti, i presidenti di società cambiano in media ogni anno e mezzo), l'opzione aumenta su base annuale. Per le società non quotate la valutazione delle azioni è difficile. In un caso si è calcolata, a titolo sperimentale, la media degli utili su base triennale. Nel Regno Unito, l'imposizione dei proventi da opzioni costituisce un problema molto arduo. Negli altri paesi europei, il problema è meno noto e dovrà essere studiato da esperti fiscali paese per paese.

Il gruppo di lavoro formula le seguenti raccomandazioni:

La Commissione delle Comunità europee dovrebbe avviare uno studio sul trattamento fiscale dell'opzione per i dirigenti negli Stati membri della CE e negli USA e dovrebbe studiare altresi' a livello teorico i vantaggi e l'impatto economico dell'opzione nonché gli ostacoli che si frappongono all'applicazione dell'approccio dell'opzione su nuove azioni.

a) I lavori della Commissione CE volti ad armonizzare l'imposizione fiscale sulle società dovrebbero considerare altresi' la retribuzione dei dirigenti tramite opzioni e diritti alla pensione e tener conto degli aspetti politici, sociali ed economici.

b) L'importanza dell'opzione quale strumento delle società di capitale di rischio esige un trattamento (fiscale) armonizzato nella CE, al fine di agevolare le operazioni internazionali.

c) L'opzione dovrebbe essere presa in considerazione non solo per l'avvio o il rilevamento azionario ma anche per le successive fasi intermedie delle finanze della società da prendere in considerazione in ogni regime fiscale.

d) La terminologia "opzione su nuove azioni" ("stock options") ha un'accezione negativa presso l'opinione pubblica e dovrebbe essere sostituita con un termine più positivo, possibilmente con DIRITTI EUROPEI DI PARTECIPAZIONE, come proposto dal Prof. SCHMIDT.

In aggiunta all'opzione, il gruppo ha discusso altresi' la retribuzione della dirigenza tramite diritti alla pensione, che sono relativamente bassi nelle quotazioni americane e - per quanto riguarda la trasferibilità delle pensioni - dipendono in Europa da accordi individuali.

Ma, innanzitutto, il concetto dell'efficacia dell'opzione dovrebbe essere presentato come fattore essenziale della crescita delle piccole imprese, perché altrimenti la "politica dell'invidia" renderebbe impossibile ogni riforma.

B) Mobilitazione degli investitori di capitale di rischio

Dapprima, il gruppo definisce il concetto di "investitori non bancari di capitale di rischio" e decide di sopprimere il termine "non bancario". I principali gruppi di investimento discussi durante la riunione sono:

- i fondi pensioni e le società di assicurazione
- i fondi industriali (p.es. società industriali)
- le istituzioni accademiche
- i fondi d'investimento e gli investitori collettivi
- gli investitori privati.

I governi e le industrie nazionalizzate non sono prese in considerazione in quanto rientrano nella competenza del gruppo di lavoro 4. Per quanto riguarda gli investitori accademici, che in Europa già partecipano ai fondi di capitale di rischio, si ritiene che la loro partecipazione sia tesa essenzialmente a stabilire stretti rapporti finalizzati al trasferimento tecnologico. Per mobilitare gli investitori di capitale di rischio, il gruppo di lavoro formula le seguenti raccomandazioni:

1. Ogni incentivazione degli investitori istituzionali di capitali di rischio deve essere correlata con il tasso di crescita potenziale della capacità gestionale dei dirigenti delle società di capitale di rischio in Europa, al fine di evitare sviluppi negativi.

2. Prima di proporre misure volte a superare gli ostacoli legali e statutari che impediscono alle istituzioni di investire in capitali di rischio, la Commissione CE dovrebbe fare un inventario positivo/negativo della normativa e del rispettivo impatto nella CE e negli USA; inoltre, potrebbe esser necessario esaminare gli ostacoli risultanti dalla struttura organizzativa delle istituzioni che effettuano gli investimenti.

3. La Commissione delle Comunità europee dovrebbe incentivare la costituzione di società di capitale di rischio di dimensione europea onde creare un dinamico mercato europeo di capitali di rischio (obiettivo: investimenti di 1-2 miliardi di dollari all'anno); a tale scopo, la Commissione dovrebbe esaminare gli ostacoli alle compartecipazioni e agli accordi transizionali. Gli investitori istituzionali, in primo luogo fondi pensioni e assicurazioni, dovrebbero essere autorizzati, incoraggiati o costretti ad investire una determinata percentuale del reddito annuale in capitale di rischio.

4. L'industria dovrebbe essere motivata ad utilizzare lo "sportello tecnologico" offerto dal capitale di rischio per incrementare il volume e l'efficienza della ricerca e dello sviluppo. Inoltre, l'industria potrebbe aiutare a designare aree industriali adeguate per gli investimenti di capitali di rischio in vista della creazione di grandi società europee.

5. La Commissione delle Comunità europee è invitata ad appoggiare lo sviluppo dell'infrastruttura del capitale di rischio al fine di ridurre i rischi per i fornitori di fondi.

6. L'università dovrebbe contribuire allo sviluppo dell'infrastruttura del capitale di rischio, promuovendo la formazione imprenditoriale, colmando la lacuna informativa esistente tra tecnologia e domanda e offerta di lavoro.

Per evitare gli effetti negativi derivanti dalla mancanza di dirigenti esperti in materia di capitale di rischio, ogni azione diretta a mobilitare gli investitori istituzionali dovrebbe avere priorità e scadenzari specifici.

RELAZIONE DEL GRUPPO DI LAVORO N. 4

Presidente : K. NATHUSIUS

Relatore : P. DOURNEL

DISPOSIZIONI GOVERNATIVE PER LO STIMOLO DEGLI INVESTIMENTI DI RISCHIO

I lavori di questo gruppo sono stati animati dalla partecipazione attiva di una cinquantina di persone. Data la vivacità della discussione presentiamo qui un resoconto tematico che ci permetterà di meglio sintetizzare quanto detto durante la seduta.

I SITUAZIONE ATTUALE

Le misure prese dai diversi governi degli stati membri della Comunità europea possono essere raggruppate in tre grandi categorie

- Misure fiscali
- Offerta diretta di capitali
- Sistemi di garanzia

A. Le misure fiscali

La maggior parte degli stati membri ha preso delle misure di riduzione fiscale per favorire gli investimenti. In quanto tali, esse non possono essere che benefiche per le operazioni di capitale di rischio. Possiamo per esempio citare la possibilità di riporto delle perdite verso gli esercizi futuri, e, quando sussista, la possibilità di dedurre queste perdite dagli esercizi anteriori (1).

Inoltre, alcuni stati membri hanno adottato misure fiscali specifiche di prese di partecipazione e di capitali di rischio. Queste misure possono interessare sia società di capitali di rischio, per esempio il trattamento della plusvalenza di cessione realizzata dalla "Sociétés Financières d'Innovation" in Francia oppure dalla "Wagnisfinanzierungsgesellschaft" in Germania, sia costituire degli incentivi ai privati per investire nei "Fonds d'Innovation" (Belgio) o nelle imprese (Regno Unito).

B. OFFERTA DIRETTA DI CAPITALI

Molti stati hanno adottato misure d'offerta di capitali per stimolare il capitale di rischio. Un esempio sorprendente è la "National Enterprise Agency" creata recentemente dal governo irlandese. L'azione degli stati in materia puo' prendere diverse forme che vanno dalla partecipazione diretta in alcuni settori, per esempio in Grecia, all'appoggio per la creazione di società che distribuiscono fondi d'origine statale o mista (Germania: Wfg., Francia: SFI,...) (2).

Bisogna comunque notare che queste misure restano limitate sia per la loro ampiezza sia per il loro impatto, non avendo evidentemente raggiumto il loro margine critico.

C. I fondi di garanzia

Anche in questo punto i diversi stati hanno applicato, in questi ultimi anni, numerosi programmi tendenti ad incoraggiare gli sforzi all'investimento. Questi programmi si possono concepire sia come ausiliari o complementari a organismi di garanzia gia' esistenti, sia come numerosi intervenienti a vocazione specifica. Citiamo, come esempi di questa ultima categoria il "P.P.M. Guarantee Scheme" olandese e la Verlustausfallgarantie des Wfg" tedesca (2).

Altri stati costituiscono fondi di garanzia nazionale misti, sostituendosi agli organismi di garanzia classici per assumere in ultima istanza i rischi del banchiere (Francia: SOFARIS, Regno Unito: Government Guarantee Scheme for Small Business Loans, Belgio: Fonds de garantie de l'Etat,...).

Notiamo che questi ultimi sono il modo di accedere piu' frequente al sostegno da parte delle PMI (2).

II ESPERIENZA E REAZIONI DEI PARTECIPANTI

Per indirizzare il dibattito, si è deciso di cercare di rispondere a una serie di domande con l'aiuto dell'esperienza dei partecipanti.

A. Quale puo' essere il ruolo di un governo in materia?

a) Esempio irlandese

La National Enterprise Agency è stata fondata verso la metà di ottobre con lo scopo d'offrire dei capitali di rischio al primo stadio della creazione di un'impresa. Una volta superati i rischi tecnologici e di penetrazione sul mercato. essa venderà le sue parti sul mercato secondario.

L'originalità di questo sistema statale consiste nell'utilizzazione delle capacità tecniche di esperti che non siano funzionari statali per porre riparo alla mancanza di esperienza degli impiegati dello stato in materia di capitali di rischio. Questi esperti saranno pagati grazie ad una parte delle plusvalenze di cessione registrate dalla NEA nel corso della realizzazione dei suoi programmi. Questa parte potrà essere del 20 % della plusvalenza realizzata dal progetto, alla quale si aggiungono gli onorari versati a titolo di assistenza alla gestione.

Questa struttura à una creazione molto originale e potrebbe servire da modello ad altri governi.

b) Esempio canadese

Questo esempio è interessante sotto diversi punti di vista. Potrebbe, fra l'altro, rispondere a una domanda rimasta in sospeso nel corso del simposio del 1982, cioè le possibilità d'intervento dello stato grazie agli appalti pubblici, specialmente in materia di difesa.

Avendo il Canadà deciso di aumentare i suoi sforzi in materia militare gli appalti si sono in gran parte rivolti verso delle società a carattere innovativo, offrendo loro contemporaneamente contratti di ricerca e sviluppo e sbocchi sicuri. Questa coordinazione ha permesso di sviluppare il capitale di rischio che conosceva i problemi abituali di scarsità di capitali per i primi stadi dell'innovazione.

B. Problemi di ambiente

I problemi di ambiente e di contesto politico-economico hanno costituito la maggior parte dei lavori Questa nozione di ambiente raggruppa i seguenti argomenti:

a) Politica fiscale

Puo', essere considerata come l'ostacolo principale allo sviluppo del capitale di rischio nell' Europa continentale. Le reazioni che suscita potrebbero essere divise secondo tre tipi d'imposta gravanti sul capitale di rischio.

- Imposte sul profitto: riducono in modo significativo la tendenza al risparmio e percio' contribuiscono all'attuale situazione di denaro raro e caro. Per di piu', davanti alla debolezza del loro risparmio, gli investori hanno piuttoso la tendenza ad investire i loro fondi in settori reputati per il loro debole rischio senza cercare di dimimuire il rischio potenziale grazie alla diversificazione.

- Imposte sulle società: l'estrema variabilità dei tassi e delle basi d'imposta sulle società nei diversi stati membri costituisce un evidente ostacolo alle operazioni internazionali, potenzialmente a alto rendimento

- Imposte sul plus-valore dei capitali: anche queste hanno un effetto negativo nella misura in cui spingono l'investitore a cercare, come hanno fatto fino adesso dei progetti ad altissimo rendimento per compensare questi prelievi; i tassi di rendimento giudicati necessari sono raramente raggiunti, gli investitori preferiscono non correre rischi.

- Da un punto di vista etico, il gruppo di lavoro N. 1 non s'è mostrato convinto dell'accettabilità di un trattamento fiscale privilegiato.

Questo concetto di trattamento fiscale ineguale alla lunga potrebbe rivelarsi pericoloso poiché attirerebbe verso il capitale di rischio imprese che necessitano di altri tipi di finanziamento, cosa che creerebbe in breve tempo un problema sulla natura delle operazioni.

Inoltre sembra pericoloso sfavorire lo sviluppo tradizionale che è generatore della maggioranza delle plusvalenze svincolate negli ultimi tempi.

b) <u>Percezione del ruolo dell'imprenditore</u>

E' un soggetto che ritorna con molta frequenza e sembra tipico del nostro continente. Infatti, al contrario degli Stati Uniti, dove l'insuccesso è considerato come parte normale del gioco, in Europa produce una reputazione a volte infamante.

Si tratta di un problema legato alla nostra cultura e alla nostra educazione, percio' non potrà essere risolto che grazie a un cambiamento di mentalità e agli esempi di successo che succedono ai casi di fallimento. Credere che esso potrà essere risolto prima della prossima generazione è perfettamente illusorio.

c) <u>Condizioni generali offerte agli imprenditori</u>

Potrebbe trattarsi di possibilità reali d'azione degli stati in materia . Queste condizioni generali possono essere viste in due modi:

- Creazioni di um ambiente economico favorevole: migliore gestione del bilancio dello stato e del debito pubblico, politica di lotta contro la disoccupazione e l'inflazione.

- Creazione di strutture favorevoli, come i "innovation centres" messi a disposizione di immobili adatti a usi industriali a basso costo. Quest'ultima azione governativa è già condotta in alcuni stati come l'Irlanda, il Regno Unito, e la Francia (2).

d) Formazione di gestionari specializzati

E' evidentemente una grave lacuna nel nostro sistema educativo. Si puo' tuttavia considerare che la soluzione sia abbastanza semplice: probabilmente basterebbe estendere le attività delle associazioni a delle conferenze e a dei corsi sul capitale di rischio. L'azione del "Piano transnazionale di sviluppo delle infrastrutture sarà certamente positiva in materia.

e) Motivazione degli imprenditori

E' evidente che un miglioramento della mobilità dei dirigenti, aggiunto ad un incoraggiamento per quelli che desiderino creare la loro propria impresa, avrebbe un effetto oltremodo positivo: creazioni di nuove imprese e assunzione di personale direttivo in sostituzione dei creatori.

III RACCOMANDAZIONI

1. Bisogna continuare a stimolare l'iniziativa privata.

2. Le società di capitale di rischio esistenti non devono accaparrarsi la totalità degli aiuti, cio' nuocerebbe all'aumento del numero degli intervenienti.

3. Il clima economico e sociale dovrebbe essere elevato per spingere all'iniziativa.

4. Dovrebbe essere intrapreso un grosso sforzo di formazione dei gestionari.

5. Si dovrebbe creare e sviluppare una infrastruttura transnazionale di sostegno al capitale di rischio.

Note:

(1) Vedi in proposito i rapporti EUR 8820 e 8821 distribuiti durante il simposio

(2) Vedi il rapporto EUR 8819

Relazione del Gruppo di lavoro 5

Presidente : C. CLEIFTIE

Relatore : R. GUTH

Infrastruttura comunitaria di collegamento tra mercati di capitali di rischio

Nello svolgere il proprio lavoro, il gruppo si è ispirato a tre semplici principi:

1. Piuttosto che presentare raccomandazioni di tipo formale, è sembrato più interessante limitarsi a tappe di riflessione, da sottoporre alle Comunità europee a mo' di "input" per un ulteriore esame.

2. Tra gli scogli tradizionali che si incontrano nello svolgimento di questo lavoro ce n'è uno che consiste nel volere a tutti i costi dar prova di originalità, con conseguenti frequenti proposte volte a dar vita a nuovi sistemi, procedimenti o organi incaricati di nuovi compiti. Di fronte alla naturale tendenza di demoltiplicazione istituzionale, il gruppo ritiene, al contrario (cio' potrebbe già costituire oggetto di una prima raccomandazione), inutile creare sistematicamente "novità" e che le istituzioni esistenti sono perfettamente in grado di presiedere alla messa in opera di un'infrastruttura comunitaria di collegamento tra mercati di capitali di rischio.

3. Qualsiasi passo concreto compiuto su iniziativa della Comunità europea dovrebbe essere caratterizzato da:

semplicità di concezione e di "modus operandi";

buona diffusione presso i destinatari, organizzando un migliore marketing presso i destinatari primari e in particolare presso le piccole e giovani imprese che sono quelle che soffrono maggiormente a causa della lunghezza dei canali di informazione;

concentrazione sulla realizzazione di un'infrastruttura e sulle condizioni-quadro adeguate, dando contemporaneamente vita ad un clima propizio all'aprirsi dei mercati di capitali di rischio. I membri del gruppo non hanno ritenuto auspicabile che le autorità europee si sostituiscano più del dovuto alle forze del mercato. Questa costituisce una seconda raccomandazione, la quale, benché non specificatamente orientata verso il tema della nostra commissione, non per questo perde il proprio valore.

I meccanismi di collegamento di capitali a rischio possono essere presi in considerazione sotto forme diverse. Dato l'orientamento di questo simposio e le qualifiche dei membri del gruppo, abbiamo evidentemente privilegiato l'aspetto finanziario. Se il tema del denaro non abbraccia tutta la problematica, è purtuttavia vero che senza denaro non ci sarebbero mercati di capitali di rischio !!

Secondo il gruppo:

1. occorre trovare urgentemente un meccanismo per facilitare l'effettiva libera circolazione dei capitali nell'ambito della Comunità. Benché cio' figuri nei Trattati, nonostante gli sforzi già compiuti le autorità europee dovrebbero operare con insistenza affinché vengano soppresse le varie e molteplici barriere nazionali ancora esistenti. Per illustrare quanto sopra mi limitero' a citare due esempi tipici:

   in Italia vige l'obbligo di depositare una cauzione senza interessi pari al 50% degli acquisti di valori stranieri o effettuati all'estero;

   le discriminazioni fiscali degli investitori, secondo la natura giuridica del loro statuto o della loro nazionalità, persona privata o pubblica, nazionale o straniera.

2. La Comunità dovrebbe ispirarsi all'esempio della EVCA (European venture capital association) e continuare ad operare secondo gli stessi principi che sono stati alla base della creazione di tale organismo di collegamento unico nel suo genere. Essa dovrebbe anche cercare di ottimizzare tutte le potenzialità che rappresentano l'EVCA come meccanismo di collegamento tra mercati di capitali di rischio, al fine tra l'altro di trarre il massimo profitto dai vari incentivi nazionali e svolgere un ruolo di tipo dinamico a livello comunitario.

Questa prima serie di modelli di comportamento dovrebbe essere rapidamente completata mediante un rinnovo dell'aiuto finanziario (sotto questo profilo il Prestito europeo per l'innovazione = PEI costituisce un primo passo interessante). In tale contesto è stata spesso ricordata l'azione della BEI. Quest'ultima dovrebbe anche rivolgersi alle società di capitali di rischio considerandole come interlocutori degni di diventare "partner" finanziari.

Il gruppo propone che l'EVCA contribuisca a riconoscere ufficialmente questa professione, rilasciando un attestato di rispettabilità nei confronti della comunità finanziaria nel suo insieme e, in particolare, nei confronti della BEI, il che autorizzerebbe i suoi membri a valersi della qualità di intermediario finanziario.

Il Gruppo n. 5 ritiene che si tratti di un provvedimento che potrebbe essere molto rapidamente messo ad esecuzione mediante l'elaborazione di regole deontologiche il cui rispetto sarebbe assicurato dall'EVCA.

Per cio' che riguarda i mercati paralleli di capitali, il gruppo ritiene irragionevole voler creare un mercato unico su scala comunitaria. Le società ammesse a queste quotazioni particolari hanno principalmente una vocazione locale o nazionale e il livello europeo non è adeguato per negoziare i loro titoli.

La dimensione comunitaria avrà senso solamente tramite l'interconnessione delle Borse valori: in tal modo, i vari mercati paralleli potranno approfittare "ipso facto" della dimensione comunitaria.

Non sembra quindi opportuno prendere in considerazione la creazione di legami europei separati, specifici ai mercati paralleli di capitali.

Il Gruppo n. 5 attira infine l'attenzione della Comunità europea su due aspetti più "spigolosi" che importanti:

- da un lato, la necessità di migliorare le tecniche di investimento dei capitali di rischio e il grado di professionalità dei "capitalisti di rischio" per conferire loro il controllo completo che richiede l'ambizione di considerare il mercato comune nel suo insieme come un mercato unico. Anche in questo caso, l'EVCA svolgerà un ruolo pionieristico che dovrebbe essere validamente sostenuto dagli organismi europei;

- dall'altro, sembra che le Istituzioni europee non abbiamo ancora rivolto sufficiente attenzione all'effettivo problema dello sfasamento tra la durata di maturazione di una tecnologia e le restrizioni imposte dai capitalisti di rischio. Questo problema, con il quale gli imprenditori hanno a che fare tutti i giorni, meriterebbe ricerche complementari per cercare di conciliare due esigenze apparentemente contradditorie.

Relazione del Gruppo di Lavoro 7

Presidente : J.D. INCLEDON

Relatore : E. PHILLIPS

Capitale di rischio attraverso investimenti collettivi

Il gruppo ha individuato in Europa una serie di fattori che rende la vita difficile alle nuove società in confronto alle società omologhe nell'America del Nord. Quantificando tale differenza, un partecipante ha precisato che le difficoltà incontrate negli Stati Uniti sono decuplicate nella Comunità europea, semplicemente perché la Comunità è composta da dieci paesi diversi. Egli si riferiva ai differenti regimi fiscali, alle differenti prassi contabili, alle differenti lingue, ai differenziali di inflazione e alle differenti monete che si incontrano viaggiando da un paese all'altro della Comunità europea.

In Europa, molte società devono affrontare questi problemi molto presto in quanto i singoli mercati nazionali sono cosi' ristretti che un'impresa cercherà di esportare già nel primo anno di esistenza. Per contro, negli Stati Uniti, ci sono molte più compagnie che possono operare per parecchi anni senza trovarsi nella necessità di esportare al di fuori dell'America del Nord.

In Europa si registra inoltre una relativa mancanza di esperienza rispetto a quanto si constata negli Stati Uniti. A titolo di esempio, è stato ricordato nel Gruppo 7 che molti imprenditori europei sembrano aver bisogno delle società di capitale di rischio per impostare i loro programmi aziendali, mentre tale prassi è del tutto corrente nella vita aziendale degli Stati Uniti. Il gruppo dubita che molte società di capitale di rischio in Europa abbiano la competenza necessaria per fornire l'aiuto di cui hanno bisogno taluni imprenditori.

Analizzando la situazione dal punto di vista degli investitori residenti in un paese della Comunità europea, il gruppo ha notato che questi possono essere restii ad investire all'estero perché temono di incontrare problemi (quali i controlli dei cambi) qualora desiderino rimpatriare il loro denaro.

Del pari, il gruppo ha rilevato una professionalità più elevata tra gli investitori americani in genere che non tra colleghi europei.

Sulla base di questi fattori, il gruppo è arrivato alla conclusione che le società di capitale di rischio statunitensi sono più evolute ed hanno un'esperienza maggiore delle organizzazioni europee. Di conseguenza, mentre alcune società americane hanno conquistato una quota rilevante del mercato europeo per i loro prodotti, gli Stati Uniti stanno ritirando nel contempo il capitale di rischio dall'Europa. Naturalmente, cio' contribuisce a rafforzare ulteriormente le società americane di capitale di rischio a scapito delle omologhe organizzazioni europee.

Sulla base di queste considerazioni, il gruppo ha formulato la prima raccomandazione:

> " Prendendo atto della relativa mancanza di esperienza rispetto alle società di capitale di rischio americane, noi dovremmo cercare strumenti atti a potenziare le organizzazioni intermediarie in Europa onde consentire loro di competere con maggiore efficienza."

Le misure espressamente menzionate dal gruppo sono: disposizioni fiscali a favore di dette organizzazioni e abolizione degli ostacoli alla libera circolazione dei capitali attraverso le frontiere nazionali.

La seconda raccomandazione del gruppo era intesa come un approccio diretto alla mancanza di esperienza tra le società di capitali di rischio e gli imprenditori in Europa:

> " Sarebbe opportuna un'assistenza selettiva per aiutare le organizzazioni intermediarie e i dirigenti delle società che ricorrono al capitale di rischio, ad acquisire le tecniche indispensabili per il successo nel loro campo".

Infine, il gruppo ha ritenuto che i mercati di capitale di rischio trarrebbero vantaggio da eventuali agevolazioni delle condizioni di investimento, particolarmente su archi di tempo ridotti di due o tre anni; in altri termini, occorrono migliori meccanismi di realizzo. Un altro modo di esprimere tale punto di vista è che, finché ci saranno cambi in tutti gli Stati membri (secondo gli orientamenti del Mercato dei titoli non quotati di Londra - London USM) che facilitano l'investimento in fondi di capitale di rischio, rimarrà difficile disinvestire a breve termine. Di qui la raccomandazione finale:

> " Occorre rafforzare il meccanismo per la realizzazione degli investimenti di capitale di rischio in una fase precoce."

Relazione del Gruppo di Lavoro 8

Presidente : I. MOMTCHILOFF

Relatore : J.M. GIBB

Gestione dei capitali di rischio

Scopo del gruppo di lavoro è definire in termini concreti le peculiarità della gestione dei capitali di rischio ed indicare le possibili linee di condotta per gli investitori. Si è prestata inoltre attenzione a certe difficoltà incontrate dagli operatori con capitali di rischio, difficoltà che potrebbero essere in parte risolte con iniziative ufficiali a livello nazionale o comunitario.

Il gruppo ha affrontato i seguenti aspetti del problema :

1. Strutture

2. a) Individuazione di progetti convenienti
   b) Criteri decisionali per gli investimenti

3. a) Controllo degli investimenti
   b) Il momento del realizzo

1. STRUTTURE

Durata di un'operazione con capitali di rischio : periodo sufficientemente lungo (almeno 10 anni).

Operatori : Possono essere :
- singole persone,
- società che operano con capitali di rischio,
- istituzioni.

Settori di investimento : due opzioni principali :

a) vasto ventaglio di settori (con conseguente ripartizione o diminuzione statistica dei rischi), o

b) specializzazione (con conseguente acquisizione di conoscenze più specifiche che comportano potenzialmente un miglior calcolo dei rischi).

Impressione comune è che la prima opzione presenti qualche vantaggio in più della seconda.

Stadio di finanziamento : Il finanziamento di progetti nella loro fase iniziale è interessante in termini di potenziale di crescita, ma più rischioso che non il finanziamento di progetti in fasi successive di sviluppo, per i quali vi è una forte richiesta. Dovrebbe essere diversificato al riguardo il portafoglio di una società operante con capitali di rischio.

Tipo di operatori. Una società operante con capitali di rischio dovrebbe essere diretta da un "team" persone con comprovata :

- esperienza di direzione aziendale ;
- esperienza contabile ;
- comprovata capacità nel settore finanziario.

Esempio di unità specializzata in operazioni con capitali di rischio :

un esperto di direzione aziendale)
)a cui affidare più o meno 5 progetti di investimento.
un esperto finanziario)

Esempio di unità non specializzata in operazioni con capitali di rischio :

un esperto di direzione aziendale)
)
un esperto finanziario)
)
+ comitato consultivo)a cui affidare più o meno 15 investimenti
+ consulenti)
+ rete di contatti)
)

Investimenti in altri paesi

Gli investimenti all'estero sono necessari per operare su un mercato più vasto e per raggiungere l'obiettivo della diversificazione, senza tuttavia dimenticare la necessaria consulenza in materia di problemi giuridici, tutela dei brevetti, normativa fiscale, ecc.

Incentivi per i membri di una unità operante con capitali di rischio

Una possibilità sarebbe quella di offrire ai membri dell'unità o "team" una partecipazione diretta agli utili ricavati. Si possono pero' presentare delle difficoltà quando l'unità in questione fa parte di un sistema istituzionale.

Un'altra possibilità sarebbe quella di offrire ai componenti l'unità un diritto di opzione sull'acquisto di azioni. Sfortunatamente, ben pochi paesi dispongono al riguardo di un'adeguata struttura giuridica.

Libera circolazione dei capitali

La libera circolazione dei capitali, essenziale per lo svolgimento di operazioni a livello internazionale, non è ancora un dato acquisito nella Comunità europea, a motivo ai controlli sui cambi in vigore in alcuni Stati membri e ad altre normative, come ad esempio la questione della nazionalità dei direttori ed amministratori delle società.

Cooperazione internazionale

Quantunque sia preferibile, come si è già accennato, operare in un contesto internazionale, non è facile conquistare e consolidare la propria posizione su un mercato straniero. E' il problema se sia o meno opportuno riunirsi in gruppi finanziari transnazionali. Al riguardo potrebbe essere forse di aiuto l'Associazione europea per i capitali di rischio European Venture Capital Association di recente fondazione.

Struttura decisionale

La scelta di fondo va fatta fra una struttura gerarchica o collegiale. Nel primo caso, la responsabilità decisionale ricade su una sola persona. Nel secondo, si assiste ad una ripartizione delle responsabilità, in quando le decisioni vengono prese sulla base di una procedura formale di voto. E' stata espressa a debole maggioranza una preferenza per il secondo sistema.

2. a) REPERIMENTO DI PROGETTI

Si puo' far ricorso ai seguenti strumenti :

- stampa specializzata ;
- università ;
- altri operatori con capitali di rischio ;
- eventuali membri del consiglio consultivo ;

- acquirenti buyers dell'industria ;
- consulenti, esperti contabili, altri esperti ;
- direttori di banca ;
- partecipazione a convegni ed esposizioni ;
- banche di dati.

2. b) CRITERI DECISIONALI PER GLI INVESTIMENTI

Occorre poter rispondere affermativamente ai seguenti quesiti :

- Appare adeguata la capacità di amministrare il rischio?
- E' disponibile un piano di investimento?
- Il piano è stato esaminato e ritenuto soddisfacente dal punto di vista commerciale, industriale e finanziario?
- E' ravvisabile un preciso, concreto vantaggio commerciale o di acquisto di proprietà?
- Gli autori del progetto si impegnano finanziariamente in prima persona?

3. a) CONTROLLO DEGLI INVESTIMENTI

Dopo aver proceduto ad un investimento, si dovrebbe controllarne la validità :

- facendosi consegnare ed esaminando delle relazioni sui progressi ottenuti ;
- garantendo, se necessario, l'aggiornamento del piano di investimento ;
- occupando, se possibile, un seggio nel consiglio di amministrazione ;
- fornendo un'assistenza concreta al gruppo direttivo.

3.b) IL MOMENTO DEL REALIZZO

Non esiste ovviamente al riguardo alcuna norma precisa e codificata, ma è preferibile ritirarsi prima che si arresti il tasso di crescita, vale a dire con un certo tempismo.

CONCLUSIONI E RACCOMANDAZIONI

Iniziative di carattere legislativo sono necessarie per migliorare il diritto di opzione dei membri delle società operanti con capitali di rischio all'acquisto di azioni.

La libera circolazione dei capitali nell'ambito della Communità europea è necessaria se si intendono raccogliere i frutti di una cooperazione transnazionale in materia di capitali di rischio.

Si dovrebbe organizzare un maggior numero di corsi di iniziazione alla gestione dei capitali di rischio.

Si dovrebbero infine sviluppare delle banche di dati sulle possibilità offerte in questo settore a livello comunitario.

QUINTA SESSIONE - RIASSUNTO DELLA RIUNIONE DEL 25.11.1983

Riepilogo del sig. I. N. MOMTCHILOFF,

General Manager, Investors in Industry Group PLC, London

Devo ora riassumere questo simposio, ma evitero' di farlo poiché si tratta di un compito quasi impossibile. Desidero tuttavia farvi partecipi di un paio di mie riflessioni personali.

La signora LEBAS ha cercato di convincerci - appassionatamente, devo dire - che cio' che conta è il sistema. Secondo me, non c'è dubbio che lo sviluppo di un mercato secondario costituisce un contributo essenziale al sistema dei capitali di rischio.

Sono un deciso sostenitore di una precisa normativa nell'ambito dei mercati, ma, a mio modo di vedere, se bisogna incoraggiare le attività riguardanti i capitali di rischio, una componente essenziale di qualsiasi sistema è costituita da un mercato secondario regolamentato con giudizio e assennatamente orientato. Cio' è necessario per colui che rischia effetivamente il suo futuro per dar vita ad una società.

Dopo tutto, durante i lunghi periodi nei quali nel Regno Unito non abbiamo avuto accesso a un mercato secondario, chiunque avesse cominciato per proprio conto o nell'ambito di un gruppo aveva solamente due modi per fare soldi in base all'investimento iniziale.

Il primo consisteva nel costituire una società di tali dimensioni, stabilità e livello qualitativo da poter accedere al mercato primario e ottenere una quotazione pubblica. Si tratto di una prospettiva scoraggiante e costantemente mutevole, poiché alcuni anni fa era possibile accedere al mercato principale con utili di 250.00 lire sterline, ma solo alcuni anni dopo erano necessari utili di un milione e ancora successivamente di un millione e mezzo. Una parte di questo aumento è devuto all'inflazione, ma -ripeto- solamente una parte. Relativamente poche società sulle centinaia che iniziano possono aspirare a raggiungere tale obiettivo.

L'altro modo in cui è possibile incassare denaro è vendere, ma molte persone che costituiscono delle società non hanno in realtà questo obiettivo. Esse danno vita a delle società semplicemente perché desiderano costituire una impresa.

L'esistenza del mercato secondario fornisce un'altra dimensione. Cio' significa che le possibilità di queste persone di procurarsi denaro altrui e di realizzare una parte del loro investimento personale (forse lo fanno per potersi permettere un'automobile, o una seconda automobile, o forse una Rolls-Royce) sono, nel Regno Unito, decisamente aumentate. Se non è possibile dare incentivi alla gente che cerca di mettere in piedi una attività, vuol dire che stiamo perdendo il nostro tempo, poiché sono queste persone che creano ricchezza. Esse devono fare soldi : coloro che li finanziano devono fare soldi ; in realtà tutti coloro che fanno parte del sistema devono avere un incentivo per assumere i rischi insiti nell'operazione. Se ci sono quindi ostacoli che si frappongono al corretto funzionamento del sistema è allora compito dei governi, della Commissione, di noi tutti darsi da fare per rimuoverli.

Il secondo punto che vorrei sottolineare è un punto al quale ho già accennato in precedenza, ma che ritengo essere tremendamente importante : vi è una maggiore necessità di 'capitale di sviluppo' in Europa di quanto non ce ne sia per stravaganti capitali di rischio. Siffatto tipo di investimento assicura stabilità e buon potenziale di guadagno. Esso non dovrebbe essere trascurato, poiché se troppi gruppi iniziano ed hanno l'ambizione di operare solamente ad un certo livello, allora molti dovranno dichiarare fallimento ed io non vorrei vedere questo fantastico sviluppo del finanziamento a reddito variabile delle società private cadere in discredito a causa di ambizioni non realistiche.

Potrebbe essere l'inizio di un altro piccolo Medio Evo. Cio' succede in America. Ricordo di aver visto a Minneapolis, non molti anni fa, una parte della sala delle contrattazioni con tre tabelloni bianchi. Chiedo che cosa sono e mi sento rispondere : 'Erano la nostra sezione Nasdaq[1]. Il mercato è morto. Sono finiti i giorni del P.E. a due cifre'.

Penso che prima o poi il mercato americano subirà un calo ; ritengo che lo stesso potrà accadere anche all'U.S.M. (Mercato dei titoli non quotati in borsa).

1) 'National Association of Securities Dealers' Automated Quotation'

La mia ultima riflessione di cui vorrei farvi partecipi riguarda l'elemento transnazionale. Tutti sanno che le nostre possibilità di attaccare il mercato europeo nel suo insieme con un prodotto o un servizio incontrano numerose difficoltà a causa di una vasta gamma di ostacoli : barriere non doganali, comportamenti diversi da paese a paese , ecc. E' purtroppo vero che il primo mercato al quale guardano coloro che intendono dar vita ad una impresa di tipo moderno sono gli Stati Uniti. Con cio' non voglio dire che gli Stati Uniti andrebbero trascurati, poiché in effetti essi costituiscono il più grande mercato del mondo, ma è un peccato per noi europei non poter disporre di un vasto mercato tutto per noi.

Per il momento, vi è una tendenza verso un sempre maggiore protezionismo. Ogni paese desidera essere considerato attivo in settori alla moda, con tecnologie di punta e si orienta ad avere la sua piccola impresa di robotica, ad esempio, da custodire gelosamente. Questo è un errore fatale.

Ritengo ora che lo sviluppo di una forte industria di capitale di rischio possa essere, in questo caso, di aiuto. Forse, coinvolgendo varie institutuzioni nel capitale di rischio e facendo lore comprendere che operano in un mercato internazionale, riusciremo a dimostrare che torna a vantaggio degli Stati membri lavorare tutti insieme.

Se si riesce a far si' che la gente affidi importanti somme di capitale di rischio, si riuscirà allora ad avere un'incidenza sulla filosofia dei governi, delle istituzioni e dell'industria. Non sarà per domani, ma nutro la reale speranza che - almeno per quelle imprese che saranno alla base del nostro futuro - dovremo approfittare dell'esistenza del mercato comune, maggiormente di quanto non siamo riusciti a fare con le imprese attualmente in via di estinzione.

LIST OF PARTICIPANTS

LIST OF PARTICIPANTS

ABBEY, J.
Secrétaire général
Fédération Internationale
des Bourses de Valeurs
22, bd de Courcelles
F - 75017 PARIS

ADAM, W.A.
Directeur
AI Management
Division Adam International B.V.
144, av. E. Plasky
B - 1040 BRUXELLES

ADAMSON, D.L.
An Investigation of Unquoted
Holdings of U.K. Financial
Institutions
Nuffield College
GB - OXFORD OX1 1NF

AIGNESBERGER, C.
Wissenschaftlicher Angestellter
Universität Mannheim
Naumannstr. 18
D - 6800 MANNHEIM

ALEXAKIS, G.
Commission des Communautés
européennes, Direction générale
"Affaires économiques et financières"
200, rue de la Loi
B - 1040 BRUXELLES

ALLEMAN, S.
Manager Financial Department
De Nationale
Investeringsbank N.V.
Carnegieplein 4
NL - 2517 KJ DEN HAAG

ALLEN, G.D.
Management Counsellors
Technology & Market Assessment
Chemical Process & Biotechnology
Industries
341, av. Louise, bte 10
B - 1050 BRUXELLES

APPLEYARD, R.
Directeur général
"Marché de l'Information et Innovation"
Commission des Communautés européennes
200, rue de la Loi
B - 1040 BRUXELLES

AREND, R.
Attaché au Département des
Crédits Internationaux
Banque Internationale
à Luxembourg S.A.
2, bd Royal
L - 2449 LUXEMBOURG

ASAKAWA, S.
Toshiba
Audrey House, Ely Place
GB - LONDON EC1

AUTINO, G.
Représentant permanent
Bureau de Bruxelles de la
Confédération Internationale
du Crédit Populaire
38, av. des Arts, Bte 9
B - 1040 BRUXELLES

AXIOMAKAROS, P.
Dipl.-Wirtsch-Ing.
Data Bank LTD
P.O. Box 76005
GR - 17110 NEA SMYRNI - ATHENS

AYRES, B.
Venture Capital International
720 So. Colorado blvd. Suite 940
USA - DENVER CO. 80222

BACHE, J.P.
Commission des Communautés
européennes Direction générale
"Affaires économiques et financières
200, rue de la Loi
B - 1040 BRUXELLES

BACHRACH, E.
Granville & Cie
27, Lovat Lane
GB - LONDON

BALL, B.
Public Servant
Dept of Science and Technology - 7FL
339, Swanston Street
Australia - 3000 MELBOURNE, Victoria

BARTHELEMY, J.P.
Conseiller scientifique
Société Cachot
11, av. Victor-Hugo
F - 75116 PARIS

BATTINI, P.
Chargé d'Affaires
SOFINNOVA
51, rue Saint Georges
F - 75009 PARIS

BECHTOLD, T.
Unternehmensberater
DVC Venture Capital GmbH
Hauptmannsreute 91
D - 7000 STUTTGART 1

BELARD, A.M.
Sous-Directeur
Caisse Centrale des
Banques Populaires
115, rue Montmartre
F - 75002 PARIS

BENELLI, N.
Direttore centrale
Cassa di Risparmio
di Trieste
Casella Postale 481 Centro
I - 34100 CENTRO

BIRGET, A.
Banque Générale du Luxembourg S.A.
14, rue Aldringen
L - 1118 LUXEMBOURG

BLACKIE, P.A.
Commission des Communautés
européennes, Direction générale
"Affaires économiques et financières"
200, rue de la Loi
B - 1049 BRUXELLES

BLOHM, B.
Redakteur
Handelsblattredaktion
Kasernenstr. 27
D - 4000 DUESSELDORF 1

BOEHM, H.
Dipl.-Volkswirtin
Kreditanstalt für Wiederaufbau
Palmengartenstrasse 5-9
D - 6000 FRANKFURT AM MAIN

BOETTGER, G.
Westdeutsche Landesbank Girozentrale
Friedrichstrasse 56, Postfach 1128
D - 4000 DUESSELDORF 1

BOLAND, M.
Conseiller à la Direction Générale
Institut National des Radioéléments
Zoning Industriel
B - 6220 FLEURUS

BOLLINO, G.
Directeur central
Istituto Mobiliare Italiano
Bureau de représentation
auprès de la CEE
67, rue de la Vallée, bte 7
B - 1050 BRUXELLES

BOTTENBERG, A.P.
Staatsbeamter
Wirtschaftsministerium
Bezuidenhootseweg 30
NL - 's GRAVENHAGE

BOUDIN, M.
Ingénieur, Directeur
COCKERILL SAMBRE
Direction Reconversion
& Développement
29, allée des Ecureuils
B - 6428 HAM-SUR-HEURE

BOUSQUET, J.
Secrétaire général
FINNOVELEC
6, Rue Ancelle
F - 92200 NEUILLY

BRAND, M.
Dipl.-Kfm.
Arbeitskreis Aktie E.V.
Berliner Allee 4
D - 4000 DUESSELDORF 1

BRASSEM, E.A.
Assistant International Tax Manager
Amro Bank
Herengracht 595
NL - 1017 CE AMSTERDAM

BURGARD, H.
Commission des Communautés
européennes, Direction générale
"Marché de l'information
et innovation"
Bâtiment Jean Monnet
L - LUXEMBOURG

CANDRIES, L.
General Manager
Candries Sports
Industry
125, Gentsesteenweg
B - 2800 MECHELEN

CARBONNEL, P.
Représentant permanent
de la Confédération Internationale
du Crédit Populaire auprès des C.E.
38, av. des Arts, bte 9
B - 1040 BRUXELLES

CARDON, V.
Ecole de Commerce Solvay
Université Libre de Bruxelles
229, av. Montjoie
B - 1180 BRUXELLES

CARLETTI, A.
Marketing
Banca Nationale dell'Agricoltura
Via dei Giornalisti 41
I - 00135 ROMA

CARRE', O.
Institut Orléannais
de Finance
294, av. du Loiret
F - 45160 OLIVET

CARROLL, N.V.G.
Associate Director
Allied Irish Investment
Bank Limited
Bankcentre Ballsbridge
IR - DUBLIN 4

CASPERS, R.
Professor
European Business School
Schloss Reichartshausen am Rhein
D - 6227 OESTRICH-Winkel (Rheingau)

CLAROTTI, P.
Commission des Communautés
européennes Direction générale
"Institutions financières
et fiscalité"
200, rue de la Loi
B - 1049 BRUXELLES

CLAUS, D.
Dipl.-Volkswirt
NORD/LB Hannover
Georgsplatz 1
D - 3000 HANNOVER 1

CLEIFTIE, C.
Directeur adjoint
Sofinnova
51, rue St Georges
F - 75009 PARIS

COCCO, S.
Mediocredito Lombardo
Via Broletto 20
I - 20121 MILANO

COLLE, F.
Directeur
Charbonnages de France
9, av. Percier, B.P. 396 08
F - 75360 PARIS CEDEX 08

COLLING, F.
Député, Ing. Dipl.
INFO Arbed
6, rue Adolphe
L - LUXEMBOURG

COLLOWALD, P.
Conseil Médical
Commission des
Communautés européennes
25, rue Archimède
B - 1049 BRUXELLES

CREPET, M.
Directeur des Credits
Chambre Syndicale
des Banques Populaires
131, av. de Wagram
F - 75017 PARIS

CROSS, N.E.
Investors in Industry plc
91, Waterloo Road
GB - LONDON SE1 8XP

DAMIEN, V.
Conseiller
Sociéte Regionale
d'Investissement de Wallonie
Rés. Concorde
19, Pl. Josephine Charlotte, Bte 1
B - 5100 JAMBES

DASKALOPOULOS, J.
Agricultural Bank
of Greece
23, Panepistimiou Str.
GR - 132 ATHENS

DE BLOCQ VAN KUFFELER, J.P.
Director
Brown, Skipley and Co. Ltd
Flanders Court. Lothbury
GB - LONDON EC2R 7HE

DE BRUYN, R.
Exec.-Financ. Probl.
Confederazione
Industria Italiana
Vile Astronomia 30
I - 00149 ROMA

Y FABLO DE LA NUEZ
Agent de change
Bourse de Valeurs de Madrid
1, Plaza de la Lealtad
E - MADRID 14

DE MAUTORT, L.
Chef de Département
C.E.P.I.I.
(Commissariat Général du Plan)
9, rue Georges Pitard
F - 75015 PARIS

DE SCHRIJVER,
Administrator
Min. van Economische Zaken
Beatrixlaan, 7
NL - 2595 AK DEN HAAG K312

DE SCITIVAUX, M.
Directeur du Développement
SOFARIS
4, rue Cambon
F - 75001 PARIS

DEAN, G.
Managing Director
Electra Risk
Capital PLC
Temple Place, Victoria Embankment
GB - LONDON WC2R 3HP

DEARING, N.
Manager, Small Business, Section
National Westminster
Bank P.L.C.
3, Rd Floor, 116 Fenchurch Street
GB - LONDON EC3M 5AN

DECLERCQ, G.
Président
INVESTCO N.V.
54, bd du Régent. Bt. 2
B - 1000 BRUXELLES

DEGNER, H.
Syndikus
Vorstand der Hanseatischen
Wertpapierbörse Hamburg
Börse, I. Stock, Zimmer 151
D - 2000 HAMBURG 11

DELIEGE, M.
Manager
Arthur Andersen & Co.
56, Avenue des Arts
B - 1040 BRUXELLES

DELVA, E.
Direttore centrale -Serv. Crediti
Cassa di Risparmio di Verona
Vicenza e Belluno, Direzione generale
Via Garibaldi 1
I - 37121 VERONA

DEMEURE, T.
Directeur adjoint
Société Générale de Banque
3, Montagne du Parc
B - 1000 BRUXELLES

DESANTI, U.
Directeur adjoint
Lavoro International Bank
25, Bd Royal. P.O. Box 286
L - LUXEMBOURG

DICKEN, N.
Journaliste
Letzeburger Journal
123, rue Ad. Fischer
L - LUXEMBOURG

DORN, G.
Wirtschaftsingenieur
Technologieberatungsstelle Ruhr
30-32, Ostring
D - 4630 BOCHUM 1

DOUMONT, M.
Attaché de Direction
Association Belge
des Banques
36 rue Ravenstein , bte 5
B - 1000 BRUXELLES

DOURNEL, P.
Expert,
DG XIII Commission des
Communautés européennes
26, Rond-Point de l'Esplanade
F - 67000 STRASBOURG

DUNCAN, M.
Fonctionnaire de Bourse
Bourse de Valeurs
de Milan
P.zza Affari, 6
I - 20123 MILANO

DUPOND, A.H.
Directeur financier
Banque Industrielle
et Mobilière Privée
22, rue Pasquier
F - 75383 PARIS CEDEX 08

DURCAN, P.
Senior Manager
Allied Irish Investment
Bank Limited
Bankcentre Ballsbridge
IR - DUBLIN 4

ELBERTSE, E.A.M.
Sekretär
Zentralverband
Niederländischer Unternehmen
Postfach 93093
NL - 2509 AB DEN HAAG

ENGELHARDT, K.
Wissenschaftlicher Leiter
Technologieberatungsstelle Ruhr
30-32, Ostring
D - 4630 BOCHUM 1

ERNST, G.
Privatbankier
Delbrück & Co
Rankestrasse 13
D - 1000 BERLIN 30

ERNST, M.
Faculté Universitaire de
Science Economique à Namur
28, rue du Centre
B - 4660 THIMISTER

FLAVIN, J.
Managing Director
Development Capital
Corporation Limited
DCC House, Stillorgan,
Blackrock
IR - Co. DUBLIN

FLEMINKS, T.
Sr. Manager Securities Division
RABOBANK NEDERLAND
169, Gildenkwartier
NL - 3503 SE UTRECHT

FLORNOY, Y.
Syndic
Chambre Syndicale
des Agents de Changes
4, Place de la Bourse
F - 75002 PARIS

FLYNN, C.
Technical Services Manager
Allied Irish Banks Ltd.
Credit Policy
& Control Department
Bankcentre, Ballsbridge
IR - DUBLIN 4

FONTAINE, P.
Ingénieur, Chef de service
Reconversion & Développement - Liège
S.A. COCKERILL SAMBRE
21, Quai Louva
B - 4200 OUGREE

FONTANEAU, P.
Professeur des Facultés de Droit
Avocat à la Cour de Paris
28, rue de Franqueville
F - 75116 PARIS

FRAGOSO, J.
Administrateur
Caixa Geral de Depositos
Largo Do Calhariz 1109
P - LISBOA CODEX

FRIGESSI DI RATTALMA, G.
Vice Direttore
Istituto per la Ricostruzione
Industriale - IRI
Via Vittorio Veneto, 89
I - 00187 ROMA

FRITSCH, U.
Geschäftsführer
Arbeitskreis Aktie E.V.
Berliner Allee 4
D - 4000 DUESSELDORF 1

FROUG, B.
Venture Capital International
720 So. Colorado blvd., Suite 940
USA - DENVER CO. 80222

FUCHS, R.O.
Schriftführer
Secretary
Amsterdam Stock Exchange
Beursplein 5
NL - 1012 JW AMSTERDAM

GASTONE, P.G.
Business Development
Air Products Ltd.
Hersham Place, Molesey Road
GB - WALTON-ON-THAMES,
Surrey KT12 4RZ

GAUTRY, P.
Institut Orléannais
de Finance
33, rue des Hautes Levées
F - 45100 ST PRYVE ST MESMIN

GENIE, P.
Inspecteur général
B.N.B.
5, bd de Berlaimont
B - 1000 BRUXELLES

GIBB, J.M.
Commission des Communautés
européennes, Direction générale
"Marché de l'information
et innovation"
Bâtiment Jean Monnet
L - LUXEMBOURG

GOODMAN, B.
Commission des Communautés
européennes, Direction générale
"Marché de l'information
et innovation"
Bâtiment Jean Monnet
L - LUXEMBOURG

GRANDI, P.
Mediocredito Lombardo
Via Broletto 20
I - 20121 MILANO

GREPPI, E.
Banque Européenne
D'Investissements
Bvd. Konrad Adenauer
L - LUXEMBOURG

GROENEVELT, B.
Manager
Eindhoven University
P.O. Box 513
NL - 56000 MB 1 EINDHOVEN

GROMMEK, S.
Unternehmensberater
Luisenstr. 11
D - 7600 OFFENBURG

GUINOT, F.
Attaché de direction
Renault Entreprises
Industrielles
Quai le Gallo
F - BOULOGNE BILLANCOURT

GUTH, R.
Commission des Communautés
européennes, Direction générale
"Marché de l'information
et innovation"
200, rue de la Loi
B - 1049 BRUXELLES

HAETRICH, W.
Professor
European Business School
Schloss Reichartshausen am Rhein
D - 6227 OESTRICH-Winkel (Rheingau)

HAHN, O.
Commission des Communautés
européennes, Direction générale
"Crédit et investissements"
Bâtiment Jean Monnet
L - LUXEMBOURG

HAMILTON, R.J.C.
General Manager
Pegasus Holdings Ltd
11 - 15, Monument St.
GB - LONDON EC3R 8JU

HANSEN, J.
Director
Federation of
Danish Industrie
18, H.C. Andersens Boulevard
DK - COPENHAGEN V.

HARMSEN, D.M.
Senior Research Analyst
Fraunhofer-Institut für
Systemtechnik und
Innovationsforschung
Breslauer Strasse 48
D - 7500 KARLSRUHE 1

HARNIER, O.
Conseil des Ministres
des Communautés Européennes
170, rue de la Loi
B - 1040 BRUXELLES

HAUG-ADRION, E.
Commission des Communautés
européennes, Direction générale
"Institutions financières
et fiscalité"
200, rue de la Loi
B - 1040 BRUXELLES

HAYDEN, J.D.
Snr. Vice President - Europe
Dataquest Lokj Ltd
144 146 New bond St.
GB - LONDON W1

HENRIKSEN, O.B.
Directeur général
Commission des Communautés
européennes, Direction générale
"Institutions financières
et fiscalité"
8, square de Meeûs
B - 1049 BRUXELLES

HEYDT,
Hoofd Adm.
Min. van Economische Zaken
Beatrixlaan, 7
NL - 2595 AK DEN HAAG K312

HODGSON, R.G.
Managing Director
Granville & Co. Limited
27-28 Lovat Lane
GB - LONDON EC3R 8EB

HUECKER, G.
Diplom-Volkswirt
Berliner Industriebank
Landecker Strasse 2-3
D - 1000 BERLIN 33

HUNGEN, R.
Regierungsdirektor
Bundesamt für Finanzen
Friedhofstr. 1
D - 5300 BONN 2

INCLEDON, J.D.
Chairman
Hilger Analytical ltd.
Suite 33, 140 Park Lane
GB - LONDON W1Y 3AA

JACOUT, O.
Consultant
Braxton Associés
10, rue de La Paix
F - 75002 PARIS

JACQUOT, J.P.
Banque Européenne d'Investissement
100, bd. K. Adenauer
L - LUXEMBOURG

JANIETZ, J.B.
Journaliste
Luxemburger - Wort
B.P. 1908
L - LUXEMBOURG

JANSSELME, A.
Chargé de Mission
Administration Française
Braxton Associés
10, rue de la Paix
F - 75002 PARIS

JONES, J.L.
Adviser International Affairs
The Stock Exchange
GB - LONDON EC2N 1HP

KALIPOLITIS, A.
Chem. Eng.
Agricultural Bank of Greece
23, Panepistimiou Str.
GR - 10221 ATHENS

KANE, E.W.
Vice President and Director
John Hancock Venture
Capital Management, inc.
P.O. Box 111
USA - BOSTON MA 02117

KAPLAN, P.T.
Partner
Weil, Gotshal and Manges
767, Fifth Avenue
USA - NEW YORK NY 10153

KARSCH, W.
Redaktion "Die Bank"
13, Gereonsdriesch, Postfach 100965
D - 5000 KOELN 1

KIRSCH, R.
Président
Société Nationale de
Crédit et d'Investissement
3, rue de la Congrégation
L - 1352 LUXEMBOURG

KOERBER, K.O.
Verbandsgeschäftsführer
Verband der Lebensversicherungs-
Unternehmen e.v.
Eduard-Pflüger-Str. 55
D - 5300 BONN 1

KRAUSE, H.J.
Dipl.-Kfm - Abteilungsdirektor
Bundesverbandes
deutscher Banken e.V.
35/41, Mohrenstr.
D - 5000 KOELN 1

KREYS, F.
Techno Venture
Management GmbH 2CoKG
57, Smaninger Str.
D - 8000 MUENCHEN 80

KRUYFF, L.
Advisor
Center for Micro-Electronics
Eindhoven, P.O. Box 128
NL - 5600 AC EINDHOVEN

KUEHR, T.
IVCP - International Venture
Capital Partners S.A. Holding
35, rue Glesener
L - 1631 LUXEMBOURG

LACOSTE, F.
Conseiller financier
35, bd d'Inkermann
F - 92200 NEUILLY

LAMBOPAY, M.
Directeur
Société de la
Bourse de Luxembourg
11, av. de la Porte-Neuve
L - 2227 LUXEMBOURG

LANGEN, R.
Geschäftsführer
Stahlbearbeitungs -
Zentrum Saarbrücken GmbH
Hochstrasse, 67 (Burbacher Hütte)
D - 6600 SAARBRUECKEN

LANNOY, J.
Conseiller spécial de la
Commission des Communautés européennes
14, route de Diekirch
L - 6705 FRASSEN-BONNEST

LEBAS, P.
Présidente, Responsable d'études
Association - Recherche sur les
Sociétés à Technologies
37, rue Serpente
F - 95800 CERGY

LEMAIRE, R.
Gérant de Stés
724, Bois d'Achelles
F - 59910 BONDUES

LEWINTRE, J.M.
Compagnie Financière
d'Epargne et de Finances BRED
18, quai de la Rapé
F - 75012 PARIS

LIEBERT, W.
Diplom-Kaufmann
Liebert & Partner
13 a, Tauentzienstrasse
D - 1000 BERLIN 30

LUECK, J.T.
Dipl.-Volkswirt
BMW Technology Partners
545, Middlefield Road, Ste 160
USA - MENLO PARK, CA 94025

LUTZ, W.
Conseiller
Groupement des Caisses
D'Epargne de la CEE
92-94, square Plasky, bte 1
B - 1040 BRUXELLES

MACK, M.
Conseiller de Direction
ABC - AFINNOVAC
148, bd Malesherbes
F - 75017 PARIS

MAQUIL, M.
Sous-Directeur
Société de la Bourse
de Luxembourg S.A.
Boîte postale 165
L - 2011 LUXEMBOURG

MARANJIAN, L.
Consultant
Creative Strategies Int'L
Banda House
Cambridge Grove
GB - LONDON W6 OLN

MATI, C.
Lic. rer. pol.
Schweizerische
Bankiervereinigung
Aeschenvorstadt 4
CH - 4002 BASEL

MATZKA, A.
Kreditreferent
Finanzierungs-garantie-
Ges.m.b.H.
Hoher Markt 9
A - 1010 WIEN

MAZZOLA, B.
Research Department
Istituto Bancario San Paolo
di Torino
Via Santa Teresa, 3
I - 10121 TORINO

MENSCH, G.
Professor
School of Management
Case Western
Reserve University
311 Wickenden
USA - CLEVELAND, OHIO 44106

METZGER, M.
Oberregierungsrat
Bundesministerium für
Forshung und Technologie
Postfach 200607
D - 5300 BONN 2

MOMTCHILOFF, I.
General manager
Investors in Industry
Group PLC
91 Waterloo Road
GB - LONDON SE1 8XP

MONDELLO, F.
Rep. Confindustria
Confederazione Generale
dell'Industria Italiana
1, av. Joyeuse Entrée, bte 11
B - 1040 BRUXELLES

MONMART, J.P.
Directeur
Bourse de Bruxelles
Palais de la Bourse
B - BRUXELLES

MOREL, M.
Soginnove, filiale de
la Société Générale
rue Boudreau
F - 75009 PARIS

MOSSING, M.
Danmarks Sparekasseforening
Købmagergade
DK - 1150 COPENHAGEN K

McGOVERN, B.
Financial analyst
Industrial development
Authority
Lansdoune house, Ballsbridge
IR - DUBLIN 4

McGRATH, M.
Project Development Executive
Entreprise House
Plassey Technological Park
IR - LIMERICK

NATHUSIUS, K.
IVCP - International Venture
Capital Partners S.A. Holding
35, rue Glesner
L - 1631 LUXEMBOURG

NEUMANN, W.
INFOBRIEF Luxembourg Sàrl
Postfach 206
L - 2012 LUXEMBOURG

NICCOLINI, M.
Ingenieur
Confindustria Segreteria G.G.I.
Via Astronomia 30
I - ROMA

NICOLAS, J.M.
Directeur Général
INNOVEST S.F.I.
3, Le Sébastopol, Quai Kléber
F - 67055 STRASBOURG CEDEX

O'HOGAN, D.
Arthur Young & Co.
Portbello House
IR - DUBLIN 8

OLSEN, J.
Assistant Commissioner
Electronic Media
Telestyrelsen
Anker Heegaards Gade 4
DK - 1503 KOBENHAVN V

ONIANS, R.A.
Director Business Development
Monsanto Europe SA
270-272, av. de Tervuren, bte 1
B - 1150 BRUXELLES

OOMS, M.
Adviser, Gewestelijke
Investeringsmaatschappij
voor Vlaanderen
1-3, Anneessensstraat, Bus 1
B - 2018 ANTWERPEN

ORTH, G.
Prognos AG Basel
Steinengraben, 42
CH - 11011 BASEL

OUZOUNIS, G.
Financial Analyst
Agricultural Bank
of Greece
25, Panepistimiou Str.
GR - 10221 ATHENS

OYARZABAL DELGADO, M.
Centro Para el Desarrollo
Tecnologico Industrial
Ministerio de Industria y Energia
C/Ramirez de Arellano S/N
Edificio GAN
E - MADRID 27

PERRY, R.
Director, Policy Analysis
IDEA Corporation
33 Yonge Street, Suite 800
Canada - TORONTO, ONTARIO M5E IV3

PETIT, P.
Directeur (Div. Etudes Economiques)
Chambre Syndicale
des Banques Populaires
131, av. de Wagram
F - 75847 PARIS CEDEX 17

PHILLIPS, B.
Commission des Communautés
européennes, Direction générale
"Crédit et investissements"
Bâtiment Jean Monnet
L - LUXEMBOURG

PHILLIPS, E.
Commission des Communautés
européennes, Direction générale
"Marché de l'Information et Innovation"
Bâtiment Jean Monnet
L - LUXEMBOURG

PICCA, N.
Directeur Général
IMI International
Holdings S.A.
63, av. de la Liberté
B.P. 1022
L - 1010 LUXEMBOURG

POUZET, G.
Banque Privée de
Gestion Financière
61, rue de Monceau
F - 75008 PARIS

PRIES, G.
Banque Générale
du Luxembourg S.A.
14, rue Aldringen
L - 1118 LUXEMBOURG

PROSSER, D.J.
Managing Director
CIN Industrial
Investments Ltd.
10, Bouverie Street
GB - LONDON EC4Y 8BA

RAPPARINI, R.
Commission des Communautés
européennes, Direction générale
"Marché de l'information
et innovation"
Bâtiment Jean Monnet
L - LUXEMBOURG

RETTAROLI, R.
Officer
Italian Banking Association
Piazza Del Gesu' 49
I - 00186 ROMA

REVELAS, K.
Commission des Communautés
européennes, Direction générale
"Crédit et investissements"
Bâtiment Jean Monnet
L - LUXEMBOURG

ROELANDT, P.
Administrator
European Venture
Capital Association
Clos du Parnasse 11F
B - 1040 BRUXELLES

ROERICHT, R.
Leiter Büro Technologietransfer
der Rheinisch-Westfälischen
Technischen Hochschule Aachen
Templergraben 55
D - 5100 AACHEN

ROSA, C.
Direttore generale
Ital-Finanziaria
Piazza Venezia 5
I - 00187 ROMA

ROSSELJONG, G.
Attaché de Direction
Caisse d'Epargne
de l'Etat
1, Place de Metz
L - 2954 LUXEMBOURG

ROTONDO', P.P.
Commission des Communautés
européennes, Direction générale
"Marché de l'information
et innovation"
Bâtiment Jean Monnet
L - LUXEMBOURG

RUECKERT, D.
Commission des Communautés
européennes, Direction générale
"Marché de l'information
et innovation"
Bâtiment Jean Monnet
L - LUXEMBOURG

RUIZ DE VELASCO, A.
Agent de change
Bourse de Valeurs de Madrid
1, Plaza de la Lealtad
E - MADRID 14

S. BERGARECHE BUSQUET
General Manager
Sociedad Bancaya de Promoción
Empresarial (Grupo Banco Vizcaya)
Po de la Castellana 110
E - MADRID 6

SCHIERMEYER, R.
Bank Kaufmann
Deutsche Bank
Berlin AG
6/16, Otto-Suhr-Allee
D - 1000 BERLIN 10

SCHMIDT, H.
Institut für Geld- und
Kapitalverkehr der
Universität Hamburg
5, Van-Melle-Park
D - 2000 HAMBURG 13

SCHMITZ, C.
Université Paris-Dauphine
(Doctorat en finance)
30, av. de la Gare
L - 1018 LUXEMBOURG

SCHMIT, P.
Attaché de Direction
Caisse d'Epargne
de l'Etat
1, place de Metz
L - 2954 LUXEMBOURG

SCHOOFS, J.
Techn. Univ. Eindhoven
Ind. Liais. Dept
Postbus 513
NL - 5600 MB EINDHOVEN

SCHOUPPE, F.
Directeur
INVESTCO N.V.
54, bd du Régent, bt 2
B - 1000 BRUXELLES

SCHUBERT, A.H.
Rechtsanwalt
Syndicus der Bremer
Wertpapierbörse
Postfach 10 07 26, Domshof 11
D - 2800 BREMEN 1

SCHULTHEISS, G.
Sous-Directeur
Société Générale Alsacienne
de Banque
8, rue du Dôme
F - 67000 STRASBOURG

SCHWARZE, H.J.
Syndikus
Berliner Wertpapierbörse
16 -18, Hardenbergstr.
D - 1000 BERLIN 12

SCHWEICKART, K.
Rechtsanwalt
Günther-Quandt-Haus
Seedammweg 55
D - 6380 BAD HOMBURG v.d.H.

SCOTTO, M.
Journaliste
Le Monde
100, av. des Hêtres Rouges
B - 1970 WEZEMBEEK OPPEM

SCOTT, P.
European Associate
Johnson & Johnson
Development Corporation
Runnymede, Malthouse
Runnymede Road
GB - EGHAM, TW20 9BO

SERBINIS, P.
Economist
Agricultural Bank
of Greece
23, Panepistimiou Str.
GR - 10221 ATHENS

SEVENANS, M.
Manager
Philips Int. Finance
Boîte postale 196
L - LUXEMBOURG

SIEGERT, G.
Wissenschaftl. Mitarbeiter
Fraunhofer-Institut für
Systemtechnik u. Innovationsforschung
Breslauer Str. 48
D - 7500 KARLSRUHE 1

SILVEIRA GODINHO, J.A.
Economist
Banco Espirito Santo e
Comercial de Lisboa
Avenida da Liberdade, 195-150
P - 1200 LISBOA

SJOEBERG, S.
President
Connova Invest AB
33, Stora Nygatan
S - 411 08 GOTHENBURG

SMITH, R.
Journaliste
McGraw-Hill
22, rue des Acacias
B - 1950 BRUXELLES

SPIERENDONK, S.P.
Divisional Manager
AMRO BANK
595 Herengracht
NL - 1017 CE AMSTERDAM

STOECK, W.
Börsensyndikus
Frankfurter
Wertpapierbörse
Börsenplatz, 6-10
D - 6000 FRANKFURT am MAIN 1

STOKES, W.F.
Senior Executive EEC Affairs
National Westminster Bank
41, Lothbury
GB - LONDON EC2P 2BP

STOLTE, H.M.
Managing Director
Gamma Holding N.V.
P.O. Box 80
NL - 5700 AB HELMOND

STORMONTH-DARLING, R.A.
Laing and Cruickshank
Mc Anally, Montgomery and Co
Piercy House, Cophall Avenue
GB - LONDON EC2R 7BE

TAHON, F.
Ingénieur
Chambre Régionale de Commerce
et d'Industrie de Haute Normandie
Palais des Conseils
Quai de la Bourse
F - 76007 ROUEN CEDEX

TAYLOR, I.C.
Executive Director
Midland Bank
Industrial Finance Limited
22, Watling Street
GB - LONDON EC4M 9BR

TELLINI, G.
Managing Director
SO.FI.PA. - Societa'
Finanziaria di Partecipazione S.p.A.
Via Saverio Mercadante, 9
I - 00100 ROMA

TROOST, C.
Assistant Director
De Nationale Investeringsbank N.V.
4, Carnegieplein
NL - 2517 KJ DEN HAAG

TSIAVOS, D.
General Manager
Investment Bank
1, Corai street
GR - ATHENS

VAHLBERG, J.
Deutscher Bundestag
Bundeshaus Room NH 1512
D - 5300 BONN

VAN ACKER, G.
General Manager
Gewestelijke
Investeringsmaatschappij
voor Vlaanderen
1 - 3, Anneessensstraat/Bus 1
B - 2018 ANTWERPEN

VAN DE VEN, F.J.J.M.
Manager Corporate Finance
Bank ITEC
Nassauplein 27, P.O. Box 308
NL - 2501 CH THE HAGUE

VAN DER STICHELE, M.
Administrateur-Directeur
s.a. PROMINVEST
24, av. Marnix 24
B - 1050 BRUXELLES

VAN DER VLUGT, H.
Commission des Communautés
européennes, Direction générale
"Affaires économiques et financières"
Bâtiment Jean Monnet
L - LUXEMBOURG

VAN HAVRE, J.C.
Director (Board)
Candries Sport Industry
125, Genstesteenweg
B - 2800 MECHELEN

VAN HOUT, D.S.
General Manager
Investments and
Corporate Finance, ENNIA NV
P.O. Box 202
NL - 2501 CE's-GRAVENHAGE

VAN OUTRYVE D'YDEWALLE, R.
President
Gewestelijke
Investeringsmaatschappij
voor Vlaanderen
1 - 3 Anneessensstraat/Bus 1
B - 2018 ANTWERPEN

VANDAMME, R.
Commission des Communautés
européennes, Direction générale
"Institutions financières
et fiscalité"
8, square de Meeûs
B - 1049 BRUXELLES

VERTENEUIL, J.
Directeur
Commission bancaire
99, av. Louise
B - 1050 BRUXELLES

VIDAL SANZ, C.
Economiste
Bourse de Barcelone
Consulado 2
E - BARCELONE

WACHTER, G.
Dipl. Kaufmann
Landeskreditbank
Baden-Württemberg
15, Schellingstr. Postf.439
D - 7000 STUTTGART 1

WALSH, T.
Divisional Manager
Entreprise Development
IDA/Ireland
Lansdowne House, Ballbridge
IR - DUBLIN 4

WATSON, D.
Commission des Communautés européennes, Direction générale "Marché de l'information et innovation"
200, rue de la Loi
B - 1049 BRUXELLES

WECKEL, P.
Assistant d'université
Université de Strasbourg III
34, rue Stoskopf
F - 67100 STRASBOURG

WEGENER, L.
Beamter, Reg.-Volksw.-Dir.
Ministerium für Wirtschaft u. Verkehr des Landes Schleswig-Holstein
Düsternbrooker Weg 94
D - 2300 KIEL 1

WILK, E.
Beamter
Bundesministerium der Finanzen
Gravrheindorter Str. 6-8
D - 53 BONN 1

WILLEMAERS, M.
Agent de Change, Associé gérant
C.C.C. Piti & Cie, SCS
22, Fond St Servais
B - 4000 LIEGE

WYLLIE, J.A.
Technology Transfer
DS Ventures Inc.
P.O. Box 1, Eccles
GB - MANCHESTER M30 0BH

XYDIAS, J.
Directeur de Banque
Credit Bank
40, Stadiou Street
GR - 10252 ATHENS

YOUNG, A.
Professor of Finance
School of Management
Syracuse University
USA - SYRACUSE, New York 13210

YOUNG, T.
Company Director
BSC (Industry) Limited
NLA Tower. 12
Addiscombe Road, Surrey
GB - EAST GROYDON CR9 3JH

ZOIS-DERTILIS, M.
Economist
Commercial Bank of Greece
11, Sophocleous Street
GR - ATHENS